KATRINA ON STAGE

KATRINA ON STAGE

FIVE PLAYS

Edited by Suzanne M. Trauth
and Lisa S. Brenner

NORTHWESTERN UNIVERSITY PRESS
EVANSTON, ILLINOIS

Northwestern University Press
www.nupress.northwestern.edu

Printed in the United States of America

10 9 8 7 6 5 4 3 2 1

Library of Congress Cataloging-in-Publication Data

Katrina on stage : five plays / Edited by Suzanne M. Trauth and Lisa S. Brenner.
    p. cm.
    ISBN 978-0-8101-2750-0 (pbk. : alk. paper)
    1. Hurricane Katrina, 2005– Drama. I. Trauth, Suzanne. II. Brenner, Lisa S.
PS627.H87K38 2012
812'.608035876335064—dc22

                                                                2011010040

∞ The paper used in this publication meets the minimum requirements of the American
National Standard for Information Sciences—Permanence of Paper for Printed Library Materials,
ANSI Z39.48-1992.

CONTENTS

ACKNOWLEDGMENTS

We owe a debt of gratitude to many people who assisted us in the planning, organizing, and editing of *Katrina on Stage*. First and foremost, we would like to thank the playwrights—John Biguenet, Catherine Filloux, Tarell Alvin Mc-Craney, Joe Sutton, Tim Maddock, Lotti Louise Pharriss, and Samuel Brett Williams—whose generous and enthusiastic contributions to this anthology created a work we, and they, can be proud of.

Aimee Hayes provided us with her personal perspective on Hurricane Katrina; we are grateful for her willingness to share this poignant story and for introducing us to other New Orleans artists. We thank John Pietrowski, artistic director of Playwrights Theatre of New Jersey, for including us in his Katrina festival of new works. Our participation introduced us to a number of plays that told Katrina stories, several of which are included in the anthology. We'd also like to thank Kimberly Gordon for acquainting us with Tim and Lotti's work.

We'd especially like to thank all of those who supported the early phases of this project: Jack Bowers, Matthias Goldstein, Eileen Trauth, Adam Shapiro, Nancy Tichenor, Michael Allen, Eileen Skarecki, Mike Finn, Ross Maxwell, Mike Peters, Bruce Cohen, and Mason Weisz.

We extend our deepest gratitude to the people of New Orleans who inspired these plays. We hope this book is a tribute to their courage, spirit, and determination. Finally, we would like to thank Mike Levine, and Northwestern University Press, for recognizing the importance of this anthology. Mike's steadfast support, patience, and ready answers to questions literally gave birth to this book. It would not have been possible without him.

On a personal note . . .

I am very grateful for the support offered by my family and colleagues as we conceived, wrote, and edited the anthology. Thanks to Montclair State University for providing the sabbatical that enabled me to begin the editing process of collecting, reading, and evaluating plays for consideration, and especially to the Department of Theatre and Dance. I am grateful to Lisa for joining me in working on *Katrina on Stage;* her critical analysis, enthusiasm, and willingness to get the details right have made this "labor of love" a special journey. As always, I am grateful for Elaine's belief in me and support through all phases of my projects.

—Suzanne M. Trauth

A special thank-you to my colleagues at Drew University, who supported me throughout this project, especially the Theatre Department, Jonathan Golden, Shawn Spaventa, and the Drew Disaster Relief Program. I am also grateful to Amy Koritz for her advice and wisdom and for connecting us to The Porch 7th Ward Cultural Organization, and to President Robert Weisbuch, who personally encouraged this work. Thank you to my family and particularly to Daniel, without whose love and assistance this anthology would not have been possible. Finally, I want to thank Sue for taking this leap of faith with me and for her mentorship, creativity, insight, and patience, which made these years of collaborating together a pleasure.

For my father, Mel Silberman (z"l), who taught me the meaning of perseverance.

—Lisa S. Brenner

INTRODUCTION

On August 29, 2005, a confluence of geological, climatic, political, economic, and sociological factors stood ready to create the most devastating natural disaster in American history. Hurricane Katrina flooded 80 percent of the city of New Orleans, killing roughly 1,800 people, destroying approximately 200,000 Gulf Coast homes, and displacing an estimated one million people. At $81.2 billion, it is also considered the nation's costliest natural disaster. More aptly, however, Katrina was a national social disaster: it was a case study in shoddy public works management, rampant neglect of environmental protections, and governmental disorganization at the local, state, and federal levels that left thousands of people stranded on rooftops and interstate highways for days without food and water.

Although the floodwaters have long receded, New Orleans still struggles to resurface. In 2010, it was estimated that a third of New Orleans's housing was still empty, and there were no indications if or when previous occupants would rebuild. Neighborhoods still vary greatly in terms of resources and their capacity to organize. The hardest hit seem to be the poor, many of whom cannot afford to live in the area due to housing costs that remain unaffordable. Moreover, neighborhoods with weak market value are subject to being bought out by speculators with no intention of revitalizing them.

During the days immediately following the storm, the majority of Americans obtained information about the hurricane through radio and television reporting. Though often heartbreaking and devastating to see and hear, these reports were mostly general in nature, limited in scope, and painted with a broad stroke. They allowed listeners and viewers to remain somewhat passive and voyeuristically removed from the event. Personal engagement was not necessary.

Closely following on the heels of Hurricane Katrina and its catastrophic destruction, however, was another, different kind of response: an artistic response. Art served as an antidote to the flow of information provided by broadcast media. Filmmakers, playwrights, actors, dancers, photographers, authors, musicians, and fine artists began to create art that documented the events of Katrina in a variety of media and that expressed a profound tangle of emotions. Artistic expressions were vital in that they allowed the individual artists to communicate personal, specific, and often contradictory reactions to the storm and its aftermath. Artists directly affected by the storm, as well as those outside the Gulf Coast region who felt moved to respond to the enormity of Katrina, interpreted the devastation in New Orleans and filtered the emotional response through their own distinctive perspective. Katrina art not only created the possibility of challenging the media's version of reality but also acknowledged those voices that had been silenced, ignored, or stereotyped in the dominant discourse.

The list of works generated, and continuing to be created, as a result of Hurricane Katrina is impressive and moving. A sampling includes documentary films such as Spike Lee's *When the Levees Broke: A Requiem in Four Acts* and *If God Is Willing and Da Creek Don't Rise,* Jonathan Demme's *Right to Return: New Home Movies from the Lower 9th Ward,* and Tia Lessin and Carl Deal's *Trouble the Water;* musical tributes like Terence Blanchard's *A Tale of God's Will (A Requiem for Katrina),* the African American rock band Living Colour's song "Behind the Sun," and *Katrina Ballads*—a ten-part musical impression composed by Ted Hearne; the short-lived television series *K-Ville* and the HBO drama *Treme,* set in post-Katrina New Orleans and produced in the city; the dance piece *Katrina, Katrina: Love Letters to New Orleans,* created by Pearson Widrig Dance Theater; *Los invisibles,* a photo exhibition of documentary photos, portraiture, and conceptual images that explore the Latino immigrant presence in post-Katrina New Orleans; and books by writers Dave Eggers (*Zeitoun*), Tom Piazza (*Why New Orleans Matters* and *City of Refuge*), and the graphic novel *A.D.: New Orleans After the Deluge* by Josh Neufeld. The range of art is as extensive as the range of reactions to the storm.

Of all the arts, however, theater has a unique ability to build an individual connection to a national tragedy and the human beings affected by it. Theater's emotional impact stems from the intimate relationship the audience experiences in being addressed by live actors who ask them to grapple with the stories they tell. At the same time, the live experience of theater has the potential to foster communal bonds, even in moments of dissension. Theater can create a shared sense of responsibility by providing a personal interaction that speaks to a varied group of people and shapes them, instantaneously, into a community who can be moved to action. Emotional and intellectual engagement with theater can produce consequences, such as a desire to advocate for accountability.

The etymology of the word "theater" comes from the Greek "theatron" for "seeing space." At its core, theater about Hurricane Katrina asks us to bear witness—to acknowledge what New Orleans went through and continues to struggle with—and to support the residents of the Gulf Coast. Plays permit us to document, dramatically, this devastation and to keep the casualties of Katrina alive in an immediate and visceral fashion.

There has been an outpouring of theatrical activity in post-Katrina New Orleans. Given the performative nature of New Orleans culture—Jazz Fest, carnivals, Mardi Gras Indian traditions, second line parades—it is not surprising that several of these projects have been experimental, interdisciplinary, and often site-specific. Kathy Randel, director of ArtSpot Productions, created *Spaces in Between,* which she performed inside the gutted home where she was raised, as well as *Loup Garou,* in collaboration with Mondo Bizarro, about the devastation of southern Louisiana's wetlands. Andrew Larimer's *Get This Lake off My House,* a modern version of Shakespeare's *The Tempest,* was performed outdoors in what was once part of the Pontchartrain Beach Amusement Park. Performance artist José Torres-Tama has been touring his one-man show *The Cone of Uncertainty* both nationally and internationally, highlighting the Latino community's experiences of Katrina, including those of immigrant workers.

Other performance events include Alternate Roots and Junebug's collaborative production of *Uprooted: The Katrina Project,* which helped organize those displaced by Katrina, and Ashé Cultural Arts Center's *Voices Not Forgotten,* a performance piece created and performed by senior citizens. *HOME: New Orleans* is a multidisciplinary project executed by teams of artists and students who are both local and living outside the region. The project aims to commemorate and energize several neighborhoods that had been devastated. Its productions have included *LakeviewS,* where bus tours took audiences to various sites in the Lakeview neighborhood to see both visual and performing arts installations. Many of these works have explored the themes of memory, loss, racism, environmental devastation, and the meaning of home.

Camp and satire have continued to jibe local politics, whether at Le Chat Noir or Southern Rep's New Play Bacchanal 2010, which featured Jim Fitzmorris's *The Thanatos Brass Band,* where the rulers of Mt. Olympus were cast as familiar political figures from the Crescent City.

While newcomers have mixed with local New Orleanians to successfully create new companies like the NOLA Project, Cripple Creek Theatre Co., Goat in the Road Productions, FourFront Theatre, and Skin Horse, for insiders dealing with the day-to-day challenges of post-Katrina life in New Orleans, outsiders coming in to create art may be viewed as circumspect. Several community-based theater projects in which participants tell their own stories have been well received, including works coordinated by Jan Cohen-Cruz and *Swimming Upstream,* a collaboration between Eve Ensler's V-Day project and the Ashé Cultural Arts Center. In their discussion of the original scenario for *HOME: New Orleans,* however, participants Ron Bechet and Amy Koritz discuss conflicting aesthetic ideologies between outside and community participants. While a great critical success, Paul Chan's staging of Samuel Beckett's *Waiting for Godot* in the Lower Ninth Ward received differing reactions from local artists, reflecting concerns regarding money or reputation made off Katrina art which may or may not support the city.

Katrina on Stage addresses these social issues while also putting a human face on a historical event of epic proportions. It documents an unprecedented time in American history, exposing issues of race, class, and government failure, as well as highlighting our collective and individual heroism. The plays create opportunities for individual actors, theaters, and universities to present vibrant, exciting theater for audiences both familiar and unfamiliar with the details and personal stories associated with Hurricane Katrina. At the same time, it can supplement the study of sociology, anthropology, political science, and history. But what this collection of plays does most meaningfully is reinforce that which live theater does most powerfully: touching audiences in a unique way both emotionally and intellectually, speaking to the hearts and minds of all who are willing to listen.

Included in this anthology is *Rising Water* by New Orleans writer John Biguenet and commissioned by Southern Rep in 2007. The first play of a trilogy about the collapse of the levees in New Orleans and its aftermath, *Rising Water* depicts a couple awakening at two in the morning to find their pitch-dark house filling with water. The play is not the product of an outsider's perspective; on the contrary, it is a personal narrative written by a local and deeply imbued with a range of emotions that confirm the author has "been there." *Rising Water* was a cathartic experience for many New Orleans residents and became the best-selling show in the theater's twenty-three-year history before it went on to be produced nationally.

Rising Water is the story of Sugar and Camille, two people "no longer young" who try to weather the consequences of Hurricane Katrina while dealing with the crises in their marriage. Both intimate and epic, the play introduces many of the issues and themes that are repeated in the rest of the anthology, and, indeed, in many of the theatrical works that have arisen as a result of the hurricane: the chaos of a dying city, destruction and survival, redemption and renewal, the juxtaposition of the personal and political.

The play is a blueprint of the physical and emotional toll of survival and loss experienced throughout New Orleans in the aftermath of Hurricane Katrina. Sugar and Camille's story is one that was repeated thousands of times in the course of that one night and serves to document the personal, human crises as well as the external, political crises that resulted in the breakdown of the couple's—and the city's—defenses. Playwright John Biguenet indicates he began writing *Rising Water* in anger but ended up writing a love story. The audience might feel moved to identify with the couple and empathize with Sugar and Camille as they confront their relationship and the devastation, but it is not sufficient to sit on the sidelines and watch the action unfold; in the final moment of the play, with the wailing of the alarms swelling and the lights brightening to a full moon, Camille and Sugar turn from each other and face the spectators. They appear to be confronting them and asking "Why?" It is a question that demands an active answer. In this powerful moment—one that can only be achieved by a live theatrical experience—the issue of claiming responsibility is front and center. The audience is invited to move beyond empathy to engagement.

Playwrights Catherine Filloux, Tarell Alvin McCraney, and Joe Sutton consciously play with the challenges posed by this invitation in *The Breach*. As the character Mac explains, "This city is ripe for predators coming in and turning it into something *typical* and we're going to have to be vigilant." Commissioned locally by Southern Rep in 2007, the play was then developed through a series of staged readings around the country, both in and outside the Gulf Coast. *The Breach* was subsequently produced by Southern Rep in New Orleans in 2007 and Seattle Repertory Theatre in 2008; the play therefore needed to take into account that it had to speak to different types of audiences. The script fuses three distinct journeys. Two survival tales, a man with MS who has to swim out of his house and three family members awaiting rescue on the roof, are juxtaposed with the narrative of a northern reporter who investigates rumors that the levees were intentionally blown. Wary of his motives, the locals are hesitant to tell him their stories and instead push him to investigate his own identity.

As the journalist named Lynch probes his interviewees, they fire back with their suspicions: "Tell why you're here. What you're after." They are not only distrustful because he is from New York, but also because he is white. The locals ask Lynch if his editor knows he is in New Orleans talking to black people, if he likes writing about black people, and whether he is a liberal with a soft spot for African Americans. Lynch's only defense is that he writes about America's racial divide because it makes him feel superior to other whites who don't want to acknowledge it. By including Lynch's story, the playwrights potentially challenge those outside the Gulf region—especially white audience members—to scrutinize their own motives. Are they interested in these issues? For what reasons?

The juxtaposition of the three Katrina tales also keeps spectators at a critical distance from which to view this tragic event. As with *Rising Water,* the story of Quan, Severance, and Pere Leon stuck on their roof awaiting help gives audiences an inside look at the fear and desperation of those trapped in the flooded city. Like Camille and Sugar, these characters are filled with regret and a desire for redemption as they face the possibility of the end of their lives. Pere Leon continually berates Severance for his lack of responsibility to his family and for his sins (the play indicates that Severance is having a homosexual relationship with a young man named Gideon), but eventually he comes to embrace his grandson as his kin and baptizes him with Katrina's dirty waters.

The scope of the play, however, widens to connect this intimate family story with larger historical events. As we see with Quan, Katrina cost innocent people their lives and left children severed from their loved ones. This is also the case in Iraq, where Mac's son is stationed. A bartender who suffers from multiple sclerosis, Mac is rescued by a man on a boat who is carrying a dead baby. This image is mirrored by Mac's fantasy sequence of his son Francis saving babies in the Persian Gulf and fighting for the freedom of the Iraqi people. It is only later—after Francis dies from a car bomb—that Mac begins to question why America is fighting this war in the first place: "We can't save our own cities and we try to save theirs?" At the same time, Lynch's interviewees push him to link Katrina with previous floods (the one in 1927 and later Hurricane Betsy) in which they believe the levees were intentionally blown to save the more affluent parts of the city.

Not only is the audience challenged by tracking three different story lines performed by actors playing multiple roles, but each story line is itself told in such a way as to keep the audience a step removed. Quan's family narrative of being trapped on the roof is simultaneously told in real time when she is seven and by an older Quan several years later as she reflects back on what happened. Mac's journey is surrealistically depicted as a battle between himself and Water, whose character later blurs with the attending nurse, Sandy. While expressing his feelings of being caught in between two worlds as he investigates the Katrina story, Lynch tells his editor, "We don't live in one country.

We live in two countries. And I'm in the other one." This idea is expressed both figuratively and literally as Lynch's conversations with his editors and fellow reporters back home conflate with his interviews with the New Orleans residents—both groups are played by chorus members. Audiences must therefore work to make connections both within and between the three story lines.

They may notice, for example, the characters' constant desire for the truth, for something in which to believe. Lynch ultimately goes home with the realization that he still doesn't understand what happened and doesn't think he ever will. There is no single truth, but only perceptions of the truth; nonetheless, these are still worthy of consideration. Does it matter if the levees were deliberately blown or failed because the Army Corps of Engineers failed to build or inspect them properly? Should we accept official versions of reality—whether about Iraq or Katrina—simply because they have been fed to us by the media, government, or military officials? When is it harmful to let our suspicions get the best of us?

Katrina brought with it the breach of the levees and also a breach of trust in one another and in the government. What kind of society do we live in if we allow for the needless deaths of innocent people? The play asks us to ponder what we believe in—what can we? what should we?—and it offers hope in humanity's ability to persevere, to learn, and to make choices. As Lynch reminds us, we need to be vigilant and to create not a mausoleum but a New Orleans that lives.

Produced at the New Orleans Arts Center, *The Trash Bag Tourist*, by Samuel Brett Williams, similarly explores themes of race and class, exploitation, and the tensions between insiders and outsiders. The play provides a snapshot of one family's struggle with trust and community as a result of New Orleans's migratory population ending up in cities across the nation. Set in his home state of Arkansas, this one-act features the perceptions of folks in a place outside Louisiana that absorbed the residents of New Orleans. Despite the seeming generosity of American towns and cities toward Katrina victims—the church takes them in, tents are set up outside the local Wal-Mart replete with sleeping bags and bug zappers—the play reveals the hostility toward these outsiders. They resent the challenges posed by absorbing large numbers of displaced people: dealing with the newly crowded stores, integrating them into the schools, and finding them homes and jobs. Dorothy reveals the real attitude toward the New Orleanians when she declares, "Everyone wants Arkadelphia back the way it wuz."

At the same time, the play demonstrates the ways in which people exploited Katrina for their own purposes. According to the "trash bag tourist" Chuck, the gymnasium where the church has put them up has little food. He uses the same words to describe the gym as Dorothy and Molly use to describe life with the Katrina refugees: crowded and smelly. The audience also learns that the church minister, Brother Eric, is the reason FEMA trailers have failed to arrive. Chuck claims he "ain't never seen a man so excited 'bout tragedy in [his] whole life." Brother Eric orders people about and treats them like bums, asking them to wash his truck for three dollars. His actions are less motivated by concern for Katrina victims than the publicity he is receiving. Eventually, we learn that Chuck himself has been exploiting the tragedy of Katrina by posing as a survivor and cashing in on government and community handouts.

It is therefore not surprising that trust becomes a major theme in the play. Molly, who was mistreated by her boyfriend and teased throughout high school, desperately wants to leave Arkadelphia and hopes that Chuck will be her ticket out—if only she can believe in him. Dorothy, whose husband left her for the rodeo and who has only her daughter to rely on, is wary of Chuck from the start. Meanwhile, homeless and jobless, Chuck clings to his trash bag of belongings as if his life depended on it; without it he has nothing left to prove that he exists. It is not until he kisses Molly for the first time that he releases his grip. Each of the characters has individual reasons for distrusting others, but Williams also suggests wider systemic issues of trust arising from racism and economic inequality.

While *The Trash Bag Tourist* explores the exodus from New Orleans, there was a simultaneous movement of people entering the city. The volunteer response to New Orleans was instantaneous and breathtaking. From firefighters, emergency workers, and religious groups to university students on winter and spring breaks, Americans from around the country stepped up to the plate. Refugees were housed, fed, and integrated into communities, and many homes were gutted and rebuilt in New Orleans.

The stories of these volunteers have become familiar; what is less well known is the story of animal rescue following Hurricane Katrina. *Because They Have No Words*, by Tim Maddock and Lotti Louise Pharriss, is based on Maddock's real-life journey into the chaos of the Gulf Coast. It was first produced at the Lounge Theatre in Los Angeles and opened September 2, 2006, just a year after Katrina struck, and in May 2008 was presented at the Piven Theatre in Evanston, Illinois. The play demonstrates in vivid fashion the extent of the damage done by the storm and the range of beings affected. While most of the volunteers came from beyond the Gulf Coast, making them outsiders as far as the catastrophe was concerned, their commitment and experiences are no less significant. As the character Tim is reminded by Nancy, who runs an animal sanctuary, "just by showing up down there, you gave everyone you met a little hope." At another point in the play, when a nurse finds out that Tim has come from Los Angeles to volunteer, she replies, "And you came all this way to help? And here we thought we'd been forgotten. It's almost enough to give me hope that things are gonna be all right." Though outsiders' motivations have been questioned since the storm, some people in the city at the time of the disaster were grateful for the assistance.

The opening dialogue of the play reminds Tim, and the audience members, that disaster relief is dangerous activity and often includes heat, humidity, debris, flooding, distressed animals, sanitation issues, and a lack of electricity and communication. His experience with Katrina's aftermath is also theirs: Tim has become their proxy, and they are thrown—in a disconcerting fashion—into the chaos and devastation with him.

The structure of the play reminds the audience that it is seeing theater, and while it might identify emotionally with Tim's and his fellow volunteers' predicaments, there is a buffer zone between characters and audience members. Actors play several roles (including animals), characters consistently address the audience directly, humor helps to balance the emotional devastation, and flashbacks/forwards allow characters to clarify story points and intentions. All of these techniques encourage viewers to maintain some objectivity as they descend with Tim into the confusion and mayhem of animal rescue.

Like *The Trash Bag Tourist, Because They Have No Words* illuminates the social fractures exposed during the city's evacuation. Tim is left to wonder whom he would become "if everything around [him] was turned upside down. If [his] routine, [his] safety and security, were all taken away . . ." The spectators are left to wonder as much about themselves, since they see the crisis as Tim sees it. Confronted with the anarchy of Hurricane Katrina, how would they react? Because of the visceral experiences that make up Tim's journey in *Because They Have No Words*, audience members are less voyeurs and more participants. At the end of the play, Tim visits a rescued wolf dog named Pete, and an animal speaks for the first and only time in the play, saying "thank you." Pete's gratitude might reflect that of other Katrina victims for the work of all the volunteers who stepped in to provide assistance.

Katrina: The K Word, by Lisa S. Brenner and Suzanne M. Trauth, broadens the scope of personal Katrina narratives. Brenner and Trauth chose to create documentary theater, or more specifically what has been defined as "theater of testimony," in which an interviewer records the words of actual people. Tracking the stories of twelve characters of different ages, occupations, and racial backgrounds before, during, and after the storm, the piece allows for a range of perspectives. The audience does not get *the* authentic Katrina experience but rather interpretations of this experience, which are, in effect, no less authentic.

Brechtian theater argues against psychological identification both between the actor and the character and between the audience and the character. Instead it aims to create distance by which the characters and their circumstances can be viewed critically. Like *Because They Have No Words*, *The K Word* utilizes many Brechtian techniques for this purpose: actors play multiple roles, the sequences of the play are announced before the action unfolds, and the characters break the narrative to debate the responsibility (or lack thereof) for specific actions surrounding Katrina. Rather than dictate which side is right and which is wrong, the play leaves contrasting viewpoints unresolved to stimulate debate. While the play represents the journeys of twelve distinct characters with whom the audience can identify (thus connecting audiences to the people behind the media headlines), the script doesn't rely on the audience's empathy alone, trying to balance their emotional investment in these characters with a degree of critical distance. This separation guards against the two dangers of theater of testimony: audiences will watch characters recount traumatic events merely for their own sensationalism, or they will identify so strongly with the narratives that they simply become distressed.

Thus the question of audience distance becomes increasingly important. By staging *The K Word* as a "disaster tour," the play situates the audience in the role of voyeurs and asks them to examine the significance of this role: are they to gawk or acknowledge and understand what occurred? To help achieve this aim, the script deliberately thwarts the viewer who might take a passive stance. As the audience members enter, jazz plays and the characters greet them and welcome them to New Orleans. However, once this prologue is finished, the character Vivie announces the start of the tour:

> Does everyone have a seat, 'cause the tour bus is ready to roll. OK?
> Good, now, listen up, here's how it works. We can't tell you every story
> out of New Orleans, I mean, my God, 250,000 people lost their homes.
> But these twelve folks you just met are gonna tell you . . .

The ensemble finishes her sentence with the words "exactly what happened." The characters pause, surprised that others think they know best what occurred. They stand wary of each other and of being made to recite the tale. By extension, the audience too should be wary: What kind of story are they expecting to hear? Can anyone tell them "exactly what happened"? Is it possible that not every character will relay the same experience? Despite their wariness, the characters continue to tell their stories since the audience "paid good money for this tour," but the play is meant to deny spectators an easy, inactive encounter.

In *The K Word*, no one character's story is privileged over another. While the characters may agree on certain topics—for instance, almost everyone states that they expected the hurricane to be merely a two- to three-day hiatus from their lives—they may not agree on others, including how many people died as a result of Katrina. By giving the audience contradictory information, the play hopes to avoid simple answers, encouraging them to discuss the contrary perspectives and even be inspired to do some investigative work on their own. Moreover, offering multiple narratives reinforces the idea that people had vastly different experiences during Katrina, often based on their resources. While the character Rachel, a professor, is able to ride out the storm at a hotel in Baton Rouge, the character Shakira ends up in the Superdome because her father did not have enough gas to leave the city.

The dramatic tension in *The K Word* does not lie in a suspenseful revelation of a turn of events—everyone knows that the storm will come and that havoc will follow. Rather, it lies within the characters' ability to come together as a community after the fact, despite class, racial, and political differences, and despite personal loss, resentment, fear, and crime. For some of the characters, Katrina solidifies their relationship with New Orleans: "Nothing made me feel like a New Orleanian, a local, than the storm." While others choose not to return: "There's a lot of things they didn't have the opportunity to do before that they're able to do now that they are living in Texas." Rather than project a utopian vision, the play encompasses fractures within the community and the challenges of the road that lies ahead. In this sense, *The K Word* examines the meaning of home, both locally and nationally—an idea highlighted by the recitation of the Pledge of Allegiance with its promise of "liberty and justice for all" as the final lines of the play are spoken.

According to Janelle Reinelt, for a public occurrence to become "theatricalized," it must fit the Aristotelian mold:

> The event must be of significant gravity to the well-being of the nation ... [It] must attract a critical mass of public attention ... have unfolded in a form of narrative that can be apprehended in terms of protagonists and plot ... and ... embody a certain kind of analogical critique of their ways of living.

Katrina undoubtedly had captured national attention, and it unfolded in narrative form—if one considers the storm as the "inciting action" that propels the various protagonists forward. However, since fall 2005, Katrina has drifted from American consciousness—the media has moved on to other events such as wars, political campaigns, and economic collapse. To continue with Reinelt's metaphor, the Katrina story seemed to lack catharsis. The "critique of our way of living" remains overwhelming—racism, class discrimination, and the government's apathy and ineptitude exposed by Katrina are perhaps too painful and are therefore easier to sweep under the rug. What is more, Katrina is a narrative without closure: the problems in New Orleans—and in our nation—are ongoing and seem to be getting worse, as the BP oil spill made disturbingly clear.

And yet, perhaps this is precisely why all the plays in this anthology refuse to offer a simple catharsis. All of these stories remain open-ended. What exactly happens at the conclusion of *Rising Water*? Will either Camille or Sugar survive their time on the roof? The ringing alarms seem to suggest the end is approaching, but there were miraculous Katrina survival stories, and this might be one. Similarly in *Because They Have No Words*, the futures of the pets Tim saved are unknown. Luna is adopted, but Gasper seems lost forever. Xena will most probably never see her rightful owner.

The Trash Bag Tourist too ends without any solutions. Although the audience knows that Chuck leaves, they are unsure where he'll go or if anyone will help him. Even Dorothy's final words cast doubt that they will. The audience also does not know what will happen to Molly except that she remains trapped with her mother, literally and figuratively broken. This lack of resolution makes sense, because the characters themselves have become crushed along with their dreams, suffering under the weight of the systemic problems of race, gender, and class to which they have fallen prey.

The Breach doesn't provide any definitive answers for the blowing of the levees; nor do we know how exactly Mac's fiancée, Linda, died, or what will happen to Quan. Instead, the audience is left to confront the significance of the levee breach—its ramifications for the future of New Orleans and also for the country as a whole. *The K Word* closes in a similar vein with the tour guide telling spectators that this story is "to be continued. Which just pisses ya off." Meanwhile, the rest of the actors lift a coffin-like box draped in a tattered American flag and recite the Pledge of Allegiance, followed by a trumpet playing "Just a Closer Walk with Thee."

These plays remind audiences that they are part of the story continuing to unfold. The danger in making Katrina an exclusively local issue is that it excuses the rest of the nation from its responsibility to its citizens—both for accountability regarding the events surrounding the storm and for aiding in sustainable, equitable reconstruction. Given that in November 2009 a federal judge found the Army Corps of Engineers directly and fiscally responsible for much of the disastrous flooding during Katrina, organizations such as levees .org maintain that "what happened during Katrina is a national infrastructure issue and not a parochial New Orleans issue." Beyond national responsibility for the extent of the Katrina disaster, the Army Corps of Engineers' involvement has implications for the rest of the country, since the Corps monitors most of the important water projects in the United States and much of the country's population lives in counties protected by levees. The twofold goals of national education and activism extend beyond charitable works; the United States neglects the lessons from Katrina at its own peril.

The plays in this anthology recognize Katrina as a national event that continues to impact all Americans even years after the floodwaters have abated. They cannot speak definitively for all New Orleanians; everyone in New Orleans has a personal stake in the Katrina narrative. With roughly 250,000 people who have lost their homes, there are at least as many accounts. Rather than tell *the* Katrina story, this anthology incorporates several Katrina stories, including those of different races, genders, ages, sexual orientations, and classes. It attempts to provide a forum for those who may not have had the opportunity to speak out and encourages listeners, viewers, and participants to remember the City That Care Forgot.

SELECTED BIBLIOGRAPHY

Andersen, Christine F., et al. "The New Orleans Hurricane Protection System: What Went Wrong and Why." *American Society of Civil Engineers Hurricane Katrina External Review Panel Report* (2007): 47–48. Accessed September 18, 2009. http://www.asce.org/files/pdf/ERPreport.pdf.

Bates, Lisa K. "Post-Katrina Housing: Problems, Policies, and Prospects for African Americans in New Orleans." *The Black Scholar* 36, no. 4 (2006): 13–31.

Bechet, Ron, and Amy Koritz. "The New Hybridity: HOME, New Orleans and Emerging Forms of Community/University/Arts Collaboration." *Community Arts Network Reading Room.* Posted in 2008, last accessed November 24, 2009. As of September 6, 2010, the Community Arts Network website has been discontinued. http://www.communityarts.net/readingroom/archivefiles/2008/09.

Cohen Cruz, Jan. "HOME, New Orleans: University/Neighborhood Arts Collaborations." *Civic Engagement in the Wake of Katrina.* Koritz, Amy, and George J. Sanchez, eds. Ann Arbor: University of Michigan Press, 2009. 162–84.

Cha-Jua, Sundiata Keitha. "Introduction to *The Black Scholar* Special Issue on Hurricane Katrina: High Tide of a New Racial Formation." *The Black Scholar* 36, no. 4 (2006): 2–6.

DeLozier, Elana, and Nina Kamp. "Hurricane Katrina Timeline." *Brookings Institution.* Accessed December 29, 2010. http://www.brookings.edu/fp/projects/homeland/katrinatimeline.pdf.

Douglas, Jack, Jr. "In New Orleans, Recovery Is Still a Distant Dream." *The Newark Star-Ledger,* August 29, 2007, 1:10.

Eaton, Leslie. "In New Orleans, Plan to Raze Low-Income Housing Draws Protest." *New York Times,* December 14, 2007, A28.

Elliott, James R., and Jeremy Pais. "Race, Class, and Hurricane Katrina: Social Differences in Human Responses to Disaster." *Social Science Research* 35, no. 2 (2007): 307.

Ellis-Lamkins, Phaedra. "Four Years after Katrina: Lessons from the Gulf Coast." *Huffington Post,* August 28, 2009. Accessed December 12, 2009. http://www.huffingtonpost.com.

Grunwald, Michael. "The Threatening Storm." *Time Magazine,* August 13, 2007, 30–39.

Harris-Lacewell, Melissa, and James Perry. "Katrina Nation." *Huffington Post,* August 26, 2009. Accessed September 20, 2009. http://www.huffingtonpost.com.

Huffington Post. "Four Years after Katrina." *Huffington Post,* August 28, 2009. Accessed September 20, 2009. http://www.huffingtonpost.com.

Hurricane Katrina External Review Panel Reports . . . June 1, 2007. "The New Orleans Hurricane Protection Systems: What Went Wrong and Why." Accessed January 21, 2011. http://www.asce.org/Content.aspx?id=7252.

Junebugproductions.org. "Uprooted: The Katrina Project." Accessed December 29, 2010. http://www.junebugproductions.org/#/original-productions-collabo/4528633751.

Landphair, Juliette. "'The Forgotten People of New Orleans': Community, Vulnerability, and the Lower Ninth Ward." *Journal of American History* 94, no. 3 (2007): 837–45.

Levees.org. "United States Counties Protected by Levees." Accessed January 21, 2011. http://levees.org/2009/12/01/new-map-shows-large-sectors-of-american-population-are-protected-by-levees/.

Long, Alecia P. "Poverty Is the New Prostitution: Race, Poverty, and Public Housing in Post-Katrina New Orleans." *Journal of American History* 94, no. 3 (2007): 795–803.

Marinello, Nick. "Diaspora." *Tulanian* 78, no. 1 (2006): 36–41.

O'Neill, Karen. "Broken Levees, Broken Lives, and a Broken Nation after Hurricane Katrina." *Southern Cultures* 14, no. 2 (2008): 89–108.

Piazza, Tom. *Why New Orleans Matters.* New York: HarperCollins, 2005.

Plyer, Allison. "Neighborhood Recovery Rates." *Greater New Orleans Community Data Center,* July 1, 2010. Accessed July 21, 2010. http://www.gnocdc.org.

Reckdahl, Katy. "Many Area Residents Face 'Unaffordable' Housing Costs, Study Says." *Times-Picayune Online Edition,* June 27, 2009. Accessed December 29, 2010. http://www.nola.com/news/index.ssf/2009/06/many_area_residents_face_unaff.html.

Reinelt, Janelle. "Towards a Poetics of Theatre and Public Events: In the Case of Stephen Lawrence." *The Drama Review* 50, no. 3 (2006): 69–87.

Rosenthal, Sandy. "Recent Ruling Shows True Tragedy of Katrina Was Federal Government's Creation of the Disaster Itself." *Huffington Post,* December 14, 2009. Accessed December 15, 2009. http://www.huffingtonpost.com.

Saulny, Susan. "New Orleans Hurt by Acute Rental Shortage." *New York Times,* December 3, 2007, A1, A23.

Schwartz, John. "New Study of Levees Faults Design and Construction." *New York Times Online Edition,* May 22, 2006. Accessed November 17, 2009. http://www.nytimes.com.

Simon, Fran. "Resuscitation." *Tulanian* 78, no. 3 (2007): 36–39.

Thevestigesproject.org. "Home, New Orleans: Performing the Neighborhoods, Rebuilding Communities." December 2006. Accessed December 29, 2010. http://www.thevestigesproject.org/web/thinktank/documents/HNOBrochure12-06.pdf.

Wallenberg, Christopher. "In Katrina's Wake." *American Theatre* 27, no. 5 (2006): 54–59.

Walsh, Bill. "Corps Chief Admits to 'Design Failure.'" *Times-Picayune Online Edition,* April 6, 2006. Accessed September 20, 2009. http://archive.stateline.org/html/2006/04/06/214_228.html.

KATRINA ON STAGE

RISING WATER

John Biguenet

PRODUCTION HISTORY

Rising Water was given its initial staged reading by the National New Play Network, where it won the 2006 Commission Award. Ryan Rilette directed the premiere on March 17, 2007, at Southern Rep Theatre in New Orleans, where it became the best-selling show in the theater's twenty-year history. Since then the play has had productions around the country in California, New Jersey, New York, Massachusetts, Missouri, North Carolina, and Lockport, Louisiana. *Rising Water* was a 2006 National Showcase of New Plays selection and a 2007 recipient of an Access to Artistic Excellence development and production grant from the National Endowment for the Arts. The play won the Big Easy Theatre Award for Best Original Play of 2007.

CHARACTERS

Camille, slender but no longer young
Sugar, her husband, no longer young or slender

ACT 1

SCENE 1

[*The dark attic of a narrow, one-story house at night, about 2:00 A.M., cluttered with old possessions. Moonlight sifts in through a vent in the roof. The sound of a folding staircase is heard being pulled down suddenly and splashing into water.* CAMILLE *clambers up from below into the attic, a lit flashlight in her hand. The bottom of her nightgown is wet.*]

CAMILLE [*shouting down the folding stairs*]: The flashlight, Sugar. Bring the light. It's dark up here.

SUGAR [*from below*]: I thought you brought it up with you.

CAMILLE: Not this light. The other one.

SUGAR [*from below*]: Which one?

CAMILLE: The one that's in the kitchen. Hurry, though. The water's everywhere.

SUGAR [*from below, sloshing through water*]: I know, I know. But I can't see a goddamn thing down here. Where'd you say you put it?

[CAMILLE *points her flashlight down the stairs.*]

CAMILLE: I didn't put it anywhere. Why would I move it? The flashlight's in the cupboard above the oven where it always is.

[*Long, anxious pause.*]

Sug?

[*Silence.*]

Is it where I said it was?

[*Silence.*]

Sugar, did you find it there?

[*Silence.*]

Sug?

SUGAR [*from below*]: I got it, yeah, I found it where you said.

CAMILLE: You scared me half to death. Now come up here. The water's rising all around the stairs.

SUGAR [*from below*]: Wait. Let me grab the photographs.

CAMILLE: Photographs? Just get up here.

SUGAR [*from below*]: The albums in the bookcase, I'm talking about.

CAMILLE: We had them on the bottom shelf. They're ruined by now. Just get yourself up here before you drown.

SUGAR [*from below*]: Then what about that box of pictures in Frankie's room?

[CAMILLE *points her flashlight down the stairs again.*]

CAMILLE: There isn't time.

[*Pause.*]

Sugar, I can see the water coming up.

[*Silence.*]

Sug?

[*Silence.*]

You hear me, Sug? Forget the photographs.

[*Silence.*]

Sugar, you scaring me.

[*Long silence.*]

SUGAR [*from below*]: They weren't there. You remember where you seen them last?

CAMILLE: I don't know. Just climb up here. The water's getting higher all the time.

SUGAR [*from below*]: There's one more place they might be—on top the cabinet in the dining room.

CAMILLE: Sug, leave them be.

SUGAR [*from below*]: Just let me look. I think I saw them there last week.

CAMILLE: The water's coming up the stairs. Will you forget those photographs? They're not worth drowning for.

[*Silence.*]

Sugar?

[*Long silence.*]

Sug?

[*Silence.*]

Sugar!

SUGAR [*from below, but more distant*]: Will you calm down, Camille?

[*Pause, then* SUGAR *is approaching the bottom of the stairs.*]

I found them where I thought they were. Just hold your horses. I'm coming up.

[*His legs wet,* SUGAR *climbs up into the attic with his flashlight on, clasping a box of photos to his chest.*]

There. You happy now?

CAMILLE: You make me crazy. Why you have to be so damn hardheaded all the time? Water's pouring in downstairs from God knows where, and you decide to go wandering around in the dark. You lucky you didn't drown or something.

SUGAR: A little water's all it is down there.

CAMILLE: A little? Think you're fooling me with that?

SUGAR: Now don't go getting all hysterical on me, Camille. We got a little water in the house is all. No point making more of it than what it is.

CAMILLE: Listen, Sug, when you woke me up with all that snoring of yours and I swung my legs out of bed, I stepped in water halfway up my knees. Scared the daylights out of me, but it couldn't've been deeper than a foot.

[*She makes her way to the folding stairs and points her flashlight down the stairs.*]

And look at it now, not five minutes later. That's got to be at least three feet of water inching up the stairs.

SUGAR: That's a damn lie.

CAMILLE: A lie? See for yourself, you think I'm lying.

SUGAR: No, not the water, woman. I mean the way you constantly complain I snore in bed. Why you always insist on going around telling people I'm a snorer when you know perfectly well you've never heard a snore come out of me?

CAMILLE: I've never heard you snore? Sug, either you snore or we've got ourselves some giant toad lives under our bed and spends the whole night croaking at the moon.

SUGAR: Go on and make fun if you want, but I've never once—not in my entire life—heard any snoring coming out of me. And the slightest little peep escaped my lips at night, I'd be the first to hear it. You know what a light sleeper I am.

CAMILLE: Oh yeah, you a light sleeper, all right. In our bedroom downstairs five minutes ago, I'm wading through water in the pitch dark, like I'm in some kind of dream or something, shouting, "Sugar, Sugar, the house is flooding." And you know what you do, you light sleeper, you?

SUGAR [*shrugging*]: Me? Why I jump right out of bed.

CAMILLE: No, that was just now—and only after I gave you a couple good whacks with my pillow to wake you up again. I tell you the house is filling up with water, I go splashing off down the hall with the flashlight to see if I can find where the water's coming from, and when I come back in the bedroom, what do I hear in the dark? That giant toad we got in there snoring his brains out again.

SUGAR: Now, Camille, you know I was up before dawn yesterday morning to see if the hurricane was still heading this way. Sure I'm a little sleepy tonight. What man wouldn't be after the day we had?

CAMILLE: But that's just it, Sugar. The rain's been over, I don't know, a good ten hours, maybe more. The hurricane's way up in Mississippi, Tennessee by now. So where's it from, all this water? It makes no sense.

SUGAR: How should I know where the water's coming from? *You* woke *me* up. I was sound asleep.

CAMILLE: You'd rather that I'd let you drown in bed?

SUGAR: All I'm saying is how am I supposed to know just where the hell it's coming from. Something sprung a leak, I guess.

CAMILLE: A leak? You really think our house is filled with water—our bedroom, kitchen, parlor, dining room—they're flooded thanks to . . . what? . . . some dripping pipe?

SUGAR: Might be the water heater or maybe something in the bathroom. You sure you jiggled the toilet handle before you went to bed?

CAMILLE: You think an overflowing toilet put all this water in our house?

SUGAR: I didn't say the toilet made it flood. It's just you never take the time to shake the handle when you're done . . . And really, when you get right down to it, such a simple thing to do. Wouldn't take you half a second. And then you wonder why our bill's so high.

CAMILLE: Well, Sugar, they come to find out our toilet's why there's water everywhere, I guarantee our bill will run a little high next month.

SUGAR: All right, all right, it's probably not the toilet made it flood.

[*Pause.*]

But by the way, as long as you and I are talking water bills, did you remember it this month? The bill, I mean. I think it's due the first.

CAMILLE: We've got a house that's filling up with water. Every stick of furniture we own and everything electrical, every piece of clothing's ruined. The two of us could drown tonight. But none of that concerns my husband. No, the thing that worries him the most: maybe I might not mail a bill on time. He wouldn't want us both to drown and not have paid our water bill this month.

SUGAR: You always put off paying them, the bills. Then every month, we've got those fees to pay. The water bill this month, it's just exactly why I have to nag you all the time.

CAMILLE: It's just exactly why you have to be a nag? Because you knew the day would come when we'd be trapped, with water lapping at the attic stairs from God knows where, and I'd forget to bring the bill. And that's "exactly why" you always have to be a pain in the neck about it every month?

SUGAR: "Exactly" in the sense of something unexpected that would come along like this, and we'd be stuck up here without our things, and then you couldn't mail the bill on time.

CAMILLE: Well, maybe I should dive into the pool that used to be our dining room and try to fish you out the bill before it's late.

SUGAR: But what's the good in doing that? By now, the bill's too soggy for an envelope.

CAMILLE: Will you forget the water bill for two seconds and tell me where all this water's coming from? No leaking pipe could fill our house just since we went to bed tonight.

SUGAR: Depends how big a leak it is.

CAMILLE: We're talking three damn feet of water, Sug, not just some bathroom mat that's soaking wet. And anyway, the water wouldn't stay. Even if we had a leak inside, the house would drain, not fill up like a tub.

SUGAR: I didn't say it's leaking from a pipe. I said I didn't know where the water might be coming from.

[*Pause.*]

And nothing about it on the radio—what stations I could get, at least—before we went to bed tonight. Of course, the batteries were nearly dead. It was hard to hear them clear, the news reports.

CAMILLE: I don't suppose that it occurred to you to bring the radio with you when you came up here?

SUGAR: You didn't bring it up with you?

CAMILLE: No, I grabbed the flashlight. The radio was on your side of the bed.
SUGAR: You want the radio so bad, I'll go down right now and get it for you.
CAMILLE: Are you out of your mind, Sugar?
SUGAR: I've waded in water way deeper than that before.
CAMILLE: I'm not letting you down those stairs again.

[*Silence.*]

SUGAR: Should've said something, you wanted the radio up here.
CAMILLE: Didn't think I needed to, something as obvious as that.
SUGAR: Nothing's obvious when you got water rushing into your house in the middle of the night.
CAMILLE: Just what I was getting at before. The water's coming in the house from somewhere else.
SUGAR: Probably the city's pumps backed up. Or maybe one of them went down. A miracle they work at all as old's they are.
CAMILLE: You telling me one broken pump put all this water in our house?
SUGAR: It doesn't work like that. One goes bad, another's got to do the job of two. So it burns out. And then a third one goes, and then—
CAMILLE: Yeah, yeah, yeah. One after another they all give out—
SUGAR: Until it floods. That's how it works. That's how everything works down here. One piece fails, the whole thing falls apart.
CAMILLE: But that makes no sense.
SUGAR: Ain't that the truth.
CAMILLE: No, I mean it makes no sense the pumps are why it's flooding now. The time the sun went down tonight, the streets were clear. That young couple from around the block—Charlene and what's-his-name—they were out walking their dog, remember? There wasn't any standing water left. Even if the pumping stations all shut down, there wasn't nothing left for them to pump.
SUGAR: Then you tell me. What else could it be?

[*Silence.*]

CAMILLE: What if you were right before?
SUGAR: What about?
CAMILLE: About a leak.
SUGAR: So now it's you thinks our bathroom's where the flood is coming from?
CAMILLE: No, Sugar, it's not about our plumbing we need to worry. What if it's the levee giving way?

SUGAR: The levee? Oh, don't talk crazy, woman. The U.S. Army built those things. The U.S. Army Corps of Engineers. You think they don't know how to hold the water back? A levee's not just mud. There's steel inside. No way a storm like what we had today could breach a levee.

CAMILLE: Yeah, we dodged a bullet when it veered away from us.

SUGAR: Dodged a bullet? I told you we had nothing to worry about. Those hurricanes that come this way, they hit the mouth of the river and always veer off to the east.

CAMILLE: But you got to admit, it was bad enough this morning. Maybe all those people left town yesterday weren't such idiots after all, now were they, Sug?

SUGAR: That'll be the day, I evacuate for some goddamn hurricane. We rode out Betsy when I was a boy, and I don't know how many other storms since. I'm not sitting twelve hours in a traffic jam from here to Baton Rouge just to wind up stuck in some motel in Houston for a hundred bucks a night. Not when you know the storm's gonna veer off anyway and hit Mississippi like it always does.

CAMILLE: Maybe so, but I'd've been a whole lot happier today sitting on the foot of a bed in that hundred-dollar motel in Texas watching it all on the TV.

[*Pause.*]

I was scared this morning, Sugar, when the storm come through. The wind clawing at the roof the way it did, shaking all the windows, rooting underneath the door—it was like some kind of beast battering the house, looking for a way in, a way to get at you and me.

SUGAR: Hell, I been through worse weather fishing down at Delacroix Island. A squall sneaks up behind you out there and day turns into night—now that'll put the fear of God in you, especially if your engine won't crank the first time you give the starter a tug or two.

CAMILLE: I hate it when you go out there alone in that little boat of yours.

SUGAR: A day like that and things go bad, another man wouldn't be the slightest bit of help—just someone else to drown with me and feed the crabs.

CAMILLE: Don't talk like that. You love to frighten me.

SUGAR: Come on, Camille, with all the fishing trips I've made alone, how many times I ever come home drowned?

CAMILLE: You think you're cute, but what's going on tonight, it's nothing to joke about. I couldn't say for sure—too hard to tell with the streetlights out and the moon behind a cloud—but when I pulled the bedroom curtain back, it looked like a river running wild outside, the water swirling over everything out there.

SUGAR: Well, no surprise in that. Makes sense, in fact. Maybe it's a water main outside that burst. Or sewers backing up from all the rain.

CAMILLE: A sewer backing up wouldn't put three feet of water in our house. It has to be the levees, Sug.

SUGAR: Camille, we got to be twelve, fifteen blocks from the levee. You have any idea how much it would take to flood the streets from there to here and then fill up our house with water three feet deep?

[CAMILLE *checks the water from the staircase opening.*]

CAMILLE: Four feet deep. It's come up another foot, at least.

SUGAR: Then four feet deep. Woman, you talking more water than you know.

CAMILLE: But that's exactly what I'm saying. Where else could so much water be coming from, it's not some levee giving way? That's Lake Pontchartrain down there in our living room, I guarantee.

SUGAR: So maybe it is the levees. I don't know.

[*Silence.*]

And anyway, what difference does it make where the hell it's coming from?

CAMILLE: We need to know what we are dealing with.

SUGAR: I'll tell you what we're dealing with—water, plain and simple.

[SUGAR *joins* CAMILLE *and points his flashlight down the stairs.*]

Lots and lots of water.

[*Silence.*]

Anyway, maybe you ought to stop worrying about what exactly happened and start worrying about what we're gonna do now we're up here.

CAMILLE: And what do *you* propose that we should do?

SUGAR: Wait until the water falls, I guess.

CAMILLE: What makes you think the water will go down? The land around here's nine, ten feet below sea level. There's nowhere lower it can run off to. And for all we know, the whole city may be flooding this very minute.

SUGAR: That's just plain foolishness to say a thing like that. Why would the city flood? The hurricane's long gone.

CAMILLE: Exactly. Something else is going on.

SUGAR: What are you getting at, Camille? You think the city's gonna sink to-night, and we all drown? If you were right, imagine what that would mean: a city under water. It's insane.

CAMILLE: You never heard of Atlantis?

SUGAR: A fairy tale for children, that's all Atlantis was. It's crazy what you saying, woman.

CAMILLE: Crazy? Things only sound crazy until they happen. But once they do, then people want to know why no one saw it coming, what went wrong.

SUGAR: New Orleans has been here for—what's it been?—three hundred years? You really think tonight's the night the city dies?

CAMILLE: I wish I knew why you're so sure it won't be tonight New Orleans disappears.

SUGAR: You hear yourself? New Orleans disappear? You act like this is Noah and the Flood we're dealing with. A little water in our house, that's all we're talking. A couple hours, it'll start to drain. You'll see.

[*Lights fade.*]

SCENE 2

[*Lights rise. An hour later.* CAMILLE *is sitting on a box.* SUGAR *is distracting himself by rooting around in the things stored in the attic.*]

SUGAR: What's all this junk we've stored up here?

CAMILLE: Think I know? Toys. Old furniture. What difference does it make? Five feet of water—most likely even more than that by now—is sitting in our house this very minute. Everything we own is gone, destroyed.

SUGAR: Not everything. This stuff is all OK. And nothing we can do about downstairs. So tell me what exactly we've got here.

CAMILLE: The things you wouldn't let me throw away.

SUGAR: You mean the things we thought we'd need again.

CAMILLE [*turning toward the attic stairs*]: The water, Sugar, the water's everywhere.

[SUGAR *picks up a toy beside him to distract her.*]

SUGAR: Like memories, sort of, stored away, these things.

CAMILLE: Yeah, like you said, just so much useless junk.

SUGAR: What's in that trunk? Your hope chest, isn't it?

CAMILLE: That's what my mother called it, anyway.

SUGAR: What hopes are lurking in that chest of yours?

CAMILLE: I don't remember. Photographs, I guess. And souvenirs. You know, just sentimental stuff you put away and never think about again.

SUGAR: Let's see.

[SUGAR *opens trunk, roots around a bit, pulls out wedding dress, and holds it up against himself.*]

Remember?

CAMILLE: Yeah, you made a lovely bride.

[*Pause.*]

Give it here.

[CAMILLE *takes the dress from him and covers herself with it.* SUGAR *looks at a wedding album from the trunk.*]

SUGAR: All morning long, the rain kept coming down.

CAMILLE: My father told me how it was good luck, to have it raining on your wedding day. And everyone was sure the rain would stop at least in time for us to go to church.

SUGAR: Except, as it turned out, they all were wrong.

CAMILLE: It rained so loud no one could hear the priest, and when we kissed, the thunder made us jump.

SUGAR: How many times I got to tell you there wasn't any thunder at the end?

CAMILLE: Yeah, I know. There was no clap of thunder. Just your heart, exploding with undying love for me.

SUGAR: At least that's how it felt when I kissed you.

CAMILLE: I've heard you tell that joke for over thirty years.

SUGAR [*offended*]: It's not a joke. How can you call it that? Exaggeration, maybe. But not much.

CAMILLE: I didn't mean to hurt your feelings, Sug. You know I think it's sweet when you say that.

SUGAR: I really was afraid my heart would burst. You looked so lovely standing there in white, your veil thrown back, your eyes about to close. I guess I couldn't quite believe my luck.

CAMILLE: You mean to have a girl like me love you?

SUGAR: More like . . . to find a girl like you to love.

CAMILLE: It wasn't 'cause I loved you half to death?

SUGAR: Oh sure. I liked the way you looked at me. But even more than that, I guess I knew I needed someone I could love. Someone like you.

CAMILLE: *Like* me? You mean you could have loved somebody else?

SUGAR: Aw, honey, you know that never crossed my mind. I wanted you.

CAMILLE: Still, as far as you're concerned, I didn't have to be the one you married, did I? Another girl would've done you just as well.

SUGAR: It's not a question of you or someone else. I was—what?—twenty-three, twenty-four when we got married. I just didn't see the point in being single anymore. I needed a reason to straighten out, you know, to get up every morning and go to work, not to come home fall-down-drunk from all those bars on Chef Menteur every night. I needed something to stop me living the way I was living in those days. Like I said, a reason to straighten out.

[*Pause.*]

You know, a wife.

CAMILLE: Well, that's about the most romantic thing I ever heard.

[*She throws the dress over his head.*]

You mean I was nothing but a cure for your hangover.

SUGAR: No, of course not. [*Thinking it over, as he hangs the dress up on a rafter*] But, yeah, in a way, you healed me.

CAMILLE: Healed you? Of what?

SUGAR: Of being me. Of being what I was.

CAMILLE: But that's the boy I fell in love with.

SUGAR: Maybe so. But you wouldn't've liked being that boy's wife, I promise you.

CAMILLE: How you know what I'd like?

SUGAR: C'mon, darling, you weren't nothing but a convent-school girl back then in that little plaid skirt you used to wear. What were you, seventeen years old when I met you?

CAMILLE: Nearly eighteen. But I knew what I was getting into with a boy like you.

[*Pause.*]

And so did my daddy.

SUGAR: Damn, he hated me at first, didn't he? And what did I ever do to him?

CAMILLE: Fell in love with me, that's what.

SUGAR: Or even worse, made you fall in love with me.

CAMILLE: Yeah, that's something he never could forgive you for.

[*Silence.*]

Didn't much care for your name, neither. "Sugar? What kind of name is Sugar for a man?" he used to say. "Sounds like a horse's name, a name like that."

SUGAR: Your mama, though, she liked me from the start.

CAMILLE: They were worried about different things, those two.

SUGAR: I guess we know how that goes, huh?

[*Pause.*]

CAMILLE: This isn't the night to get into all of that again.

SUGAR: No, you right. We got other things to worry about right now.

[*Pause.*]

Like how damn hot it is. It's sweltering up here, isn't it?

CAMILLE: Yeah, it's some hot. I can barely stand it.

SUGAR: I think it's kind of cozy, you and me up here alone.

[CAMILLE *fans herself with something she's found.*]

CAMILLE: I'm dying. Must be a hundred degrees at least.

SUGAR: Try to think of something else, Camille.

CAMILLE: Then why don't you tell me one of your stories, Sug, like you used to do when we first met?

SUGAR: What kind of story?

CAMILLE: I don't care. Something scary, something to make me shiver and cool me off.

SUGAR: My daddy told me a ghost story once.

CAMILLE: You never told me any ghost story before.

SUGAR: It's too sad. I never thought you'd want to hear it, sad as it is.

CAMILLE: Well, if ever there was a night for sad stories, Sugar, this is it.

SUGAR: Yeah, you right about that.

[CAMILLE *settles sideways onto a rocking horse.*]

CAMILLE: So how's it go, this ghost story of yours?

SUGAR: There was this freighter three days out of New Orleans, loaded with cotton and on its way to Panama. They're out there in the middle of the Gulf when the wife and the daughter of the ship's captain both die, a couple hours apart, of this fever they'd had since their first day at sea.

CAMILLE: Mother and daughter both?

SUGAR: I told you it was a sad story. The old-timers, they tell the younger hands it was all his own fault, the captain. Bad luck to bring a woman aboard a boat.

CAMILLE: Some old myth or something?

[SUGAR *looks at her as if she's simpleminded.*]

SUGAR: Just good sense, that. You put a woman on a ship and the men fall to fighting over her, everybody'd wind up dead or drowned long before they ever make it back to port again. So it was only as a special birthday present to his little girl, the captain taking her on a run like that. "Damn fool couldn't deny her anything," that's the way Daddy explained it. But mother and child, they both get sick their first day out. Probably just seasickness, the captain tells himself—

CAMILLE: But you don't get fever from that.

SUGAR: And you don't get seasick on a river where you got shoreline on both banks to keep you steady. So after a while, he sends the second mate to see to them. The sailor tends the woman and the girl best he can, but when they get too weak to swallow the aspirins he's taken from the medicine locker, all he can do is crush the pills under his thumb in the bowl of a spoon and add a few drops of water so they can drink the medicine. It doesn't do any good, though.

CAMILLE: The poor captain.

SUGAR: They wrap the bodies in canvas and bury them at sea. It's the custom for the ship's navigator to shoot the sun and fix the spot where the bodies are slipped over the side, so he notes it on the ship's chart and brings it to the captain for entry in the log.

CAMILLE: Why would anybody care? It's not as if you could put up a memorial out there in the middle of the ocean.

SUGAR: I guess it's just too sad the other way, abandoning the dead to an unmarked grave, even if it is the sea. Anyway, the freighter makes port in Colón and offloads its cotton bales and takes on its cargo, probably coffee, then retraces its route back home.

CAMILLE: The captain must have been a hard man to survive the loss of his whole family.

SUGAR: Not hard enough for what happened next. Two days out of Panama on their way back to New Orleans, an officer calls the captain to the bridge. Fifty yards off the starboard bow, the water has risen up—

CAMILLE: Risen up? You mean a wave?

SUGAR: No, the water rises up in the shape of two figures—one a bit taller than the other—and just sort of hangs there in the air. The captain drops his binoculars. "Sir," the navigator whispers, "we're very close to the spot, very close."

CAMILLE: Oh, you making this all up.

SUGAR: It's my father's story, not mine. As the ship slides past, the figures tremble there in the sunlight. Finally, the watch sees the two columns of water collapse after the stern has passed them by.

CAMILLE: What does the captain do?

SUGAR: By the time the ship docks a few days later in New Orleans, the captain's been locked in his cabin. Two orderlies from De Paul's lead him down the gangplank in a straitjacket.

CAMILLE: Now who'd believe a story like that?

SUGAR: Well, even being a boy, I didn't believe him yet, either. So Daddy tells me the rest. In a big port town like New Orleans, with boats coming and going every day, a story like that gets around in a hurry. So when the ship sets sail again a week later on the same run, the old newspaper, the *Item*, it sends a photographer along.

CAMILLE: And what happens when they pass the spot?

SUGAR: Same thing. These two watery figures rise up and shimmer there in the sunlight until the ship passes by. The paper, the *Item*, it runs the photo on the front page, and by the end of the week, the seafarers' union is threatening to strike, the shipping lines don't change the route to Panama.

[*Pause.*]

You know, they got that photograph—the picture of those two columns of water, the one that ran in the paper—they got it in some kind of archives on the third floor of the main library down on Tulane Avenue.

[*Silence.*]

CAMILLE: So did they?

SUGAR: Did they what?

CAMILLE: Did they change the route to Panama?

SUGAR: Hell yeah. The owners of the four shipping lines out of New Orleans, they had dinner that Sunday afternoon in one of those private dining rooms on the second floor of Antoine's. While they're sipping their coffee, waiting for the baked Alaska to come out, they take a napkin and plot a new course for their ships.

[*Pause.*]

Daddy said they still got that napkin in one of those display cases at the restaurant. And it's a fact the new route they plotted at lunch that day has been followed ever since.

CAMILLE: And no one ever went out there again? I mean where the woman and her little girl were buried.

SUGAR: In all that time, more 'n fifty years now, no ship has passed within ten miles of the spot. So whether the sea is calm there or whether a mother and her daughter have risen up like pillars of water every day since, no one can say.

[*Silence.*]

CAMILLE [*shuddering*]: Even hot as it is right now, it gives me goose bumps, thinking of that woman and her baby waiting out there in the middle of the ocean all alone.

SUGAR: Waiting for what? That's what I don't understand. What were they looking for?

CAMILLE: You don't think the dead have a claim on us?

SUGAR: Yeah, sure they do. But what is it they want, the dead?

CAMILLE: Whatever it is we haven't got to give 'em.

SUGAR: Man, the things scare you witless when you small, they just make you sad when you get old, don't they?

[*Silence.*]

CAMILLE: Well, it's a good story, but I'm still hot.

SUGAR: All the heat gets trapped up here.

CAMILLE: Come noon, this attic's gonna turn into an oven.

SUGAR: We'll be out of here long before then.

CAMILLE: What makes you think so?

[SUGAR *checks the depth of the water at the stairs.*]

SUGAR: Come see. It's better, isn't it? Not quite so deep.

[CAMILLE *joins him and points her flashlight down the hole.*]

CAMILLE: No, the water is still coming up.

SUGAR: But don't you think it's slowing down, at least?

CAMILLE: Four steps were dry last time I looked, and now there's only three that I can see. That doesn't look like "slowing down" to me.

SUGAR: Well maybe it's not done yet coming up. But how much longer can it flood like this?

CAMILLE: Until the water finds its level. Lake Pontchartrain's a few hundred square miles of water on a normal day. You add Katrina, no telling how deep it's gonna get before it stops.

SUGAR: I can't believe the levees failed.

CAMILLE: You think it's more than one?

SUGAR: I don't know, but why would one collapse and not the others? Those levees, they're all made the same. It makes no sense. The Corps of Engineers have promised beaucoup times the levees they'd hold against a Category 3. Katrina couldn't have been any more than that. The time she got here, after crossing Plaquemines and St. Bernard, how much of her could there've been left? We've had winds as bad before.

CAMILLE: And more rain. Remember that flood in May ten years ago? Just a summer rainstorm, but the city got twenty inches in eight hours. And still it didn't flood half as bad as this.

SUGAR: Maybe it's not the lake. Maybe something else went wrong that we don't know about.

CAMILLE: Like what?

SUGAR: Could be a ship or barge broke loose from its moorings in the Mississippi. Punched a hole in those river levees up near the zoo or along the French Quarter somewhere. Or could be something else we're overlooking. I don't know where it's coming from, all this water. But maybe we'd be smart to find a way up on the roof in case we need to get there later on.

CAMILLE: You think the water will get as high as that?

SUGAR: No, probably not. Still, just to be on the safe side, we ought to look around up here for tools, something I could use to cut our way out of here we need to. Wouldn't hurt to find some food as well, or maybe something we could drink.

CAMILLE: Good idea. About the tools, I mean. If ever there was any food up here, though, the roaches would have feasted on it long ago.

SUGAR: Yeah, but you never know what you're gonna find once you start looking.

[CAMILLE *turns away to search another part of the attic.*]

CAMILLE: Then be careful what you look for, Sugar. There's usually a good reason things get hidden.

[SUGAR *puts on a bull's head mask from a box and turns to* CAMILLE *with his flashlight shining on his mask from below.*]

SUGAR: Hey, look at this.

[CAMILLE *turns and laughs.*]

I found a box of our old costumes left from Mardi Gras.

[*He brings a sexy feathered mask from the cardboard box to* CAMILLE.]

Here.

[CAMILLE *puts on the mask.*]

CAMILLE: It's been a long time since we went in masks to Carnival.

[SUGAR *turns his light on her mask.*]

SUGAR: I don't know what it is, but there's something about a woman in a mask I've always liked.

CAMILLE: Well, there's something about wearing a mask sets a woman free.

SUGAR: You thinking of that Mardi Gras before we married?

CAMILLE: You imagine I might forget that night?

SUGAR: We were so drunk.

CAMILLE: Not half as drunk as we pretended.

SUGAR: Where was it?

CAMILLE: Your uncle's house.

SUGAR: My uncle's? No, it was Emelda's place, wasn't it? Not Uncle Duncan's.

CAMILLE: Sure it was your uncle's. Just off Prytania. That big white house.

SUGAR: Yeah, that's right.

CAMILLE: We walked there after the parades when the rain began to fall. It was getting cold all afternoon, remember?

SUGAR: You started trembling in that flimsy costume you were wearing. You went as—what was it?

[CAMILLE *veils the bottom of her face with the back of her hand.*]

CAMILLE: A harem girl.

SUGAR: Yeah, yeah. That was quite an outfit that you made.

CAMILLE: My father, he threw a fit that morning when he saw me in it. But Mama reminded him I was already engaged. She said the only thing mattered was whether you approved.

SUGAR: Oh, I approved, all right.

CAMILLE: I found out later just how much you did.

SUGAR: We had to get you warm somehow. I didn't want you catching cold.

CAMILLE: But how'd we wind up in that bedroom with your uncle downstairs?

SUGAR: You don't remember? He left us in the house all alone and told us lock the door behind us when we were done changing into something warm.

CAMILLE: Oh yeah. He had a party in the Quarter he was late for.

[*Pause.*]

Your family never guessed that he was gay?

SUGAR: Sure they knew. Just no one ever said. Mardi Gras wasn't the only day people went around in masks back then.

CAMILLE: I tell you, I look in the mirror these days, sometimes I think it's a mask staring back at me.

[*She touches her cheek.*]

How'd this face get old so fast? 'Cause underneath it, I feel just the same I always did.

SUGAR: You don't look old behind that mask you got on now.

CAMILLE: Then shall I keep it on for you?

SUGAR [*laughing*]: Think I don't remember that? You lying naked on Uncle Duncan's bed—with just that square of yellow silk across your face.

CAMILLE: I wouldn't have had the nerve without my mask. It let me play that I was some harem girl called against my will to be your concubine.

SUGAR: Where'd you ever learn a word like that?

CAMILLE: The nuns at school. It's somewhere in the Bible.

SUGAR: You looked at me when I came in and whispered, "Shall I keep it on for you, my mask?" I'll tell you, we came pretty close that night.

CAMILLE: But you were such a gentleman. Too much the gentleman, as far as I was concerned.

SUGAR: I thought that's how you showed a girl respect.

CAMILLE: It wasn't respect I was looking for just then.

SUGAR: It gets to be a habit in a hurry, don't it, the way you treat a person that you love? And so you never see when she's asking something different than you're used to giving.

CAMILLE [*teasing*]: I think maybe you were just too scared of what my daddy would've done, he'd found out I'd been your concubine.

SUGAR: Scared of your daddy? Me? No way.

[*Pause.*]

But disappointing your mama, that I wouldn't've liked.

CAMILLE: Yeah, I miss her, too.

SUGAR: She was some sweet, that woman.

CAMILLE: Loved you more than she loved me, I think.

SUGAR: Only 'cause she knew how much I loved her daughter.

CAMILLE: You flirtin' with me?

SUGAR: It's that mask you wearing.

[*He takes off his shirt.*]

Take off your gown, Camille.

CAMILLE: What, here? Tonight? With water rushing up the stairs? Are you out of your mind?

SUGAR: Why not? You got something better else to do? Let's go back to that night at Uncle Duncan's house. You leave on nothing but your mask, and I promise this time I won't be such a gentleman.

CAMILLE: Where would we even—

SUGAR: Right here. On your hope chest.

CAMILLE: With all that water coming up the stairs?

SUGAR: We might not have another chance.

CAMILLE: You said we'd be all right up here.

SUGAR: We'll be fine, I promise you.

[*He takes the wedding dress and spreads it over the chest like a sheet.*]

Let's go back to the beginning, Camille. We're in Uncle Duncan's bedroom up the stairs. The windows are all fogged up with rain. There's not much light. The room is full of shadows. And you, you're wearing nothing but a mask.

CAMILLE: Sug, this isn't the time for foolishness like that. The world outside is being washed away.

SUGAR: Maybe it's not the end of the world that's going on outside. Maybe it could be for us a new world just beginning.

CAMILLE: You talking crazy.

[CAMILLE *takes off her mask and hands it back to* SUGAR *along with his shirt that she's picked up.*]

Put your shirt back on, old man. And put away this foolish mask.

[SUGAR *is still shirtless, but he takes off his mask if it's still on at this point.*]

SUGAR: Camille, we may not get another chance.
CAMILLE [*more gently, as she folds the wedding dress and puts it away*]: Sugar, put your shirt back on. We wouldn't want you catching cold.

[*Lights fade.*]

SCENE 3

[*Lights rise. Another hour later.* CAMILLE *is huddled in a corner of the attic, dozing.* SUGAR *is stretched out on the floor, snoring loudly.* CAMILLE *is startled awake by* SUGAR's *snoring.*]

CAMILLE: Sug? Sugar. Wake up. We fell asleep again.

[SUGAR *is shaken awake by* CAMILLE.]

SUGAR: What? What's wrong?
CAMILLE: You were sleeping.
SUGAR [*half awake*]: Sleeping? Me? No, you crazy, woman. I'm wide awake. I was just resting my eyes is all.

[*He sits up and stretches, yawning loudly.*]

The water start to go down yet?
CAMILLE [*checking the stairs*]: Oh God, it's up another foot at least. Maybe more. What will we do if it keeps rising?

[SUGAR *joins her at the stairs.*]

SUGAR: I don't know. But even if it stays right where it's at, nobody knows we're in here. The sun come up tomorrow morning and the water hasn't fallen yet, as hot as it already is, this attic's gonna roast us to a crisp.
CAMILLE: Forget tomorrow morning. What are people doing tonight, Sugar, the ones who can't get in their attics like we did?
SUGAR: Standing on their chairs by now, I guess, climbing up on tables, countertops.
CAMILLE: But how long can they last like that, alone in the dark, water up around their throats?

SUGAR: You'd be surprised what people can survive when there's no other choice that's left to them. A lady down in St. Bernard, she stood three days on a kitchen chair when Betsy flooded everything out east.

CAMILLE: And she survived?

SUGAR: Oh yeah, she made it through till somebody heard her screaming there. They said her legs by then were swollen up the size of an elephant's. But she survived.

CAMILLE: If the water keeps on rising, Sugar? If it gets up ceiling high?

SUGAR: It can't go on all night.

CAMILLE: But if it does?

SUGAR [*turning away from stairs*]: It gets that high, a kitchen chair won't be enough.

CAMILLE [*following him*]: But wait a minute, Sugar. If inside water's six feet deep already, then, Jesus, it must be eight feet in the street. Our place is raised, but what about Miss Jeanfreau's house next door? It's on a slab. A slab house, it's only eight feet to the ceiling from the floor.

SUGAR: But Miss Jeanfreau, she's got an attic. Remember? She asked me go up there last winter and light her heater. I'm sure she's safe up there by now.

CAMILLE: Oh, Sugar, the woman's seventy-five years old. And she can't walk without a cane.

SUGAR: I'm sure she's fine.

[*Silence.*]

CAMILLE: Who could bear to think of such a thing? Miss Jeanfreau, all those people in pitch-dark rooms, balanced on a chair, a coffee table, standing on their mattresses with water up around their mouths—old people, parents holding up their kids against the ceiling—can you imagine what's going on right now? It's unbelievable. How many lives, one by one, are being lost this very minute? Here, in New Orleans, in our own city. How many men, how many women, how many children—children, Sugar—trapped in rooms so dark they can't even see the water drowning them?

SUGAR: But we don't know for sure what's going on. We have to keep our spirits up, Camille. Divert ourselves. Think of something else.

CAMILLE: It's horrible the things will happen here, the water keeps on coming up tonight.

SUGAR: Whatever happens, we've got to trust it's all God's will.

CAMILLE: So it's God's will all those little children drown, the cripples in wheelchairs, the folks too old to climb their attic stairs?

SUGAR: It's not for us to understand. It's a night to put our trust in faith.

CAMILLE: That would take more faith than I've got left.

[*Long silence.*]

SUGAR: Listen, did you hear that? Shouts, I think, or screams.

CAMILLE: No, nothing. I didn't hear a thing.

[SUGAR *goes to stairs and cranes his neck to hear better.*]

SUGAR: Are you sure? I thought I heard something.

[CAMILLE *joins* SUGAR *at the stairs.*]

CAMILLE: Just the water sloshing against the house, most likely. Or maybe a cat up a tree.

[*Silence.*]

Nobody's coming for us, Sug.

SUGAR [*turning away from the stairs*]: Then we'll just have to put our trust in God to get us through this.

CAMILLE [*still staring down the stairs*]: You mean the God that's drowning all those innocent people tonight in this city.

SUGAR: If He didn't test our faith, it wouldn't grow, our trust in Providence.

CAMILLE [*crossing from the stairs*]: Providence? There's a good eight feet of water in the street. You think God is getting ready to send his angels down here to fly through the city and carry us all off to high ground? You think that's what's going on outside right now?

SUGAR: Don't blaspheme, Camille.

CAMILLE: You know, a sky full of angels saving the faithful. Listen. You can hear their wings fluttering in the dark. In fact, that's probably what you heard just now—angels hovering in the night, coming to save us all from a watery grave.

SUGAR: Mock all you want, if ever there was a night for faith, this is it.

CAMILLE: If ever there was a night to question your religion, this is it. How can you worship a god who'd do this to us?

SUGAR: Oh, don't talk foolish, woman. You think it's God did this to us. This water is probably just somebody didn't do his job. Some terrible mistake somebody made and didn't care enough to set it right.

CAMILLE: Then that's even worse than God did this to us. You and me, we've lost everything we own. How many people drowned in their own bedrooms since the sun went down? And it's all because somebody cut some corners, didn't pay attention to some detail, decided things were close enough to right and let it go at that? You telling me that's why we're trapped here in our own attic in the middle of the night with water lapping at the stairs? That's the reason we could die tonight, you and me?

SUGAR: If it's our levees broke, they didn't fall down all by themselves, Camille. If it's the levees giving way, there's somebody responsible.

CAMILLE: Well, if it's not God responsible, then the men did this to us, I hope they never lie down in bed they don't hear the ghosts of those they drowned tonight crying out for help. I die tonight, I'll never let them sleep, those murderers, I promise you.

[*Long silence.*]

SUGAR: We're not going to die. Not if we find a way out onto the roof.

[*Silence.*]

We need something sharp. Or maybe something we could use to pry the boards loose.

[*He looks around.*]

If I could just work that vent free over there, we wouldn't have to cut a thing. Slip out through the hole instead.

CAMILLE: Can you knock it free?

SUGAR: The screws in its base must be loose. It rattles whenever the wind blows hard.

CAMILLE: So that's the thing we always hear at night?

SUGAR: See you can't find something back there I could use like a screwdriver.

[CAMILLE *searches through some boxes in the back of the attic.*]

CAMILLE: There's nothing here.

[SUGAR *also searches the attic.*]

SUGAR: Now watch where you step in the dark over there. The floor is soft in spots.

CAMILLE: Where?

SUGAR: Everywhere up here we don't have flooring. It's nothing but sheetrock between the joists. You'll fall right through the ceiling, you put your weight in the wrong place.

CAMILLE: You mean I could fall through the ceiling and drown?
SUGAR: Just be careful where you step.

[*Pause.*]

Isn't that Frankie's toy toolbox?
CAMILLE: Where?
SUGAR: There . . . behind that table lamp.
CAMILLE: It is. It's Frankie's toys.
SUGAR: What's he got there in his tool kit? A screwdriver, maybe?
CAMILLE: Yeah, but tiny.

[*She holds it up.*]

SUGAR: Don't worry. That'll do.

[*He takes the screwdriver.*]

CAMILLE: And look, his baseball cap.

[SUGAR *starts to slowly unscrew the vent in the roof with the little screwdriver.*]

SUGAR: It barely fits, but it'll do. The screw is turning. [*With effort*] Slowly, but it's turning.

[CAMILLE *handles child's baseball cap.*]

CAMILLE: Remember how he wore this thing twenty-four hours a day when he was small? Wouldn't even take it off long enough for me to wash it. I'd have to wait until he was sound asleep before I could ease it off his head at night.
SUGAR [*working on the vent*]: Yeah, and remember the afternoon he lost it at the picture show? The way he cried, you'd have thought the world was ending.
CAMILLE: It took five minutes just to calm him down enough to get him to tell us what was wrong.
SUGAR: And then we had to go back in again to find his hat.
CAMILLE: You on your hands and knees in the dark, crawling behind the row that we'd been sitting in.
SUGAR: Reaching underneath the seats, searching for his hat—
CAMILLE: Until you grabbed that woman's ankle in the dark.
SUGAR: Good thing his cap was underneath there, too.
CAMILLE: Her, screaming like a rat had bit her leg or something.

SUGAR: Me, crawling backwards out of there, waving the cap over my head, whispering like a crazy person, "I was looking for a hat, I was looking for a hat."

[*Silence.*]

CAMILLE: The things you do, you got a child.
SUGAR: The things you should have done.
CAMILLE: Not tonight, Sug. We're not talking about all that tonight.

[SUGAR *is having trouble with the vent and turns to* CAMILLE.]

SUGAR: What did we ever do to him, made the boy so angry?
CAMILLE: I used to think it was us responsible, too. But now I'm not so sure.
SUGAR: How could it not be the parents' fault, things turn out the way they did?
CAMILLE: You think it's all your parents' doing, you turned out the way you did?
SUGAR: I think the way I treated Frankie, it wasn't so different from how my father treated me.
CAMILLE: That boy adored you, he was small.
SUGAR: And I was small, I thought my daddy hung the moon.
CAMILLE: A father can only do what he thinks he ought to do.
SUGAR: That don't absolve him, things go wrong.

[*Silence.*]

CAMILLE: Maybe it's just plain easier for us to imagine we're the ones responsible. It would be a whole lot worse thinking that what's wrong with Frankie, he never can outgrow.
SUGAR: I outgrew the life I lived when I was young.
CAMILLE: You never took up the habits Frankie's got.
SUGAR: Only 'cause you came along in time.

[*Silence.*]

CAMILLE: People think it's up to them, how their lives turn out. But when you get right down to it, how much luck—how much blind luck—decides which one of us gets to laugh and which one cries?

[SUGAR *tries to go back to work on the vent.*]

SUGAR: Well, we could use some luck tonight, I'll tell you that.

CAMILLE: Compared to some tonight, we've maybe had our share of luck already.

[SUGAR *works on the vent with difficulty.*]

SUGAR: Then I think we need a second helping.
CAMILLE: You having trouble?

[SUGAR *gives up on the vent in exasperation.*]

SUGAR: My hands are too damn big for this toy screwdriver.
CAMILLE: Let me try.
SUGAR: I loosened all the screws. It shouldn't be too hard to do.

[CAMILLE *starts unscrewing the vent.*]

CAMILLE: They're coming easy.
SUGAR: I'm starving. You sure there's nothing here to eat?
CAMILLE [*unscrewing vent*]: The roaches would have found it long ago.
SUGAR: Not if it's inside something sealed up tight.
CAMILLE [*unscrewing vent*]: I wouldn't have stored any food up here.
SUGAR: I'm talking just by accident. You know, something you might put up here by mistake, thinking it was something else.
CAMILLE [*unscrewing vent*]: Don't waste your time looking. I swear there's nothing here to find. Come hold your light so I can see the screws. I think the vent is nearly free.

[SUGAR *shines his light on the vent.*]

SUGAR: You're almost there. Just another turn or two.
CAMILLE [*loosening vent*]: I think I got it, Sugar. The vent's come loose.
SUGAR: Wait, let me see.

[SUGAR *struggles with the vent until it gives way. Moonlight streams in through the hole.*]

Yeah, it's free.
CAMILLE: Oh, thank God.
SUGAR: Let's get you on the roof.

[*They move the hope chest beneath the vent.*]

A boat comes by, and no one's there to call for help, they'll just go on and won't come back till who knows when.

[SUGAR *helps* CAMILLE *up onto the chest.*]

CAMILLE [*on the hope chest beneath the hole*]: You coming, too, aren't you?
SUGAR: Yeah, right behind you. Just let me check how high the water is.

[SUGAR *goes to the stairs.*]

CAMILLE: How deep is it?

[SUGAR *dips his hand into the water and lifts it up dripping wet.*]

SUGAR: It's bad, real bad. Nearly in the attic now. It's time we got up on the roof.

[SUGAR *crosses to the chest.*]

CAMILLE: We'll be all right, won't we, Sug? Once we're on the roof, we'll be all right?
SUGAR [*as he begins to lift* CAMILLE *through the hole*]: Woman, after what we been through and survived tonight, how could things get any worse?

[*Blackout.*]

ACT II

SCENE 1

[*The dark roof of the house in moonlight. The sound of water sloshing.* CAMILLE *begins to emerge from the hole where the vent had been.*]

CAMILLE [*with only her head out, surveying the scene in wonder*]: Oh, Sugar, you won't believe the way it looks out here.

[*Silence.*]

Boost me up.

[*She climbs out of the hole and onto the roof. Silence.*]

The water stretches off to the horizon. There's nothing but roofs and tree-tops left.

[*Silence.*]

They look like boats floating on the water, the roofs. Like some wrecked fleet of ships, all upside down, adrift in the middle of the ocean.

SUGAR [*unseen*]: Anyone else made it to a roof?

CAMILLE: No one I can see from here. And not a single light, as far as I can tell. Even with the moon out, I've never seen a place as dark as this.

SUGAR [*unseen*]: Shout and see anyone answers back.

CAMILLE [*shouting*]: Anyone there?

[*Silence.*]

Anybody hear my voice?

[*Silence.*]

SUGAR [*unseen*]: Someone answer?

CAMILLE: No one. It's deadly quiet out here, Sugar. Nothing but the sound of water lapping at the roof.

[*Silence.*]

No dogs, no motors, no human voices. Nothing.

SUGAR [*unseen*]: Try again.

CAMILLE [*shouting*]: Hello? Hello?

[*Silence.*]

Anybody there?

[*Silence.*]

Miss Jeanfreau? Anybody?

[*Silence.*]

SUGAR [*unseen*]: Any luck?

CAMILLE: Not a sound. No wind. No birds. Nobody knocking. Nothing but the sloshing of the water.

SUGAR [*unseen*]: Everyone's probably still sitting in their attics, waiting for dawn before they get up on their roofs.

CAMILLE: The ones made it to their attics, maybe. But how many people you think already drowned in all this water?

[*Silence.*]

Sugar, come up here. I'm frightened to be alone the way it is.

[*Silence.*]

It's all so still, so dark, so quiet. As if it's me alone survived what's happened.

[SUGAR *sticks his head through the vent hole.*]

SUGAR: You're not alone. I'm right here beside you. [*Pausing as he looks around*] Jesus God.

[*Silence.*]

CAMILLE: Come up here on the roof with me.

SUGAR [*still only his head visible*]: This hole is smaller than I thought it was.

[SUGAR *struggles to squeeze through.*]

I don't know if I can squeeze my body through. [*Still struggling*] It's tight, this opening. [*Wincing*] And sharp.

CAMILLE: Come on, Sugar. If I could do it, you can, too.

SUGAR [*still trying to squeeze through*]: No, the hole's too small for me.

CAMILLE: You'll fit. Just squeeze your shoulders like I did.

[SUGAR *is apparently stuck.*]

SUGAR: I tell you it won't work, Camille.

CAMILLE: Then make the hole wider.

SUGAR [*with just his head and one arm visible*]: With what? All I've got me are those toy tools of Frankie's.

CAMILLE: I'm not staying out here by myself, Sugar. You got to find a way to get up here.

SUGAR [*still with just his head and one arm visible*]: Hang on a minute. Let me see what I can find to widen this.

[*He descends back into the attic.*]

CAMILLE [*shouting down the hole*]: You need some help? I'll come back in.

SUGAR [*his head emerging through the hole*]: No, you stay up here, no matter what. A boat comes by, and there isn't one of us to flag it down, we'll miss our chance. We'll just keep talking, you and me, until help comes. They must be on their way by now, the rescue boats and helicopters.

CAMILLE: I'd like it better you were here with me up on the roof.

SUGAR [*laughing with only his head visible*]: I'm here with you—just not all of me. [*Pausing as he looks around*] My God, it's beautiful though.

CAMILLE: What is?

SUGAR [*only his head visible*]: The moonlight on the water.

CAMILLE: And so, so still. I haven't heard another sound—no breeze, no animals, no baby crying in the dark. It frightens me for it to be so quiet.

SUGAR: The people, they'll come out when there's some light. They're huddled in their attics now. The roofs are just too thick for us to hear them there.

CAMILLE: That must be it. We're surely not the only ones who made it through all this.

[*Silence.*]

SUGAR: I'd forgotten what it's like before the sun comes up. How calm, how peaceful everything can seem.

CAMILLE [*sitting*]: I don't know you and I ever watched a dawn together.

SUGAR: Not that I remember—but that can't be. How can two people spend so many years together and never see the sun come up?

CAMILLE: When I was a little girl, I always thought the rising sun would look like the golden sail of some big ship coming to carry me away, swelling bigger and bigger the nearer it got.

SUGAR: Well, you stay up here and keep a lookout for that boat with a golden sail—and anything else floats by. Something comes this way, you start shouting for help, y'understand? I'm going to see what I can find to cut myself out of here.

[*He disappears down the hole.*]

CAMILLE: It's just so dark and silent here tonight, it feels as if there's no one else alive. Like being marooned alone on some small island or—I don't know—the sole survivor of a sunken ship, drifting in a lifeboat all night long. Wouldn't that be awful, Sug? To be the sole survivor when your ship goes down. With no one else alive but you. Just you and all that water.

[*Silence.*]

It makes me nervous—waiting all alone up here for you.

[*Silence.*]

I'm talking to you, Sugar. Did you hear what I just said?

SUGAR [*unseen*]: I heard it, every word, Camille. Don't worry, I won't be long in here. There must be something in the attic would do the job.

[*His arm and then head emerge through the hole.*]

And, look, you sure there's nothing we can eat up here? Hard candy, maybe? That would do me fine for now.

CAMILLE: You could stand to go a whole night without food for once, you know, and maybe lose a little of that weight. You didn't stuff yourself on silver bells and goldbricks all the time, this hole'd be big enough for you the way it is.

SUGAR: Yeah, well, it's not just me I'm worried about when it comes to starving.

CAMILLE: Who you think you foolin', Sug? I'm not the one keeps a stash of jelly beans beside the bed.

SUGAR: I wish I'd thought to bring them up the stairs with me tonight.

CAMILLE: It's no mystery how you come by your name, I'll tell you.

SUGAR: How many times Mama told you they called me Sugar 'cause everybody said I was the sweetest baby New Orleans ever saw?

[*Pause.*]

CAMILLE: Was there ever a baby born into a world like this? I don't recognize a thing about it.

SUGAR: Old world or new, I still need to eat.

CAMILLE: I promise you there's not a scrap of food in there. Not with all the roaches we would have. Go just find a saw or something you can use to get yourself out here. What if a boat comes by and you're still stuck in there?

SUGAR [*disappearing again*]: All right, let me look and get this done.

[*Silence.*]

CAMILLE: You know, what you said before, I'm beginning to think you might be right. In this moonlight, everything looks so strange, so fresh. Maybe it's not the end of the world, this rising water.

SUGAR [*unseen*]: I can't hear you. Somebody coming?

CAMILLE [*louder*]: No, no sign of anyone. [*Softer*] I was just saying, though, maybe you were right before. It looks so different up here now. Maybe you and me, we could go back and start again.

[*Silence.*]

I mean, with everything disappearing—our house, our things—like you said, our past is being washed away. It's left us sort of standing on a mountaintop up here, like Noah's Ark coming to rest after all that rain.

[*Silence.*]

Oh, Sugar, you really think it's possible? You really think two people—the two of us—we could begin again?

SUGAR [*an arm and then his head emerging through the hole*]: You calling me?

CAMILLE: What? No, I was just thinking out loud about what you said before.

SUGAR [*only his arm and head visible*]: What's that?

CAMILLE: About us going back to when we met and starting over fresh.

SUGAR: I was just teasing you, Camille, that's all. How's it possible, that, anyway, after all we've been through, you and me? How could we ever forget what we already know?

CAMILLE: But isn't that what people mean, they talk about forgive and forget? You let it go, all the anger, the hurt—

SUGAR: And then you spend the rest of your life pretending to forget.

CAMILLE: Isn't that what I had to do with you?

SUGAR: Camille, that was a long time ago.

CAMILLE: But never long enough. [*Sighing*] I guess you right about forgetting. Neither one of us forgot it yet, what you done to me, even after all these years.

SUGAR: Well, it don't come up so much as it used to anymore.

CAMILLE: For you, it don't, maybe.

SUGAR [*slamming his hand on the roof*]: Nothing I can ever do to make that right, is there?

[*Silence.*]

How many times you want an apology for one damn night? I've spent my whole life ever since saying I'm sorry for what I did to you that evening.

[*Silence.*]

You know, you're not the first woman to feel a belt across her back. And I haven't laid a hand on you in all this time. I haven't touched a bottle once. I've come home every night for thirty years. How many ways I got to prove to you I learned my lesson?

CAMILLE: Learning the lesson don't change needing that lesson in the first place.

SUGAR: Husbands have done far worse to wives and been forgiven.

CAMILLE: You still don't understand the way a single night can change everything between two people, do you?

SUGAR: You think that's something I don't know? The whole damn world can change from dusk to dawn. Go to bed thinking everything's OK, thinking you survived the worst; wake up with water filling up your house.

CAMILLE: But that's exactly what I'm saying, Sug. Tonight's a night that maybe everything could change between the two of us.

SUGAR: So you finally ready to forget what it was I done?

CAMILLE: Forget? No, you right about that. Nobody ever forgets nothing. Not really. But choosing what to remember, that's something we could do.

SUGAR: And what is it exactly you'd choose, Camille? What's the thing that you'd remember, you had your choice?

CAMILLE: Me? Yeah, our first Mardi Gras, I guess. A girl doesn't forget a night like that.

[*Pause.*]

And other things . . .

SUGAR: Like what?

CAMILLE: Like that other thing you always say I ought to put behind me.

SUGAR: If anything needs forgetting, it's that.

CAMILLE: You think a mother could ever forget something like that?

SUGAR: But how long can a person hang on to grief, Camille? The anger burns itself out, like a candle you cover with a glass. It flares, but then it eats up all the air inside and suffocates.

CAMILLE [*angrily*]: When you hear me bring up anything about it last?

SUGAR: Just try to get that glass off the table, then. It's a vacuum, stuck so tight it won't budge—but with something burned-out still inside.

CAMILLE: Yeah, maybe I was like that for a while—stuck fast to what had happened. But you were just as bad the other way. Refusing to admit—

SUGAR: There wasn't nothing to admit. We didn't do anything wrong, Camille. Some things, there's nothing anyone can do to stop them happening.

[*Silence.*]

You don't think I would've rather died myself than anything happen to that little girl of ours. But you can't spend your whole damn life saying good-bye, Camille. Sooner or later, you got to stop looking over your shoulder. It'll turn you into a pillar of salt, just like Lot's wife, looking back all the time.

CAMILLE: Lot's wife must have been somebody's mama. That's what it means to have a child—spending the rest of your life always looking over your shoulder to be sure they're still trailing after you.

SUGAR: You live that way too long, Camille, after a while, it's like I say. All that's left of you is salt for rubbing into a wound that's always open.

CAMILLE: I'm not the one went searching for those pictures in the flood downstairs.

SUGAR: And I'm not saying I don't think of Suzie every day. But it's wrong to make of her this, I don't know, this little anchor still holds us fast to some awful morning thirty years ago.

[*Silence.*]

CAMILLE: It can't be done, can it? I mean, pretend the past is not some anchor keeping us in place?

SUGAR [*sighing*]: Yeah, it's not that we can't go back and start again. It's that we can't help but go back, over and over again. You think your boat is get-ting somewhere, making headway, but really, you're chained to the bottom and just don't know it. We're sailing in a circle all the time.

CAMILLE: Oh, Sugar, what's ahead of us, you and me?

SUGAR: We went to bed tonight, I thought I knew.

CAMILLE: So did a lot of people already dead since then.

SUGAR: Well, we're not that.

CAMILLE: Not yet, at least.

[*Silence.*]

But tell you the truth—if that's what it is we're finally doing—I don't feel like I'm alive, either. In fact, I haven't felt like I'm alive in a long, long time now. Not like it felt when we first met.

SUGAR: You think it's any different for me?

[*Silence.*]

Probably the same for everyone. Just nobody ever dares put it into words.

CAMILLE: Suzie gone. Frankie lost. I don't know I feel I even deserve to be alive, you get right down to it.

SUGAR: How can we feel it's not all our fault, the things that happen?

[*Pause.*]

But maybe you right. Maybe this is some second chance for us tonight.

[*Silence. Lights fade.*]

SCENE 2

[*Lights rise. An hour later, now about 5:00 A.M.* CAMILLE *is lying on the roof.* SUGAR *is still in the hole.*]

SUGAR: I never knew dying could be so boring.

CAMILLE: I thought you said we're gonna be OK up here.

SUGAR: Just a figure of speech, Camille. All I mean is, it's so damn boring stuck up here all night long.

CAMILLE: Well maybe if you'd thought to bring the radio up with you from downstairs, we'd have something to listen to right now.

SUGAR: The batteries were nearly dead already the time we went to bed.

[*Pause.*]

And anyway, they're not playing music on the radio tonight.

CAMILLE: No, they probably trying to figure out what in the hell's going on around here, just like us.

[*Silence.*]

SUGAR: I tell you, my back is killing me, stuck here in this hole. Let me change arms.

[*He descends and then the other arm emerges, followed by his head.*]

CAMILLE: Be careful, Sug. You move too much, those jagged edges there will cut you to ribbons. Then what would we do, you bleeding to death on this rooftop without a boat in sight.

SUGAR [*struggling a bit in the hole*]: Yeah, you right. I'm wedged in here too tight to climb up any higher. But damn my back is getting sore. I'd go lie down in the attic for a while, but I can feel the water around my feet. It's still inching up, I think.

CAMILLE: We got to entertain ourselves, that's what we got to do. Keep our minds off everything.

SUGAR: Entertain ourselves how?

CAMILLE: I don't know.

[*Pause.*]

We used to play a game when I was small. "Secrets," they called it.

SUGAR: Secrets?

CAMILLE: Yeah, you go back and forth, telling each other secrets you're not supposed to say.

SUGAR: What kind of secrets?

CAMILLE: Ones you don't want me to know about.

SUGAR: Then why would I tell you?

CAMILLE: Because we might as well be honest with each other if we're going to die tonight like you said before.

SUGAR: But what if we don't die? Then where would I be? You'd know my secret.

CAMILLE: What secret?

SUGAR: I mean if I had a secret.

CAMILLE: But you do have secrets.

SUGAR: What secrets?

CAMILLE: I don't know, like that time you walked in on Tina taking a bath.

SUGAR: You know about that?

CAMILLE: Of course I know about that. Tina was my best friend. She told me you really got an eyeful, too. She was afraid you were going to sit down on the edge of the tub and have a little chat with her.

SUGAR: I got flustered, that's all. It's not easy to back out of a room.

CAMILLE: Yeah, I bet it's hard when you can't even turn your eyes to find the doorknob.

SUGAR: It was an accident, walking in like that. How was I to know she was in there?

CAMILLE: And she told me about that other time you saw her naked.

SUGAR: I don't remember that.

CAMILLE: How could you forget? It was that weekend we went down to Orange Beach and shared the cabin with her and Buddy. Come on, Sugar. This is our chance to reveal—after all these years together—to really reveal what's been going on inside us, who we really are.

SUGAR: I don't think that's such a good idea.

CAMILLE: Well, if you're too chicken, then I'll have to start.

SUGAR: It's really not a good idea.

CAMILLE: When we used to, you know what I mean, in bed, I'd pretend you were Sean Connery.

SUGAR: The actor?

CAMILLE: Of course the actor.

SUGAR: But he was so much older than you.

CAMILLE: Yeah, I liked that.

SUGAR: Why did you have to pretend at all? I was strong, handsome.

CAMILLE: Handsome? No, I wouldn't say handsome. Solid, maybe.

SUGAR: Solid? You mean chunky?

CAMILLE: Well, not solid. Not exactly. But, you know, rugged. How's that? You were rugged.

SUGAR: Rugged? Yeah, that would be OK.

CAMILLE: And so was Sean.

SUGAR: Sean? You called him by his first name?

CAMILLE: Well, what do you think I was pretending? "Oh, Mr. Connery, you're divine, you're wonderful." Of course I called him "Sean."

SUGAR: And what did he call you?

CAMILLE: I don't know. You were playing him. What did you call me?

SUGAR: I wasn't playing anybody. I was playing myself. I mean, I was just myself.

CAMILLE: But you must have been pretending I was somebody else.

SUGAR: No, I wasn't.

CAMILLE: Liar.

SUGAR: Oh sure, the night I walked in on Tina in the bathtub, maybe she crossed my mind.

CAMILLE: You slept with Tina!

SUGAR: No, of course not. But it was only natural, seeing her, you know, leaning back in the tub with her eyes closed. How could I not think of her that night?

CAMILLE: Just the one night?

SUGAR: Well, maybe a couple times after that. I don't know, it was all so long ago.

CAMILLE: So when was the last time you were thinking about my best friend like that?

SUGAR: I don't remember the last time—

CAMILLE: You thought about her every time, didn't you?

SUGAR: No, not every time.

[*Pause.*]

Sometimes I'd think of Madonna.

CAMILLE: The singer? The one who wears those funnels on her breasts.

SUGAR: They're not funnels. It's a costume.

CAMILLE: So I'm lying there thinking you're whispering, "Oh, my darling, my darling," and you're really sighing, "Oh, Madonna, Madonna."

SUGAR: No, of course not. That sounds stupid. "Oh, Madonna, Madonna." I call her "Louise."

CAMILLE: Louise? Why Louise?

SUGAR: That's her real name. Madonna Louise Veronica Ciccone.

CAMILLE: I can't believe you've been unfaithful to me with a girl who wears funnels on her tits.

SUGAR: They're not funnels. They're just part of her costume. And anyway, it's your own fault if I had an affair with a beautiful rock star.

CAMILLE: My fault? You cheat on me with a girl with tin tits and somehow I'm the guilty party.

SUGAR: Once you stopped singing to me in bed, I had to find someone else to take your place.

CAMILLE: I never sang to you in bed.

SUGAR: Sure you did. Remember? You used to lie in the dark afterwards, when everything was so still, and you'd sing those funny little songs to me.

CAMILLE: What songs?

SUGAR: You know. [*Singing*] "If ever I cease to love."

CAMILLE: Oh, you're out of your mind. It must have been Madonna that used to sing to you.

SUGAR: Come on, sing it with me.

CAMILLE: No, I won't sing it with you. It was some other girl used to sing to you in bed.

SUGAR: You know there's never been another girl in my bed. Just you.

CAMILLE: And Tina. And—what do you call her?—Louise.

SUGAR: Come on. Sing to me.

CAMILLE: I don't even know how it goes, your stupid song.

SUGAR: Sure you do. [*Singing*] "If ever I cease to love."

CAMILLE [*without enthusiasm*]: "If ever I cease to love."

SUGAR: Remember? [*Singing*] "The moon would turn to green cream cheese, if ever I cease to love." [*Speaking*] Now sing the whole thing to me, the way you used to.

CAMILLE: This is stupid. I'm not singing it.

SUGAR: But you do remember singing to me in bed, right?

CAMILLE: No.

SUGAR: Don't be angry with me. I told you this was a dangerous game, telling secrets.

[*Pause.*]

So you got any other secrets you been keeping from me?

CAMILLE: None you ever gonna find out about.

SUGAR: Now that's enough to make a husband worry the rest of his life, something like that coming out of his wife's mouth.

[*Silence.*]

CAMILLE: All you need to worry about is how much I love you. And I love you plenty. You know that.

[*Silence.*]

SUGAR: Be honest with you, I can't say I know why you love me at all.

[*Pause.*]

CAMILLE: I'll tell you, then.

[*Pause.*]

Just after Frankie left the last time, stormed out of the house for good after the fight the two of you'd had that night, I saw you standing in the hallway, closing the door to his bedroom. You pulled it shut so gently, you broke my heart. And I couldn't shake the sight of you, standing there before his door, like someone lost, not knowing where to go.

[*Silence.*]

SUGAR: I have to pull the door shut every night on Frankie's room to have a chance of getting any sleep at all. I can't bear to see them in the dark, his things. The model planes still on his desk, the posters curling on the walls.

[*Pause.*]

I can't sleep I know his door is open.

[*Silence.*]

CAMILLE: I think love's got a whole lot more to do with pity than people are willing to admit.

SUGAR: Pity? That's what you think love is?

CAMILLE: How many times you've taken pity on me, Sug?

SUGAR: When I ever show you any pity?

CAMILLE: How many times just tonight you pitied me how scared I was? How many times you pitied me getting old and lied how pretty I still look? How many times you pitied our boy, out there somewhere doing what he does? The heart don't break for someone it don't love.

SUGAR: Well, I know I give *you* plenty to pity. I guess that's what makes me so lovable, huh?

CAMILLE: I'm not joking, Sugar. You said you'd rather've died than it was Suzie we found that morning. You think that's not taking pity, you'd rather die than someone else? And the longer two people been together, the more you feel it, don't you, that sympathy for what the other person's going through?

SUGAR: I don't know I'd call all that pity.

CAMILLE: I don't mean you feel better than the other person—you know, superior, something like that. Just your heart breaks for them, don't it, somebody you love? That's what I'm talking about, I guess. That kind of pity.

SUGAR: So it was nothing but pity, then, you taking Sean Connery into your bed?

CAMILLE: Yeah, just like it couldn't've been anything but pity, Madonna letting you sleep with her.

SUGAR: You know, woman, you some bad.

CAMILLE: Lucky for you.

SUGAR: And lucky for Sean Connery.

[*Silence.*]

SUGAR [*looking up*]: The stars are out tonight.

CAMILLE: I know. It's so dark with all the power off, you can see them, every one. When you think the last time was anyone could see so many stars over New Orleans?

SUGAR: Go back a hundred years, at least.

CAMILLE: Oh, more than that. Two hundred, maybe more.

SUGAR: All those stars, and so much water.

CAMILLE: All the way to the horizon.

SUGAR: Reminds me of where my father and I used to fish—when I was a boy, I mean—down in the marsh. That's where he told me that ghost story of his.

CAMILLE: I can't believe he'd tell a little child a story like that. Hot as it is up here, just thinking of that mother and her baby makes me shiver.

SUGAR: Well, it gave me more than goose bumps, hearing it the way Daddy told it.

CAMILLE: It wasn't like the way you said to me?

SUGAR: To be the same, I'd have to whisper it so close to your face you could smell my breath—but in darkness so black you couldn't even see my lips.

CAMILLE: How's that possible?

SUGAR: We were deep in the marsh, way back down one of those winding canals off the ship channel, fishing speckled trout. It was already nearly three, so my father tried to start the engine. He pulled on the cord till I thought he would rip the top off the motor, but it didn't even cough.

CAMILLE: How old were you?

SUGAR: I don't know. Nine. Maybe ten.

CAMILLE: You were just a baby.

SUGAR: No, I wasn't a baby. I was ten years old.

CAMILLE: Oh, you were a baby. Ten years old.

SUGAR: OK, then, I was a baby. Anyway, bobbing there in our little boat, Daddy changed the spark plugs, cleaned the lines, went through the whole drill. But when he popped the cover back on and tugged the cord again—nothing. We were stuck. And hunkered back in the marsh the way we were, we hadn't seen another boat in a couple of hours.

CAMILLE: So what did your father do?

SUGAR: What he always did. He pulled a bottle out of the ice chest.

CAMILLE: But what about you? You must have been frightened, a little child like you.

SUGAR: There used to be a saying when I was a boy: "Nobody but God can whup my daddy, and God better watch his step." As long as Daddy was leaning back against the bow drinking Dixies, it was just another fishing trip as far as I was concerned. I knew Mama would be upset, our being late and all—and I was worried about that because I knew what would happen if she made too much of a fuss when we got home. But afraid of being stranded out in the marsh? I didn't have the slightest idea how much trouble we were in.

CAMILLE: So what did you do?

SUGAR: My father and I sat there till dusk. Every once in a while, Daddy would stand up on the bench and look for another boat, but nobody else was still out, and we were too far off the channel to catch a tow with the shrimp boats coming in from the Gulf. He was still in a pretty good mood, though. After he'd take a look, he would say, "I'd better send up a flare." And he'd unzip his pants and take a piss, standing on the seat. I guess it was all the beer he'd been drinking.

CAMILLE: And what about you?

SUGAR: Me? I'd had a little too much sun by then. Hot as it was, I started getting chills. Fever, I suppose.

CAMILLE: Keep a child out there on the water all day till he gets sick?

SUGAR: I was sick all right, but we had a bigger problem to deal with. I could already hear them lifting out of the grass before I could see them. At first, I thought it was an engine. But there weren't any boats when I looked, just small dark clouds hovering, twitching over the mudflats. I didn't know what they were—smoke, fog? But as the roaring got louder, I looked down at my hands. They were seething with mosquitoes.

CAMILLE: Mosquitoes?

SUGAR: It was weird, I hadn't felt a thing. Maybe it was the fever, I don't know, but I watched these bugs crawling all over themselves like it was somebody else's hands they were biting. And then, calm as could be, I plunged both arms into the water. With my face close to the canal, the racket from all those little wings overhead was unbelievable.

CAMILLE: And what was your father doing all this time?

SUGAR: Daddy had fallen asleep in the bow. So I crawled beside him, and when I got close enough to see him in the dark, his face and neck were so thick with mosquitoes he looked like he'd grown a black beard. I tried to call out to wake him, but my mouth was full of them before I could even say his name. I choked on mosquitoes, spitting them out into the water. My coughing woke him up. By then, they were in our eyes. I think my eyelids were starting to swell shut from all the bites. Next thing I know, Daddy throws me overboard and jumps in beside me.

CAMILLE: My God. I can't believe you never told me this before.

SUGAR: He's spitting the bugs out even while he's shouting at me. He gets his shirt off and throws it over our heads like a little tent. Then he pulls us underwater—to kill the mosquitoes still trapped under the shirt. "Vicious little bastards, aren't they?" he shouts at me even though he's just inches away when we come up again. Daddy says the edges of the shirt have to stay in the water. But it's so dark you can't tell where the water begins.

CAMILLE: That's horrifying.

SUGAR: It's the strangest feeling, floating there in this absolutely pitch-black darkness. Every now and then, I start to panic. Then he talks to me, calms me down. I get used to it after a while, I guess, because I'm falling asleep when something brushes my leg and makes me jump. I ask Daddy, "Did you just feel anything?" But before he can answer, something hits us both at the same time, coming between us, I think.

CAMILLE: An alligator?

SUGAR: Alligator? No, a shark, most likely. That afternoon, I'd seen one easing through the water, maybe fifty feet out, sliding back and forth as easy as you please. It wasn't all that big a shark—five, six foot—but big enough, I knew. So there I am, floating in the dark, remembering what I'd seen that afternoon. Not to mention Daddy, he's not under the shirt with me any-more. I call out for him and start paddling forward, trying to find him. But then I hear his voice shouting to stay still. That's when I feel it again, its side scraping my leg like sandpaper. I'm crying, with Daddy half whisper-ing, "Hush, hush, they'll hear you." That really scares me. It hasn't occurred to me there might be more than one shark. "And don't take a crap," he warns. "They love the smell of shit."

CAMILLE: So what happens?

[*Pause.*]

SUGAR: Nothing.

[*Pause.*]

We don't move for a minute or two—in the dark inside that shirt, all by myself, it felt like hours—and that was it. Gone. Daddy reaches out and grabs me and gets us organized again under the shirt. Only this time I'm hanging on to his neck so tight he says I'm gonna choke him.

[*Pause.*]

So that's when he tells me the story.

CAMILLE: You were just ten years old?

SUGAR: Worse things happen to kids. It did make me sad, though, the story. I didn't know who I felt worse for, the captain or his little girl. But that's how we got through the night. That and the singing.

CAMILLE: Singing?

SUGAR: After all those hours in the water, my father's having a hard time staying awake, I think, because all of a sudden he starts singing. In his whole life, it was the only song I ever heard him sing.

[*Pause.*]

Let me see I remember it.

[SUGAR *starts singing.*]

If the ocean were whiskey,
And I were a duck,
I'd swim to the bottom
And never come up.

But the ocean's not whiskey,
And I'm not a duck,
So I'll play the jack of diamonds
And trust to my luck.

[*Speaking*] He just keeps singing those same verses over and over again, like a chant more than a song, really. Then I start singing.

[*Pause.*]

It must have sounded strange out there in that dark marsh, those two voices carrying across the water. We kept at it a long time, waiting for the light.

CAMILLE: The whole night in the water?

SUGAR: The whole damn night. Then, when the sun finally rises, we haul ourselves up into the boat and try the motor again. There's nothing doing, though, so Daddy ties a line to a bow cleat and, with water up to his chest, drags the boat along the shelf of the mudflats for hours, it seems, until he's hauled us to the mouth of the canal. Out in the channel, we see a shrimper heading in after a night of trawling. We get up on the benches and swing the life vests over our heads, shouting like crazy people. "Hey, over here, over here."

[*Silence.*]

I've never known another feeling like when that shrimp boat, still a hundred, two hundred yards out, swung its bow toward us. You'll see when the rescue boats show up here. There's nothing else like it—seeing a boat coming to save you after you've survived a night on the water.

CAMILLE: My God, what a night.

SUGAR: So that's how I heard my father's story about the captain who buried his wife and daughter at sea.

CAMILLE: He say anything else about it, his story?

SUGAR: Yeah, one other thing. Years later, just before he died.

CAMILLE: What's that?

SUGAR: He said they all end the same way, sea stories—in madness or in death.

CAMILLE: And what about this story?

SUGAR: It's not a story. It's true.

CAMILLE: But how does it end?

SUGAR: End? With the singing, I guess, with the two of us singing, singing about whiskey and cards and a drunken duck—adrift in that black water, in that dark marsh, the mosquitoes hovering over our heads like death, and the two of us singing, singing until the sun comes up.

[*An alarm goes off in the distance.*]

CAMILLE: What's that, Sugar? Is someone coming? A rescue boat?

SUGAR: I don't see anyone. Not from down here. You see anything?

CAMILLE [*looking in all directions*]: No, nothing.

SUGAR: Might be, it's just a house alarm going off in somebody's attic.

CAMILLE: Why now?

SUGAR: They'll all start wailing, one after another, as the batteries go down. It's meant to be a warning the system's dying.

[*More alarms go off in the distance.*]

CAMILLE: It sounds like moaning when it's far away.

SUGAR: And like screams up close.

CAMILLE: I can't stand the sound of it.

SUGAR: They say it's full of fire, not water, but that's what I'd guess it sounds like down in hell.

CAMILLE: They must be on their way by now.

SUGAR: Who?

CAMILLE: The boats. They'll be here soon, won't they, Sug? Help's got to be on its way by now. The sun's nearly up.

SUGAR: Those boats, they'd better be here soon. A couple hours, that rising sun will turn the attic hotter than an oven and make this roof one sizzlin' skillet, we're still trapped up here.

CAMILLE: You wait and see. The sun comes up, the sky will fill with helicopters, and the water's gonna be so thick with rescue boats, we'll be able to walk to high ground we want to.

SUGAR: It's nearly dawn and no sign yet of anybody.

CAMILLE: The only thing you need to worry about is what you want for breakfast once they save us.

[*Pause.*]

SUGAR: At least we'll finally get to watch the sun come up together, you and me.

[*Silence.*]

CAMILLE: Let's sing, Sugar. Like you and your daddy did. Let's just keep singing till the sun comes up and those boats get here.

SUGAR: Sing what?

CAMILLE [*singing*]:
    If ever I cease to love,
    If ever I cease to love,
    The moon would turn to green cream cheese,
    If ever I cease to love.

SUGAR [*laughing then singing*]:
    If ever I cease to love,
    If ever I cease to love,
    May cows lay eggs and fish grow legs,
    If ever I cease to love.

[CAMILLE *joins in with him. More alarms go off and begin to drown them out as they continue to sing to each other.*]

    If ever I cease to love,
    If ever I cease to love,
    We'll all turn into cats and dogs,
    If ever I cease to love.

[*They stop singing and look at each other. Wailing alarms grow louder and more numerous, and light slowly brightens to full noon as they wait for help that does not come. They turn to face the audience. The alarms reach a crescendo. Blackout.*]

THE BREACH

A STORY ABOUT THE DROWNING OF NEW ORLEANS

Catherine Filloux, Tarell Alvin McCraney,
and Joe Sutton

PRODUCTION HISTORY

The Breach was developed through a series of staged readings both in and outside the Gulf Coast region. It was produced by Southern Rep Theatre in New Orleans (directed by Ryan Rilette) in 2007 and by the Seattle Repertory Theatre (directed by David Esbjornson) in 2008.

STAGING

The Breach is a highly theatrical piece that relies on devices such as double and triple casting. The actor transformations that result will take the audience from one story line to the other, all in a blink of an eye. This strategy allows the story to move via an actor's altered stance, a shift in posture, or a costume piece.

Please avoid set changes.

The primary consideration for casting remains transformational ability. We trust that the audience will learn to see the forty-year-old actress as a seven-year-old character.

Because the play is language-driven we ask you to resist the impulse to replace the spoken image with the literal fact; to change the language of rain into its literal incarnation. That said, there are specific stage directions that should be followed. For instance, "the sound of wind and rain" and the use of a wheelchair for Mac.

CHARACTERS

The Breach is a play made up of three interlocking story lines designed to be played by a company of six actors, all of whom are asked to take on multiple roles. The roles are grouped in the following manner:

Actor 1, Black man, fifties, to play *Pere Leon, Charlie,* and *Chorus 1*

Actor 2, Black man, early twenties, to play *Severance, Lancaster,* and *Chorus 2*

Actor 3, Black woman, late thirties, early forties, to play *Quan, Water* (and *Nurse & Poet*), and *Chorus 3.* Ability to move.

Actor 4, Black woman, thirties to forties, to play *Quan Older, Woman,* and *Linda*

Actor 5, White man, fifties, to play *Mac* and *Chorus 4*

Actor 6, White man, twenties, to play *Lynch* and *Francis*

Note: Chorus members take on a number of anonymous roles.

Place: Mostly New Orleans, though at one point Iraq.

Time: The first days and weeks after Hurricane Katrina.

Setting: A neutral space—which could be literally empty, or could, by flooding an empty space with water, be characterized but unchanging.

ACT 1

[QUAN *sits in a square of light humming "Soldier in the Army of the Lord." Enter* QUAN OLDER (QUAN *fourteen years later). She stands outside the square of light.*]

QUAN OLDER: It was water that woke us up that morning.

[*The sound of wind and rain is heard.*]

Rain and water pounding on our windows and slamming into our doors. Water rising wetting my seven-year-old chest. My brother Severance was there . . . He got us.

[*Lights fade on* QUAN OLDER *and come up on* PETER LYNCH *standing in a pool of light.*]

LYNCH [*dawning outrage*]: Are you watching this, I ask? Can you believe what's happening? And my friend says, "Oh yes." The two of us are watching television, I'm in my apartment, he's in his, and we're seeing images we never thought we'd see. People on rooftops. People in lines. Just masses of 'em. People outside the Convention Center. And I'm thinking how did the cameras get in? You know? How are we seeing this? How is it that reporters in trucks are slow driving past the crowds and the government isn't there? [*His outrage growing*] The police aren't there? The goddamn National Guard isn't there??? Where IS everyone? You know? How is this happening???? [*Beat, trying to rein himself in.*] And my friend says, "Wait . . . just wait . . . [*Long beat.*] . . . it'll get worse." [*Long pause.*] And he was right. [*Beat.*] He was right.

[*Lights out on* LYNCH *as* SEVERANCE (SEV) *enters pulling* PERE LEON *into the space. As gingerly as he can he sets* PERE LEON *down.*]

SEV: Granddaddy Leon, you all right?
QUAN OLDER: He pulled us up on that roof. Made sure I was OK, went back to get my granddaddy. Told me to . . . Sev say:
SEV: Be still, Quan, don't move. Just be still.
PERE LEON: Lord God!
QUAN OLDER: My granddaddy pulled up there lying on his stomach.
SEV: Let me help you.
QUAN OLDER: Breathing heavy.
PERE LEON: Severance. Gone from me. Gone from me, Severance.

QUAN OLDER: Getting wet from the still falling rain . . .

PERE LEON: I said gone now.

QUAN OLDER: He slipped a little.

PERE LEON: Uh!

QUAN OLDER: But Severance was there.

SEV: I gotcha! I gotcha, Pere.

PERE LEON: Just sit me down then turn me loose, Severance.

SEV: Granddaddy, let me . . .

PERE LEON: No! I say set me down and leave me alone. Don't want to talk to you.

QUAN OLDER: Rain and storm.

SEV: You serious?

PERE LEON: I said it.

SEV: Granddaddy, it's, it's stormin', man. It's raining . . . Sorry I pushed you up here, but I had to what . . . You hurt?

PERE LEON: I don't want to talk to you now, hear? Gone from me.

SEV: Why? What's wrong with you?

PERE LEON: I ain't explainin'. Just gone head now.

SEV: Gone where! We on the damn roof!

PERE LEON: Don't cuss me.

SEV: I don't believe this!

PERE LEON: What you keep on for, huh? You don't care 'bout nobody no way. You don't care bout nothing 'cept Severance so don't act like you got all this here concern. Much obliged for pulling my arm out of joint but I said don't speak to me.

[QUAN *hums*.]

SEV [*to* QUAN]: Get close . . . Close to Pere Leon . . . Come on.

QUAN OLDER: I couldn't move.

SEV: Eh now, listen to me, you got to cut out this . . . Come to me!

SEV AND QUAN OLDER: Come to Severance.

QUAN OLDER: Severance. My older brother. My only brother.

SEV: That's right.

QUAN OLDER: And he carried me.

SEV: That's right. Right here now you be still I be right back.

QUAN OLDER: Severance moved to go back.

PERE LEON: Eh, boy!

SEV: What?

PERE LEON: Where you going to?

SEV: In the house . . .

PERE LEON: You got sense to you? What you going in there for?

SEV: We getting wet out here. I'm going before . . .

PERE LEON: You get wet in there too. Ain't nothing in that house gone be good enough to help us out here.

SEV: Just be still.

PERE LEON: Sev!

SEV: I'll be right back.

PERE LEON: Boy, don't go in that house!

SEV: Don't get up!

PERE LEON: I said don't go, Sev! I said no!

QUAN OLDER: He reached for Sev. Sev throw his arm back.

SEV: Be still. Be still.

[SEV *disappears. Lights shift to morning sunlight streaming through a window as the character of* WATER *slides in unseen.*]

WATER [*displaying herself*]: Water.

[*Beat.*]

Seepin' through the cracks—dark and muddy.

[MAC, *fifty, in a wheelchair—a real character—claps his hands, victorious.*]

MAC: Yep, yep, yep. What'd I tell you? Katrina's veered east. All those brave survivors of the National-Weather-Service-hype are going to need a cocktail! [*Chuckling*] I got a customer who needs her Sazerac and no one coats the glass with Herbsaint like I do. She's a famous poet and she didn't evacuate—she's no pussy! But first things first—I'm callin' Linda! Time to propose!

[*He quickly wheels over to his phone, taking a deep breath.*]

MAC: OK, the big plunge!

[*He speed dials. Lights come up on the woman he imagines,* LINDA, *facing out.*]

MAC [*getting the answering machine, excited*]: Hey, Linda, there's something about survivin' a hurricane that makes you see the big picture, and you know what I see? *You*, baby. You are the moon and stars. *Fate's* gotten into me. Dodgin' storms does that. Linda, will you please be my wife? I'm down on my knees.

[*He isn't on his knees.*]

Figuratively. Look, now I don't know if I can afford to pay those drug companies that fuckin' money to get some crapshoot stuff injected. And Novatrone? Your piss comes out blue. But FINE! [*Singing*] "I'll do it for you, I'll make my piss blue." Hurry and say YES, Francis might be trying to call—it's nighttime in Mesopotamia. My boy's bringin' democracy to the little towel heads! Can your mom get some shuteye now that Katrina's gone?

[*Lights out on* LINDA. *Audience hears the faint sound of water.*]

Tell your mom New Orleans is protected!

[WATER *talks to* MAC, *who can't hear or see her.*]

WATER: Oh *really.*

[*The water sound starts to get louder, beginning to rumble.*]

MAC: Shit, what was that? [*Calling into phone*] Linda, say YES! We'll have a big weddin' soon as Franny gets back from savin' Iraq! Hello?
WATER: The phone's dead.

[MAC *feels water all around him.*]

MAC: That's water, holy shit. Water doesn't rise this fast. Hey, I got a bar to open, what the fuck is this? The aftermath?
WATER: The after *bath*?
MAC [*calling into phone again*]: Tell me you're rushin' to your attic, Linda—give me a sign.

[*Suddenly* WATER *takes hold of* MAC's *wheelchair, pushing him toward the window.*]

What the hell! [*Resisting, under his breath*] Shit, I've dodged *four* bullets now—I can survive this . . .
WATER: Have you, Macko? Let's count 'em. One?

[MAC *quickly turns his wheelchair around.*]

MAC [*frightened*]: I survived Betsy.
WATER: Your family's survived *every* hurricane.

[MAC *wheels to the door, gathering his courage.*]

MAC: That Virgin in the window? Grandpa carved that—biggest drunk I ever knew, but Mary is *protection*.
WATER: Was.

[*Struggling,* MAC *pulls himself out of the wheelchair.*]

MAC: We go all the way back to the Jesuits . . .
WATER [*overlapping*]: And *Jesus* could walk on water.

[*Legs so weak,* MAC *holds himself up with the doorknob, trying to open the door.*]

MAC: We've survived hurricanes, floods!

[*Sound of water now grows louder as he opens the door.*]

WATER [*laughing*]: I'm everywhere!

[MAC *falls back into the wheelchair.*]

MAC: It's up my freakin' legs. [*Looking around in shock*] Where'd this come from?
WATER: Levees broke.

[MAC *quickly wheels back toward the window.*]

[*Whispering*] Better break the window.

[MAC *picks up a dumbbell, throwing it through the glass.*]

MAC: Lucky I been liftin' weights.
WATER: Hum, how strong actually are those arms, big guy?
MAC [*looking around, panicking*]: This house was built raised on purpose . . .
WATER: You were given an order to evacuate.
MAC: Three generations lived here. All roaring drunks. *I* licked it.

[MAC *is trying to be brave, looking out the window.*]

WATER: Second bullet you dodged, Mr. Invincible?
MAC [*bolstering himself*]: AlCOhol! I'm the only one who beat it. Swimming out my window's nothing compared to kicking that lethal habit!
WATER: Sure, twelve easy steps! [*Skeptical*] The first one: give up your chair.

[*By now* WATER *is pushing* MAC *hard against the windowsill, her "sound" getting louder still.*]

MAC [*shouting*]: Hello, I'm in here, can anyone hear me???

[WATER *makes a faint sound—a woman screaming.*]

WATER: "Maaaaccc!!!"

MAC: Mrs. LeBlanc?

WATER: With all her cats?

MAC [*urgently*]: MRS. LEBLANC, CAN YOU HEAR ME? GO TO YOUR ATTIC!

WATER: Maaaaaaacccccc!

MAC: AND FROM THE ATTIC, STICK YOUR HEAD OUT THE WINDOW AND SCREAM!

WATER [*the sound of cats*]: "Meow, meow."

MAC: Your cats! They're still alive, Mrs. LeBlanc!

WATER: Victory!

MAC: As soon as this stops we'll save the cats! I've lived through much worse—

WATER: The third bullet, Mac?

MAC [*overlapping*]: Guy in my bar—high as a kite—points a gun to my head!

[WATER *mimes putting a gun to his head.*]

WATER [*slurring, irate*]: Why don't you stand up when you pour? You a fuckin' sissy?

MAC [*false bravado*]: I stayed calm as a lamb, and then Franny came in!

[WATER *mimes knocking gun away.*]

WATER [*now playing* FRANCIS]: "Sissy sure beats Nazi," he said.

MAC: Francis knocked that gun right out of his hand! Scared that chicken-shit off.

[WATER *by now is tipping* MAC'*s wheelchair hard against the windowsill.*]

WATER: And where is Franny when you need him most?

MAC [*overlapping*]: Best soldier ever.

WATER: Knew it from the minute he rescued the little girl's kitten in the tree.

MAC [*revving himself to go*]: Don't worry, *I* got some of that soldier in me.

WATER: Never should've let him go, chump.

[MAC *is nearly out of his wheelchair,* WATER *continuing to tip him.*]

MAC: Now the fourth bullet—KaTREEna.

WATER [*amused*]: Always a new name.

MAC: And let me tell you, I'll be here for the next gal!

WATER [*overlapping*]: What made you so cocky?

MAC: It's now or never!

WATER [*singing Elvis*]: "Come hold me tight."

MAC: Swimming out my window—FUCK—

[MAC *jumps out of his wheelchair, pushing himself through the window—the water sound growing louder still. Blackout. After a beat, lights come up on* LYNCH, *who turns in astonishment to the voices all around him. He can't believe what he's hearing, and they, like furies, enjoy tormenting him.*]

LYNCH [*exploding, astonished*]: He said what??

CHORUS 2: That the levees were blown.

LYNCH: Intentionally blown???

CHORUS 1: Intentionally blown, yes.

LYNCH [*sputtering, beside himself*]: Farrakhan *said* this? In a speech?

CHORUS 2: Yes.

LYNCH: You're kidding me. [*Then, after a moment, alarmed*] You're not? [*Then, immediately*] This is possible?

CHORUS 2: He said there was a twenty-five-foot hole.

CHORUS 1: He said that at the base of the levee there was a twenty-five-foot hole.

CHORUS 2 [*following, fast and furious*]: He said that they had sent divers down, there was a diving team there . . .

CHORUS 1: . . . and one of the divers had come back with a piece of charred concrete.

LYNCH: Charred how?

CHORUS 2: With explosives.

LYNCH [*exploding*]: And they found this???

CHORUS 1: They found this, yes.

CHORUS 2: But the diver who found it was told to throw it back in.

CHORUS 1: To not mention it.

CHORUS 2: To pretend that it hadn't been found.

LYNCH: But instead he spread the word.

CHORUS 1: Instead he spread the word, yes.

[LYNCH *is quivering almost—absolutely incredulous at this information.*]

LYNCH: And what is the explanation for this? What . . . I mean . . . why would somebody DO this?

CHORUS 1: Who knows?

CHORUS 2: To save the white part of town.

CHORUS 1: The tourist part of town.

CHORUS 2: Who knows?

LYNCH: Oh, well, that's ridiculous.

CHORUS 1 AND 2: Is it?

[LYNCH *is aghast.*]

LYNCH: Yes! I mean . . . who told him this? Where did he hear this? What—

CHORUS 1: He got it on good authority, he said.

CHORUS 2: Very good authority.

LYNCH: *What* good authority?

CHORUS 1: The mayor.

LYNCH: The mayor told him this!?!

CHORUS 2: The mayor told him about the hole, yes.

CHORUS 1: He didn't mention the explosives.

CHORUS 2: But he told him about the hole.

LYNCH: Well, who told him about the explosives?

CHORUS 1: He got that from a website.

LYNCH: What website?

CHORUS 2: Hal Turner's website.

LYNCH [*his head spinning now*]: Who's Hal Turner?

CHORUS 1: Hal Turner has a talk show, a radio talk show.

CHORUS 2: He's also got a website.

CHORUS 1: This is from the website.

LYNCH: And this makes sense to you? This . . . [*apoplectic*] . . . I mean, this makes sense???

CHORUS 2: Does to me.

[*With this,* CHORUS 2 *exits.*]

LYNCH: Does—

CHORUS 1: Hey! [*Slight beat.*] He's just putting two and two together. Something we should have been doin' . . . he tells us . . . [*his voice low, suddenly menacing*] . . . for a long, LONG time.

[*Lights shift to the rooftop.* QUAN *and* PERE LEON *sit watching, waiting. Lights include* SEV.]

SEV: Uh!

QUAN OLDER: Severance, breathing heavy, holding a tarp.

PERE LEON: Lord God, boy!

SEV: Granddaddy—

PERE LEON: Don't call me grand nothing!

SEV: Don't move, be still.

PERE LEON: I told you not go back down into that house! Didn't I say it!

SEV: I heard you . . .

PERE LEON: You heard me! You heard me?

SEV: I had to . . . Eh, don't move!

PERE LEON: Had us up here waiting in the rain—

SEV: Listen, man . . .

PERE LEON: Worrying! No! You don't listen, Sev. You hear me, you don't listen! I asked you not to do something, and you out and out in my face denied me. Like you do. Like you always do!

SEV: I wasn't gone long.

PERE LEON: I told you not to go at all. I asked you to stay. Huh. Last time you hear that from me. That's for damn sure.

SEV: What?

PERE LEON: I'm sick of worrying on you after I tell you not to do something. You grown enough to go out disobey me. Then you grown enough to reap what you sow.

SEV: I was in the house.

PERE LEON: I tell you what, Sev. Don't worry bout it. I mean, just brush it off like you do.

Tell you this. When these Waters come down, whenever we get off this roof, don't you take stock of nothing. Just get your sopping wet clothes and get from round me. Just gone. Huh. 'Cause I'm sick of it. I really am, Sev. I truly am.

QUAN OLDER: He stood there. Hurt. You could see it all over.

Even in the wind and the too early—it's—still—dark rain. You could see Sev was hurtin' from what granddaddy just said. He just standing there holding that tarp.

SEV: I . . . I brought this . . . so we could . . .

QUAN OLDER: Rain. Storm dripping off all our faces.

SEV: We can stay under it 'til the water go down.

QUAN OLDER: Rain and Wind.

SEV: 'Til it stop raining. Me and Quan sit right here . . . Next to you Gran . . .

QUAN OLDER: Pere shot him a look.

SEV: Pere Leon. We sit next to you so right now. Before the waters go down we all stay dry. C'mon Pere.

QUAN OLDER: I scooted next to Sev.

SEV: Yeah, c'mon, Quan.

QUAN OLDER: Pere Leon look like he would move to . . .

SEV: No, stay there. We'll move to you. We'll come over to you.

QUAN OLDER: But he wasn't listening.

And he slipped.

PERE LEON: Huh!

SEV: Pere!

QUAN OLDER: My grandfather slipped and disappeared in the dark still rising water.

[*Blackout. The lights come up on* CHORUS 4 *and* LYNCH. *They sit across from each other.* CHORUS 4 *is an editor.*]

CHORUS 4 [*loud, incredulous*]: Say again.

LYNCH: Intentionally.

CHORUS 4: Did this??

LYNCH: Yes.

CHORUS 4 [*giving vent*]: They intentionally blew up the levees???

LYNCH: That's what people say, yes.

CHORUS 2: Who did?

[*This last comes from a younger editor who is also quite outraged and making* no *attempt to hide it.*]

LYNCH: It's unclear.

CHORUS 4: Well, what *do* they say?

LYNCH: They don't.

CHORUS 4: The mayor?

CHORUS 2 [*angry*]: Because the mayor is black!

LYNCH: They don't say.

CHORUS 2: Well, what do they say? I mean, this rumor you're spreading—

LYNCH: I'm not spreading a rumor.

CHORUS 4: Well, what are you doing?

LYNCH: I'm reporting a story.

CHORUS 2: And the difference? What exactly is the difference?

LYNCH: They don't need me to spread the rumor. [*To* CHORUS 4] You need me to report the story.

[*Beat.*]

CHORUS 2: Why? Why do we need you to do that?

LYNCH [*still on* CHORUS 4]: Because it's the truth. To some number of people out there . . . it's the truth.

CHORUS 4: Yeah, but again, who? I mean, for this event to have occurred, somebody must have done it. Who was it?

LYNCH: The powers that be.

CHORUS 4: And who is that?

CHORUS 2: The mayor is black!

LYNCH: Still.

CHORUS 2: Still what? I mean, what kind of sense does that make?

CHORUS 4: That's what is said?

LYNCH: Yes.

CHORUS 4 [*despite himself, intrigued*]: "The powers that be?"

LYNCH: Yes.

CHORUS 2 [*incensed*]: This is from that woman, isn't it?

LYNCH: What?

CHORUS 2: That woman, what's her name, the one in the Seventh Ward.

LYNCH: I . . . don't—

CHORUS 2 [*to* CHORUS 4]: Whatshername? With the ribbons in her hair. We saw her on television.

CHORUS 4: I—

CHORUS 2: Oh, Christ . . . what . . . [*impatiently*] . . . well, whatever. She is a rabble-rouser. A race-baiting, self-serving rabble-rouser!

LYNCH: And?

CHORUS 2: And I don't see why we have to pay you for a story she is a part of.

LYNCH: Because it's important. [*With empathy*] Because too many people out there . . . it's important. [*Beat.*] And she isn't a part of it because I have no idea who "she" is.

[*He turns to* CHORUS 4—*and* CHORUS 4 *stares back at him.*]

CHORUS 4 [*grudgingly*]: I'll pay your expenses.

LYNCH: Just my expenses?

CHORUS 4: That's all I can promise.

CHORUS 2: And even that's too much.

[*Beat.*]

LYNCH: But you'll take a look? When I bring it to you . . . [*trying to nail him down*] . . . you'll take a look.

[*Beat.*]

CHORUS 4: I'll take a look.

LYNCH: OK. [*Beat.*] OK. [*Beat.*] Thanks.

CHORUS 2: Hey!

[LYNCH *had started to turn away.*]

CHORUS 2: Who are you going to talk to?
LYNCH: Anyone. Anyone who believes it. [*Slight beat.*] Anyone.

[*Lights fade out . . . They come up on* MAC *and* WATER *now floating out in the street.* MAC *tries desperately to stay afloat. He still cannot see or hear* WATER.]

MAC: HELP!
WATER [*mocking him*]: God, I *love* swimming.
MAC [*facing his house*]: The Virgin Mary's floatin' out my window!
WATER: Better give her a quick prayer. "Hail Mary full of grace . . ." Oh, she's
   gone.
MAC [*using his arms*]: Let me get to that tree. I can hold on . . .
WATER: The magnolia tree's algae now.

[MAC *tries to swim to tree.*]

MAC: Grandpa planted it . . .
WATER [*overlapping*]: On one of his *good days* . . .
MAC [*arms weakening*]: For Franny, my hero! I'm thinkin' of you, son.
WATER: Did you ever think you'd be floatin' through your neighborhood?
MAC [*struggling*]: Water keeps rising, I can't . . .
WATER: Tree's a mile away now. There go your family roots.
MAC: Hey, I followed doctor's orders—kept up my arm strength.
WATER: You get your exercise pouring and mixing drinks.
MAC: MY LEGS ARE DEAD WEIGHTS. Franny, help!

[MAC, *struggling with* WATER, *hears the sound of clanging metal beneath and all around him. He breaks free.*]

MAC: What is that swimming around in this foul drink?
WATER: Oh, no! You're being pursued by a garbage can.
MAC [*dodging it*]: Is this what I'm destined for?

[WATER *gashes him with her nails.*]

WATER: Agggghhh. The trash heap.
MAC: Owwwwwwwwwwwwww!
WATER [*ironic*]: Why you always have to be the martyr, Mac?

[MAC, *delirious, begins to hallucinate. He can now see and hear* WATER.]

MAC: Who are you?

WATER: Customers always look at you in your wheelchair and you say . . .

[*He defies her.*]

MAC: "What *you* got?"

WATER: Sickness is a mirror, and they always tell you what they got.

MAC: Always better to turn it around! Works every time. Bartender's secret.
　[*To himself*] Holy shit, I'm talkin' to Water!

WATER: *Denial* ain't just the name of a river.

MAC: No one wants to hear about me, nerves misfirin' in my body and sending
　wrong signals.

[*She suddenly dunks him under.*]

WATER: And then sending NO SIGNALS AT ALL.

[MAC *comes to the surface, gasping.*]

MAC: Save me, Francis! Saint Francis, my son, of Assisi!

WATER: *Don't be a sissy.* Tell me "what *you* got"!

MAC [*starting to lose consciousness*]: Shackles for legs.

WATER: That's right.

MAC [*to himself*]: How dare God do this to me.

WATER: Don't you have *faith*?

MAC [*screaming*]: Yeah, in Francis . . . !

[MAC *hallucinates as lights shift to a different part of the stage where* FRANCIS *and
another soldier,* LANCASTER, *watch an overcrowded bridge in Baghdad. Audience
hears screaming.*]

FRANCIS [*alarmed*]: Why they jumping off the bridge, man?

[*The sounds grow louder, chaotic.*]

LANCASTER [*laughing*]: They're flying into the river! We've died and gone to
　hell!

FRANCIS: Call in the stampede, Lancaster.

MAC: See? Look at Franny. All action!

LANCASTER: Fuckin' hajjis, let's all cut ourselves and jump! SUICIDE LEAP!
　[*Into radio, exiting*] "Echo5Lima. Aima Bridge."

FRANCIS: Oh my god, there's a baby drowning. [*Pointing*] Look!

[FRANCIS *runs forward, into the river, while off to one side,* WATER *scoops up a baby who has fallen from the bridge.*]

WATER [*to the baby*]: Down through the air, to a safer world in the water . . .
FRANCIS: Gotta get it.

[*Moving down and through the water . . .*]

Gotta . . .

[*Then, nearing it . . .*]

Hey, hey, hey, little baby . . .

[WATER *and* FRANCIS *struggle over the baby,* WATER *talking to it as* FRANCIS *tries to grab hold.*]

WATER [*to baby*]: Come, I'll take you to a happier place.
FRANCIS [*to baby*]: It's OK, doll . . .
WATER [*to baby*]: The swift river, Tigris, chasing the Euphrates . . .

[FRANCIS *yells to people in the river.*]

FRANCIS: I'm getting your baby. Your wife will drown if she doesn't stop screaming.
MAC: HE'S SAVING EVERYONE!
WATER: Except you. Race you to the Gulf . . .

[FRANCIS *wrangles the baby from* WATER, *saving her.*]

FRANCIS: OK, little girl, you're fine.

[FRANCIS *turns the baby upside down, thumping her, calling again to her parents in the river.*]

FRANCIS: I have your baby. [*To baby*] It's all right, honey. [*Then, to the parents, miming*] Pull your wife and swim. I need to get the baby onshore.

[*Taking the baby to shore,* FRANCIS *gives her CPR.*]

MAC: He got the baby's breath! She's safe.
WATER: And you're comin' with me, to the marshes . . .
FRANCIS: Who knows what seas you'll cross? [*Tenderly*] Who knows what you'll do?

[*The baby cries.*]

WATER [*to* MAC]: Don't cry.   FRANCIS [*to baby*]: Don't cry.

[FRANCIS *grabs hold of the baby—exiting—as* MAC *tries to get away from* WATER.]

MAC: Francis?
WATER: Franny's got his hands full.
MAC: With a baby!
WATER: What an imagination!
MAC [*fighting*]: Let go! I'm coming to save you, Linda.
WATER: Hasn't swum in twenty years, but he's comin'.
MAC: She built me a bar. I proposed to her!
WATER: Bad timing. Your heart's slowing down.
MAC [*hearing his own heartbeat*]: Bum, bum. Bum, bum.
WATER: Bloop, bloop, bloop, bloop . . .   MAC: Bubbles in the water . . .
WATER: Your own damn fault you stayed behind, Mac. "What *you* got?" TELL
    ME NOW.

[*She presses his wound.*]

MAC [*whimpering*]: Leg hurts so bad.
WATER: And what do you want?
MAC: Make love to Linda . . .

[*She starts to pull him further into the current.*]

WATER: How 'bout a vacation south of Grand Isle? There are the phantom
    boats loaded with pirate money? Want to gamble for your life?
MAC: I don't gamble!
WATER: You do *and* you got a handicap.
MAC [*to himself*]: I can still make love . . .
WATER: I got my eye on you, and that's why I want this honeymoon. Isn't it
    time we go?
MAC: With Linda I feel her through the numbness, because I love her . . .
WATER: She made the deal: *Alcohol*–"it's either the Co or Me."

[*Suddenly* WATER *throws water in his mouth.*]

    Drink!

[MAC *starts to go under.*]

MAC: I just got a mouthful of . . .
WATER: Poison-Passion.

MAC: A petrol cocktail.

WATER [*starting to sing*]: "Our man Mac is a swimmer . . ."

MAC [*joining in, for courage*]: "A dolphin of a man . . ."

WATER: "A dolphin of a man . . ."

MAC AND WATER: "A dolphin of a man was he!"

WATER: Grow a fin.

MAC [*grabbing his heart*]: Bum . . . Ahhhh! Bum . . . Ahhhhhh!

[MAC's *eyes shut. And for a long moment the lights stay on him as he starts to drown. Lights come up on the rooftop.* SEV *sits in the middle.* QUAN *on his right and* PERE LEON *on his left sleeping. They hold a tarp overhead.*]

QUAN OLDER: It kept us awake now this rain. Not
As hard as when it first come but
Gentle like playing baby finger across
The top of that tarp. Pere Leon Lay on
His back Breathing Heavy. Sev had again
Gone into the waters and brought him up.
Now he lay between us. Heavy breathing.
Breathing heavy.

[PERE LEON *snores.*]

We sat there for a while.

[PERE LEON *snores.*]

For a long time.

SEV: Pere . . .

QUAN OLDER: The rain and storm stopped.

SEV: Pere Leon . . .
Pere. Wake up. Pere?

QUAN OLDER: He woke with a start . . .

PERE LEON: Huh!

SEV: Whoa, man, you got to be more careful. I can't
Keep running in that water after you. You heavy.

PERE LEON: Lord, boy, don't you know not to scare no
Body awake when they sleep on a roof.

SEV: It stopped raining. I'm a move the . . .

PERE LEON: Do what you please.
You gone do that anyway.

SEV: Granddaddy . . .

PERE LEON: I done told you 'bout that. I told you not to
    Let that come out your mouth. Hell, don't
    Know why I'm acting surprised you don't
    Listen. Now I'm not listenin' to my own self.
    Must be catchin', disease like.
SEV: I told you I was sorry for going in the house.
PERE LEON: Yeah, you sorry, all right.
SEV: Stop moving.
PERE LEON: Boy, I ain't falling no more.
SEV: Aight 'cause . . .
PERE LEON: What you gone let me fall in and not come to catch?

[SEV *stares off.*]

    Wouldn't surprise me none, Sev, 'cause I didn't
    Expect you to be there the first time. In fact when
    That water come up on me like that this morning.
    When I stepped down and felt wet from shin to waist,
    I said to myself, Lord, let me get Quan, 'cause who know
    Where Severance is!
SEV: What you doubting me for?
PERE LEON: That's the kind of man you turning into. Doubtful.
    You know what it's like not to be able to trust your own.
    To know that in a heartbeat you abandoned for sin.
SEV: I ain't no abandon you.
PERE LEON: You always do.
    Every time I ask your butt to get in the house a certain . . .
    Be here at a decent hour, Sev, I look round and you still
    Out or done gone without telling me. That's your record.
    That's your track, it's what you do. Hell,
    I barely got you to put the board on the windows.
SEV: I put them up.
PERE LEON: What good they do us?
SEV: Hell, how I was gone know this was gone come.
    Nobody told me.
PERE LEON: I knew. I knew it could get bad. I seen't it. Yes, sir
    Bared witness to it.
SEV: Granddaddy, man, I'm sorry but I don't really
    Need to know 'bout you havin' visions again.

PERE LEON: Why? Boy, the Lord speaks . . .

SEV: Here he go. The Lord told you that it might flood like this?

PERE LEON: Nah, well, yeah, through MSNBC.

SEV: Who?

PERE LEON: MSNBC. The news, boy. You was busy sleeping
    Off your drunken Saturday night, but on Sunday
    They ran some models and specials about what
    This storm could do. Had you got up from your
    Rehab . . .

SEV: I wasn't drunk.

PERE LEON: You smell like armpit and Ned the wino
    When I come by your room that morning. Huh.
    I come down there to say, Sev, the Rev called wanna
    Have a prayer meeting this morning 'fore the storm.
    But I get to the door, and it already smell like
    Dewar's white label beating me back.

SEV: Somebody spilt a drink on me. You know I don't drink.

PERE LEON: Severance, I don't know what you do. Huh?
    Truly I don't. I do know that whatever it is
    Keep you out 'til all hours of the night. Whatever
    It is kept you gone all night long Saturday when I asked
    You to be here at a reasonable hour with me and your sister.
    You stumbled in here. Sound like you was crying
    And while me and your younger sister sitting in the living room
    Watching them track Ms. Kat Rina up and down the coast
    You in your room. The whole time. The whole day.
    Ain't come out once to say nothing to us. Just in
    There talking on the phone to whoever. Probably same
    Hoochie you was running around with the night before.

SEV: I was talking to Gideon.

PERE LEON: Who dat? That yellow boy from the Ninth?

SEV: You know Gideon.

QUAN OLDER: I knew Gideon.

PERE LEON: I barely know you!
    Did y'all have fun?

QUAN OLDER: They always did.

PERE LEON: I mean y'all was giggling on the phone so.
    Did you have a good time?

SEV: Gone, Pere Leon, man, just lay back.

PERE LEON: Nah. I wanna know. What y'all do, go head.
I mean, I been there. I know ain't nothing to
Shock me. It's all low and common. What y'all ride around
Scoopin' up some shawty's sippin' on some hip
And hen?

[SEV *laughs.*]

PERE LEON: No matter how good it feel right now.
It's all sin. You better get right
With the Father.
SEV: Man, we just went out, that's all.
I told you I don't drink.
PERE LEON: Let me try to put it to you another way. You a grown
Man. The man of your family 'cause your mama left
You. Who knows who your daddy is. So it's you and your
Sister. That's it. She your only sister. What if somebody say
Eh, they might come by and snatch her up in the night. Just come
In like the wind through a window and take her away far
Away so you never see her again. Somebody warn you of
This. They say this may be come in two days. What you do,
Sev?
PERE LEON AND SEV: "C'mon, Pere . . ."
PERE LEON: Don't wanna hear your brother man talk.
SEV: I . . .
PERE LEON: You what.
SEV: I watch her.
PERE LEON: Yeah? That's what you say you do, but how come you ain't do it.
I say, Severance, a bad storm supposed to come through here.
SEV: And I say we should leave.
PERE LEON: And go where?
SEV: Stay up in Thibodaux with Aunt Shun.
PERE LEON: Please, boy, during a storm you wanna
Go further out in the Bayou? You think
We got water what you think they got? Besides
Ain't no room for us over there. They got a one
Bedroom shotgun smaller than ours and
Big Nasty, that husband of your Antie, walking
Around, with his gut scrubbing the ground, ain't nothing
I want to see in the midnight hour. Man know

He nasty. Walking around lifting his leg up
So he get the good farts out.

SEV: So we stayed and I put up the boards like you
Said.

PERE LEON: But you was . . .

SEV: And I was here. This morning, when you woke up.
When the water got you and me and her up, I was here.
So stop griefin' me about the other times 'cause they
Don't count. The time it come for me to be
Here cause you needed me here Pere Leon I was here. I
Got you and her out and up. So yeah, man,
You welcome I was here.

PERE LEON: Where were you, Sev, all Saturday night?

SEV: Gone, Pere.

PERE LEON: What was so impressive about you and Gideon . . .

QUAN OLDER: You had to see them.

PERE LEON: Hanging out all Sat night.

QUAN OLDER: Seem like Sev only happy when they together.

PERE LEON: You had to, just had to.

QUAN OLDER: Only time I ever hear him laugh 'til he cry.
Only time I ever see him truly get mad was about Gideon.

PERE LEON: I just don't understand it, Sev. Even
With your family in danger. Something
You had to do! I just don't understands it!

SEV: Well, maybe it ain't for you to understand. Maybe it's a geriatric
Gap between you understanding
And me explaining, but all I know is this shit is
Irrelevant! We on the roof. I'm on a roof here with y'all. And
You safe cause I was here. So fuck Saturday, fuck
Before! What's now is this roof. What's
Real is this heat and that water.
Wish y'all just lay the fuck down!
Wish y'all be the fuck still.
Maybe I go swim over to the next house see if . . .

[PERE LEON *laughs*.]

What?

PERE LEON: Just keep proving me right, Sev. Go on. You say
You ain't had no time to sin. Honor thy mother

And thy father. Heard that one? I tried to teach
It to you. Yeah, I ain't your mama. But I took
You in and fed you. Just listen to me, Sev. If
People ain't up on they roof, they still in they
House. And that water, high up above ceiling.
Don't go looking for nobody. If we can't see
Them on the roof, then they gone on already.
They somewhere else. Leave it . . . just leave it, Sev.
You be still, be still.

[*Lights stay up on* SEV *and* PERE LEON *for another moment then cross-fade to* MAC, *as* WATER *tries to hold him under.* MAC *hears a boat's motor in the distance. Opening his eyes, gasping, he yells . . .*]

MAC: OOOOVER HEEEEEEERE!!

[*Offstage we hear a man's,* CHARLIE'*s, tortured groan.*]

CHARLIE'S VOICE [*to himself*]: Damnit, not again. [*Shouting*] I SEE YA.
MAC [*trying to get away from* WATER]: Can't make it . . .
CHARLIE'S VOICE: Now I gotta get over to you.

[*Lights cross-fade—this time coming up on* LYNCH *and a well-dressed black woman at the very moment he has just stopped her. His hand splayed out in front of her chest, it's as if he's assaulted her. And she is startled. It's outside.*]

WOMAN [*alarmed*]: What?
LYNCH [*scrambling*]: Sorry, I overheard you over there. What you were saying.
    With your friends.
WOMAN: Yes?
LYNCH: And I'd like to talk to you.
WOMAN: Do I *know* you?
LYNCH: No, I . . . no.
WOMAN [*abrupt*]: I don't think so.
LYNCH: Please!

[*This last comes out stronger than* LYNCH *had intended, and the woman—who had been turning away from him—now turns back.*]

    Look, I'm a writer. I'm . . . you know, I'm trying to understand this.
WOMAN: Are you from New Orleans?
LYNCH: No.
WOMAN: Well, then you can't understand this.

LYNCH: I'd like to try!

[*Again she had started away, but again, perhaps due to the determination or even the desperation in his voice, she turns back.*]

WOMAN: Why?

LYNCH: It's . . . [*Not knowing how to explain*] . . . I don't know. [*Beat, earnestly.*] Please?

[*At this, he half turns, gesturing to a table behind them. And finally, reluctantly, she starts over with him.*]

WOMAN: I don't have long.

[*The two soon take their seats.*]

LYNCH: Would you like a drink?

WOMAN: No. [*Almost sharply*] Just tell me what you want to know.

LYNCH: Why you would . . . I mean, what you said. Why you would say that?

WOMAN: Say what?

LYNCH: What you said!

[*Now it is* LYNCH *who seems edgy.*]

WOMAN: You'll have to be more specific.

LYNCH: About the levees. You said . . . "Well, we know what THAT'S about."

[*There is a pause. The* WOMAN'*s face has turned cold.*]

WOMAN [*wary*]: Yes?

LYNCH: What did you mean by that?

WOMAN: What do you think?

LYNCH [*almost sharp*]: Well, I know what I think . . . but I'd like to hear you *say* it.

WOMAN: Why?

LYNCH: Why not?

WOMAN: I don't understand. Why—

LYNCH: I—

WOMAN [*angry*]: Who are you again?

LYNCH: I'm a writer. [*Slight beat.*] I'm just a writer.

WOMAN: What kind of writer?

LYNCH: Magazines, mostly. Newspapers. Freelance.

WOMAN: And you're writing . . . ? [*Really pissed*] I mean, what exactly are you writing?

LYNCH: I don't know. A story, I guess. About what's happened. Down here.
WOMAN: And? What do you think happened?
LYNCH: Well, that's what I'm trying to find out.

[*Suddenly the* WOMAN *pushes away from the table.*]

WOMAN: Well, you don't need me to tell you.
LYNCH: I do, though! I . . . that's what I'm trying to say! I do!

[*She looks down at her arm, which* LYNCH *has impulsively taken hold of. He lets go of it—embarrassed.*]

I'm sorry.
WOMAN: You really don't have a clue, do you?
LYNCH [*beat, hurt*]: Maybe not.

[*She stares at him. Then, after a moment, she reaches into her bag, taking out a business card.*]

WOMAN: Call me. That's my cell phone. Call me after ten.
LYNCH: But—
WOMAN: Call me.

[*And with that, the* WOMAN *exits. When she does,* LYNCH *turns to Chorus Editor, who appears across the stage from him.*]

CHORUS 4: And?
LYNCH: And I think she's going to give me something.
CHORUS 4: Great.
LYNCH: Look, you're . . . I don't think you understand what I'm after here.
CHORUS 4: You're right.
LYNCH: I . . . [*then, impatiently*] . . . look, we live in two countries. We don't live in one country. We live in two countries. And I'm in the other one. And I'm getting a report.
CHORUS 4: Great.
LYNCH: And I'd like you to publish it!
CHORUS 4: Look . . . I told you. I—
LYNCH [*suddenly*]: Shit, it's after ten! I'll call you back. [*Aggressively*] Hello?

[*This last he does instantly, the* WOMAN *appearing across the stage.*]

WOMAN [*wary*]: Hello.
LYNCH: From New York, the writer? [*Beat, then more insistently*] I'm the writer from New York.

[*The lights fade on the editor.*]

WOMAN: Oh. Yes. [*Cold*] Hello.

LYNCH [*tentative*]: Can . . . can I speak to you?

WOMAN: Go ahead.

LYNCH: I mean . . . in person.

WOMAN: No. I don't think so.

LYNCH: Please!

[*Beat.*]

WOMAN: Why do you want to talk to me?

LYNCH: I just . . . I have a "sense" about you. That you'll . . . that you'll tell me what I need to know.

WOMAN [*amused*]: A sense, huh?

LYNCH: Yes.

WOMAN: Well, you tell me about you. 'Fore I tell you about me, you tell me about you.

LYNCH [*thrown*]: What do you want to know?

WOMAN: Who you are.

LYNCH: I told you, I'm a writer. [*Unable to think of something better*] I'm . . . I'm a writer.

WOMAN: Who you ARE!

[*Pause.* LYNCH *is genuinely puzzled.*]

LYNCH: I don't know what you mean. I'm a . . . I'm single, I'm—

WOMAN [*amused again*]: You're single?

LYNCH: Yes. [*Beat.*] I'm single, I live in New York. I write articles, I'm . . . What do you want to know???

WOMAN: Is this difficult?

LYNCH: Pardon me?

WOMAN: To answer my questions. [*Slight beat.*] Are you finding this difficult?

LYNCH: I am, yes.

WOMAN: I see.

[*A moment passes, and* LYNCH *realizes the irony.*]

LYNCH: Oh. Yes. I see. [*Beat.*] Well, what do you want to know?

WOMAN: What I asked you. Who ARE you?

LYNCH: Can I meet you? To say?

[*The* WOMAN *considers this for a moment.*]

WOMAN: All right. [*Pause.*] Come to my house.

LYNCH: Where's your house?

WOMAN: Do you know the city? Do you have a map?

LYNCH: No.

WOMAN: Well, you'd better get one, hadn't you?

[*Beat.*]

LYNCH: I . . . I have one, I . . . I don't know why I said that. I have one.

[*Beat. She wonders about this. Then . . .*]

WOMAN: Well, I'm over near St. Roch. Near Bywater. Near . . . do you know Bywater?

LYNCH: No . . . [*Then suddenly, seeing it on a map*] Oh! Yes!

WOMAN: Well, I'm over in there. Near the tracks. Drive on over. Call me when you're near.

LYNCH: But—

WOMAN: Call me then.

[*Instantly the lights come up on the editor . . .*]

CHORUS 4: And?

LYNCH: And I'm driving over.

[*. . . and go out on the* WOMAN.]

CHORUS 4: Is there a reason you're keeping me posted like this?

LYNCH: No.

CHORUS 4: Are you gonna tell me when you're going to the bathroom next?

LYNCH: I'm—

CHORUS 4 [*suddenly frightened*]: Are you OK???

LYNCH: Yes, I'm . . . yes. [*He takes a moment, looking around, driving.*] It's just so dark. [*Beat.*] Dark and silent. Very silent. [*Beat.*] Eerie. [*Then, after a moment, resolute*] But I'm fine.

[*Lights then fade on* LYNCH. *Again we hear the sound of the motor boat, and lights come up on* CHARLIE, *a driller, who appears soaking wet in his boat, an unmoving baby held fast in his arm.* MAC, *in the near foreground, flails against* WATER.]

CHARLIE [*calling to him*]: OK, hold on. Hold on. [*Looking around*] This is a fucking joke.

[CHARLIE *tries to grab hold of* MAC.]

OK, give me your arm, man. Come on!

[MAC *tries to give him his arm.*]

MAC: Ahhhh . . .

[WATER *tugs on* MAC.]

WATER: Hey, we're headed south to the coral reefs . . .
CHARLIE [*to* MAC]: Come on! Move closer to me, man!
WATER [*pulling* MAC]: Where the skeletons underwater cut your feet.
CHARLIE [*looking around*]: What did I do to deserve the apocalypse?
WATER [*answering* CHARLIE's *question*]: Breathe?

[MAC *extends his arm.*]

MAC: Ahhh arm.

[CHARLIE *grabs hold, pulling hard.*]

CHARLIE: Help me, buddy, I don't have all day. Got to get to Houston. [*Looking down at the baby*] Fuck, fuck.

[MAC *extends his arm.*]

MAC: Ahhhhh.
CHARLIE: I can't do this alone. You're gonna have to help me, buddy! I've been down in there once. I am not repeating it. HEAR ME?

[WATER *pulls* MAC.]

WATER: See, everyone's too busy, Mac. [*To* CHARLIE] He's not worth it.
MAC [*swallowing water*]: Ahggghhhh.   WATER: The language of drowning.
CHARLIE: You're draggin' me in, man! [*Shouting for help*] THERE'S A MAN DROWNING! ANYBODY OUT THERE? [*Back to* MAC] Look, asshole, I'm going to give you *one more chance*! USE YOUR FUCKING LEGS!
MAC [*mumbling*]: Fast asleep.
CHARLIE: Move 'em back and forth and tread water, pal!
MAC: M . . . S.
WATER: Sssssssinking.
MAC [*fighting*]: NO, I'M NOOTTTT!
CHARLIE: OK, got you, pal, come on.

[CHARLIE *starts pulling* MAC *aboard. As he does,* WATER *caresses* MAC *from outside the boat.*]

MAC [*sputtering*]: MS.
CHARLIE: WHAT?
WATER: See, no one understands you but me.
MAC [*breathy*]: Use wheelchair.

[*And finally* CHARLIE *has him on board.*]

CHARLIE: All right.
WATER [*angry with* MAC]: Don't count on getting far with this guy.

[*After a moment,* CHARLIE *again starts the motor as* MAC, *recovering, continues to gasp for breath. Meanwhile,* CHARLIE, *glancing down at the baby, is beginning to fall apart.* WATER *trails behind.*]

CHARLIE [*looking at baby*]: *One thing I am not doing is leaving this baby somewhere ugly.* You can be goddamn sure of that.
MAC [*trying to explain*]: Multiple sclerosis.

[MAC *starts coughing, violently, turning away.*]

CHARLIE [*in response, understanding*]: Oh, is that what YOU GOT?
WATER [*pressing* MAC'*s leg*]: Gash took your pant leg right off. Beautiful legs.
MAC: OWWWWW. [*To* CHARLIE, *faintly*] Help . . .

[CHARLIE *continues driving the boat while* MAC *tries to show him his wound.*]

It was a garbage can. PLEASE HELP ME.
CHARLIE [*looking ahead, determined*]: Can't.
MAC [*noticing the baby, frightened*]: What is that?! The baby?
WATER [*overlapping*]: Abandon ship while you still can, Mac!

[WATER *pulls at him.*]

MAC [*panicking*]: IS THAT BABY SLEEPING?

[MAC *starts moving erratically to escape while* CHARLIE, *only half-noticing him, looks at the baby again, shaking his head.*]

CHARLIE: Wish I would've had some goddamn water for her. FUCK.
MAC [*coughing*]: I've had enough . . . Is it breathing?
CHARLIE [*starting to explain*]: I see a lady on the roof with her baby . . .
MAC [*a sudden pain, delirious*]: Uhhhh.

[CHARLIE *stares at* MAC's *condition.*]

CHARLIE: Geez, nobody bothered to give you a fucking ride out of town?
MAC: Water came up so fast . . .
WATER: That's what happens when you live below sea level.

[WATER *laughs.*]

CHARLIE [*looking back at the baby*]: The levee must've crumbled . . .
MAC [*suddenly horrified*]: WHAT HAPPENED? IS THAT BABY DEAD?
CHARLIE: SHUT YOUR TRAP, YOU HEAR?
MAC: Didn't you give it CPR?
CHARLIE: Yes, I tried. Shut your fucking mouth!
MAC: My son's in Iraq! He saved . . .
CHARLIE [*referring to the baby*]: I got to get her to Houston, OK? No little girl should have this happen to her—never.
MAC [*feverish, to himself*]: Linda's alive in her attic or waiting on the roof.
WATER: Don't think about her.

[WATER, *now at* MAC's *side, near the boat, again presses at* MAC's *wound.*]

MAC: Don't!

[*We hear the sound—incongruously of sawing—as* CHARLIE *is driving the boat.*]

[*Almost in shock*] What's that noise?

[*The pain of the wound overwhelms* MAC, *who calls to* CHARLIE.]

It's STINGING!

[*But* CHARLIE *can only stare out at the water.*]

CHARLIE [*nodding*]: There's gasoline down there and fucking cables shorting.
MAC [*suspiciously*]: Whose boat is this anyway?
CHARLIE: Mine. My wife and kids evacuated—I was supposed to work . . .
MAC [*sarcastic*]: Tell me about it.

[*Beat.*]

CHARLIE [*continuing to stare out*]: Thursday, calm before the storm, my little girl is giggling 'cause she put green food dye in the ice cream. It was her birthday. Her mom lets her do it for special occasions. Looks like this water . . .
MAC AND WATER: Green . . .

CHARLIE: I was supposed to leave the next day for a month. Who wants to spend summer in the middle of the Gulf on an oil rig? Then the levees broke and everything—ballistic. World turned upside down. You know how they fucking inspected the levees every year? With binoculars, then went out for a five-hour lunch. Got smashed off their ASSES.

[CHARLIE, *looking at baby, has begun to cry, and* MAC *notices.*]

Just wasn't fast enough.

MAC: Is that baby yours?

CHARLIE [*shaking his head*]: No. Lady's. I see the lady on the roof with her baby. The baby's falling. The lady jumps. I double back, I swim down. The mother's stuck under a car. Laced around the tire like a sea horse. All this tangled cable shorting out. I grab the baby. POOR LITTLE GIRL DIDN'T HAVE A CHANCE. *She's going to be buried.* I can tell you that right now. Those fuckers aren't going to get away with this.

[CHARLIE *cuts off the motor, as he and* MAC *have arrived at the interstate.*]

I-10. This is the best I can do. Someone will pick you up.

[*He reaches for* MAC, *grabbing hold of him and dumping him onto the asphalt—the hot asphalt in the bright sun.* CHARLIE *shakes his head pitifully, exiting, as we watch* MAC, *writhing in pain. After a moment* CHARLIE *reenters and places a piece of paper in* MAC's *shirt pocket.* CHARLIE *exits, and the sun gets hotter and hotter—its rays getting brighter and brighter on* MAC. *Then the stage goes black. And immediately a pair of spotlights come up on* LYNCH *and the* WOMAN, *the two facing out as if speaking on the phone.*]

LYNCH [*shouting*]: Hello?

WOMAN: Hello.

LYNCH: I think I'm near. I'm on Claiborne.

WOMAN: Claiborne and what?

[*He looks around, spotting a sign.*]

LYNCH [*blurting*]: Elysian Fields.

WOMAN: You're near. Two more blocks. On Claiborne.

LYNCH: Two—

WOMAN: And you're here.

[*And with that, he is suddenly before her. And she opens the door.*]

Come in.

[*She then gestures for him to come in, and after a moment, he does. What he finds is a darkened room, filled with the* CHORUS, *all of whom look at him intently, glowering almost, each actor holding a candle beneath his face, creating the impression of a mask.*]

LYNCH: Hello.

[*This last he says to the room.*]

WOMAN: This the man I was tellin' you about. Writer from New York.
LYNCH: Hello.

[*Again he says this to the room—and again there is silence.*]

So . . . I guess I'm . . . uh . . . [*while turning*] . . . huh . . . nowhere to sit, huh?

[*He looks back, and the* WOMAN *looks at him impassively, and he nods his head—a joke—before turning back to the rest of the room . . . which again is silent and eerily lit. There are candles everywhere.*]

So . . .

[*Again he waits for another to speak.*]

Are you . . . ? [*Then, to the* WOMAN, *uncomfortably*] These are your friends?
WOMAN: Yes. These are my friends.
LYNCH: I see. Well, that's . . . uh . . . [*Beat.*] And you told them what I'm asking about?
WOMAN: I did, yes.
LYNCH: And? [*Hesitant*] Did anybody . . . ?

[*He turns to the room.*]

Did anybody have an opinion?
WOMAN: About?
LYNCH: What I'm asking about. [*Nervous*] What I'm . . . what I'm after.
WOMAN: Ask it again. [*Eyes twinkling*] Let's see.

[*He looks at the room, unsure how to proceed.*]

LYNCH: The levees.
CHORUS I [*sharp*]: What ABOUT them?

[CHORUS I *has stepped forward. His tone is aggressive.*]

CHORUS 3 [*intense*]: Do you KNOW what you're asking? When you start talking about the levees?

[CHORUS 3 *has also stepped forward.*]

CHORUS 2 [*angry*]: 'Bout the levees. 'Tentionally blowin' the levees? Do you KNOW what you're asking? [*Beat.*]
LYNCH [*nervous*]: I think so.

[*There is a silence.*]

CHORUS 1: What?

[*Slight pause.*]

LYNCH: I—
CHORUS 2: Tell him about Betsy.
CHORUS 3: Ain't Betsy you should be talkin' about. Tell him about '27.
CHORUS 1 [*hot, almost angry*]: Do you know about '27? 1927?

[*Beat.*]

LYNCH: No.
CHORUS 1 [*nearly overlapping*]: Levees was blown.
CHORUS 3: Intentionally blown.
CHORUS 2: You believe what she's telling you?
LYNCH: I—
CHORUS 2: Tell him.
CHORUS 1: Men in a room.
CHORUS 3: WHITE men in a room.
CHORUS 2: Not one man elected.
CHORUS 1: All of 'em bankers.
CHORUS 3: Man named Butler, from the Canal St. Bank, biggest man in the city. He say—
CHORUS 1: "Gentlemen—"

[*He reaches for a hat.*]

CHORUS 2 [*interrupting, impatient*]: Look here, we don't need no dress up. Just say what the man say.
CHORUS 1 [*annoyed*]: Man say—
CHORUS 2: This the most powerful man in the city. A damn banker! The mayor kiss his damn ring!

CHORUS 1: He say—

CHORUS 2: And look here, you don't have to take our word for it. It's all in a book. It's all in *black and white*. In a book!

[CHORUS 2 *is now waving a book around. Furious.*]

CHORUS 1: He say—

CHORUS 2: He say, listen up, we are getting calls from our brother banks—

CHORUS 1 [*correcting him*]: Our correspondent banks.

CHORUS 2: Our correspondent banks—asking if we gonna survive this . . .

CHORUS 3: The city was facin' a flood at this point. A Mississippi River flood!

CHORUS 2: He say—

CHORUS 1 [*interjecting*]: "Gentlemen!" [*And here he looks over at* CHORUS 2, *angry at having been interrupted*] . . . if you don't mind . . . [*Then, to* LYNCH, *in Butler's voice, instantly*] . . . "much as we want to answer that yes, in the affirmative—"

CHORUS 3 [*in his own voice*]: Say yes, our city WILL survive . . .

CHORUS 1: "We gotta answer another question first. What are we gonna do to MAKE it survive?"

CHORUS 2 [*to* LYNCH]: You understand?

CHORUS 1: And this is where they come up with whats-his-name, that Army Corps general.

CHORUS 3: General Beach.

CHORUS 1: General Beach. Who say . . . this was years ago now—

CHORUS 2: Just blow a hole in it.

[*Slight beat. They want to make sure* LYNCH *understands.*]

CHORUS 1: He was talkin' about water, if water threatened the city.

CHORUS 2 [*angrily*]: Just blow a HOLE in it. The levees. Don't matter what people there is. Just blow a damn hole in it!

[*Beat.*]

CHORUS 1 [*also angry*]: And so that's what they did. Butler and them others. They remembered what that Army Corps general had said, the advice he had given, and they said you know what? That's what we're gonna do. We're gonna intentionally blow a hole in the levee, flood out part of our town.

[*Slight beat.*]

CHORUS 3: Only question was where.

CHORUS 2: Which is always the question.

CHORUS 1: And they chose St. Bernard Parish. Over near where Chalmette is now. Poor whites mostly. Trappers then.

LYNCH: And they *intentionally* blew a hole in the levee???

CHORUS 1: And you know who knew about it, ahead of time, and gave his permission? President of the United States. [*Beat.*] Calvin Coolidge. Said, "Hell yeah. You want to flood out part of your people, kill off some poor, save New Orleans? Absolutely, by all means, you have my permission." [*Beat.*] And so that's what they did.

CHORUS 2: Course they come in . . . [*Suddenly, to the others*] . . . remember they come in, with a promise.

CHORUS 1: That's right—

CHORUS 2 [*to* LYNCH *now*]: A PROMISE!

CHORUS 3 [*nearly overlapping*]: Say we gonna pay you all back.

CHORUS 1 [*nearly overlapping*]: That lost property.

CHORUS 2: But they never did. [*Beat.*]

CHORUS 3 [*very sadly*]: They never did. [*Beat.*]

CHORUS 2: Which takes us to Betsy, forty years later.

CHORUS 3 [*protesting*]: Let's not do Betsy.

CHORUS 2: Where AGAIN they blew the levee.

CHORUS 1: Now, we don't know that.

CHORUS 2 [*voice ragged, crying out, enraged*]: How else do you explain it? Water fourteen feet deep. My gran'daddy kickin' out them boards in his attic, kickin' 'em out with his bare feet—nails all up in them boards, his feet bleedin', bleedin' so you couldn't see nothin' but red—how ELSE do you explain it?

[CHORUS 2 *is very emotional, his volume raised, near tears now.*]

CHORUS 1: We ain't sayin' it didn't flood.

CHORUS 3: We sayin' we don't know that they blew the levees.

CHORUS 2: How ELSE . . . do you explain it?

[*Pause.*]

LYNCH: So you're saying—

[*Suddenly a phone rings, and* LYNCH *grabs for his cell, flipping it open.*]

What? [*Beat.*] [*Annoyed*] No, I'm . . . look, no, I'm fine. I'll call back when I'm out of here. [*Beat.*] [*Angry*] I'm fine! [*He turns back to the room.*] Sorry.

WOMAN [*irked*]: Who was that?

LYNCH: Friend, just—

WOMAN: You tell him you were coming here? [*Mocking*] Black part of town. Dark part of town.

LYNCH: I told him I was coming to see you. [*Beat.*] But come on, let's—

WOMAN: Meaning?

LYNCH: What?

WOMAN: What did you tell him?

LYNCH: He's my editor. I—

WOMAN: You tell him you're down here talking to black people? Getting their story?

LYNCH: I just . . . [*Exasperated*] Look, this story here is not me. And my editors. The story here is the levees. And I'm interested in what you were just saying. [*Turning quickly to* CHORUS 3] You're tellin' me the levees were blown, what, once, twice?

CHORUS 1: Once.

CHORUS 2: Twice.

LYNCH: Once in '27.

CHORUS 2: Once with Betsy.

LYNCH: Hurricane Betsy.

CHORUS 2: That's right.

LYNCH: And—

CHORUS 2: And I'll tell you somethin', if it wasn't blown, everybody sure thought that it would be. Had armed guards walkin' all up and down. My daddy remembers it. Armed guards, night and day. We knew they'd try and blow it.

LYNCH: And they did?

CHORUS 2: They did, that's right.

LYNCH: With the armed guards there?

[*Beat.*]

CHORUS 2 [*trapped, angry, defensive*]: Look, I'm not sayin' how they did it. I'm just sayin' they did.

LYNCH: I see.

[*Beat.*]

CHORUS 1: Do you know who else posted armed guards? All up and down the levee? In '27?

LYNCH: No.

CHORUS 1: Everyone.

[*Again there is a long pause*—CHORUS I *wanting the idea to sink in.*]

From Cairo, Illinois, all the way to down here. On both sides of the river. All of 'em believin' the very same thing: that the man on the other side of the river, if he can get away with it, will kill you. He'll drown your children. He'll wipe out your land. He'll take your home from you. Now is it true? Is it true that man—that other side of the river—will do those things? I don't know. But I know we all believe it. Which is why we post them armed guards.

[*Pause.*]

LYNCH: Still—

ALL [*outraged*]: STILL?????

CHORUS I: Did you say *still*?

LYNCH: I did, yes.

CHORUS I [*incensed*]: Still what?

LYNCH: Just because we fear such a thing . . . that doesn't mean that it happened.

[*Beat.*]

CHORUS I [*regretfully*]: True.

LYNCH: And—

WOMAN [*cutting him off, her voice angry*]: You know . . . you still haven't said why *you're* here. [*Beat.*] Weren't you gonna do that?

LYNCH: Do?

WOMAN [*aggressively*]: Tell why you're here. What you're after.

LYNCH: I did. I—

WOMAN: Why you're here. [*Beat.*] I understand what the story is. [*Beat.*] I understand what you're writing about. [*Beat.*] I don't understand why.

LYNCH [*shifting, uncomfortable*]: I don't know what you mean.

WOMAN: Why aren't you writing about Bush? Or Iraq? Or fashion shows in New York?

LYNCH: That's not what I do.

WOMAN: What do you do?

[*Pause.*]

LYNCH: Look, I—

WOMAN: Is that difficult to answer?

LYNCH: In a way. Yes.

WOMAN [*harsh*]: You like writing about black people? [*Beat.*]

LYNCH: I write about a lot of things.

WOMAN: But you like writing about black people.

LYNCH: I . . . [*Beat.*] . . . look—

WOMAN: Why is that difficult to answer? I mean, look, man, I'm trying to find out who you are. Why you're asking me things. You want me to answer all these things, you tell me who the fuck you are!

[LYNCH *looks at the others in the room. He is clearly embarrassed.*]

LYNCH: I'm often writing for *The Nation* . . . liberal publications. Places like that.

WOMAN: Uh-huh. So you're a liberal.

LYNCH: I—

WOMAN: Is that what you are? You're a liberal? You got a soft spot for black people?

LYNCH: I am a journalist. I am a journalist interested in stories that . . . cut across . . . [*Then, saying it differently*] That are about things that are important. [*Beat.*] That tell us something about where we are as a society, as a nation. I am particularly interested in the divide, yes. The degree to which our communities, the black community, the white community . . . see things so differently. See the same thing . . . so differently. [*Self-flagellating*] And why is that, why . . . [*About to continue the thought, he instead stops himself*] I don't know. Maybe I want to feel . . . better.

CHORUS 3: Better?

LYNCH: Yes. That I'm . . . I don't know. [*Beat.*] Superior.

CHORUS 1: Superior?!?!?

LYNCH: To other white people! To . . . not to black people. To other white people. Who don't want to see! Who aren't interested. Who . . . I don't know, maybe "superior" is the wrong word. Maybe I just . . . [*Finally, giving up*] I don't know.

[*The* WOMAN *is staring at him.*]

WOMAN: So you want to be superior.

LYNCH: That's the wrong word. I didn't mean that.

WOMAN: What did you mean?

[*Long pause—he is really trying to think it through.*]

LYNCH: I . . . [*Again giving up*] You know what, I can't explain it. And it doesn't matter WHY I'm . . . you know, whether I'm messed up or not, it doesn't change the fact that what I believe, what I THINK . . . is true. We do have . . . things ARE fucked up here.

CHORUS 1: It doesn't sound like you think "things" are fucked up at all. It sounds like you think "we" are fucked up.

LYNCH: No, I . . . that's—

CHORUS 2: Then why you got to challenge us? All the time? Everything we say. Every goddamn thing. "Still."

LYNCH: The story I'm writing . . . I'm trying to divide fact . . . from fiction. And what I'm hearing from you . . . a lot of what I'm hearing . . . here . . . [*Beat.*] . . . is fiction.

CHORUS 3 [*enraged*]: Is—

CHORUS 1 [*enraged*]: What!

CHORUS 2 [*more enraged*]: Who the fuck are YOU to say that?

LYNCH: I'm—

CHORUS 2 [*to the* WOMAN, *outraged*]: Are you listening to this?

WOMAN [*also outraged*]: Oh, yes.

CHORUS 2: Who the fuck are YOU?

LYNCH: The 17th Street Canal, right? Other breaches?

CHORUS 2: Oth— [*Practically screaming*] WHAT?!?

LYNCH: How do you explain those??

CHORUS 2: How—

CHORUS 1: Hey! It don't matter.

LYNCH [*continuing, caught up*]: Those are white people, right? But their neighborhoods flooded. How do you explain that?

CHORUS 2: How—

CHORUS 1 [*shouting*]: I SAID . . . [*Trying to control the group, getting their attention*] It don't matter. [*Then, turning back to* LYNCH] What he say . . . [*his voice dripping with contempt*] . . . it really . . . *really* don't matter.

[*With that, he and others slowly withdraw from the room,* CHORUS 1 *stopping just as he's about to leave. He then looks over at* LYNCH *one last time . . .*]

It don't matter.

[*And then he exits, leaving the* WOMAN *and* LYNCH *alone. And there is a long, long pause . . . before she too says . . .*]

WOMAN: It don't matter.

[*. . . and the lights then slowly fade to black.*]

ACT 2

We hear the sound of QUAN, *crying in the darkness, before lights come up on* QUAN OLDER, *who appears onstage alone.*

QUAN OLDER: I was a little girl about seven on that roof. And I barely
Slept.
The one time I did . . . The one time I fell asleep I dreamt.
Dreamed a dream so strong.
I dreamt that the world was crying, that it had
Eyes and that it somehow started sobbing and weeping
Crying so loud, so hard,
That it hurt my ears and made my eyes sore to see it.
I bent to put my hands over my eyes, to cover my ears,
But my hands wouldn't move. My hands wouldn't move
Towards my ears to stop the
Sobbing that I heard.
And when I woke from this dream . . .
SEV [*in black*]: It's all right, Quan . . .
QUAN OLDER: I was being pulled out of dark water back onto the rough rooftop by Severance.

[*Lights come up now on* QUAN *in* SEVERANCE'S *arms, crying.* SEVERANCE *is standing there, holding her even though he is tired.* PERE LEON *is lying on his back, breathing heavily.* QUAN *is crying.*]

SEV: All right now . . . I gotcha.
QUAN OLDER: Rocked me in his arms.
SEV: I gotcha, lil momma . . . it's all right.
QUAN OLDER: He tried to put me down . . .

[QUAN *screams.*]

SEV: Come on, Quan, now, I got to put you down.

[QUAN *cries.*]

It's all right. You just got to be more careful.
I'll watch you. I'll watch you close. But
I can't hold you 'cause then we both might fall.

[QUAN *cries.*]

> Hey, hey! Listen, listen now. I'm tired. Just like you tired.
> I can't hold onto you. We been up here too long
> For it. Now you got to get down and stay still.
> Cut out that crying.

[QUAN *is quiet.*]

> Come on now. Here we go, get down.

QUAN OLDER: One Foot . . .

SEV: There you go.

QUAN OLDER: Two . . .

SEV: Now sit down, lil Quan.

> C'mon, sit down.

[QUAN *hums.*]

QUAN OLDER: I was so tired.

SEV: Quan, baby, it's gone be all right.

QUAN OLDER: OK.

[QUAN *sits.*]

SEV: It's gone to be all right.

QUAN OLDER: So tired.

SEV: All right?

QUAN OLDER: All right.

[QUAN *lies down.* SEV *sits next to her.*]

SEV: Good, Good.

[QUAN *hums.*]

> Yeah . . .
> Just hum.

[QUAN *hums.*]

> You know I love you, Quan?
> You know that?
> You my favorite sister.

QUAN OLDER: I'm his only sister.

SEV: I bet you didn't know that.

QUAN OLDER: Yeah. I knew it.

SEV: QUAN QUANNA!

[QUAN *laughs*.]

QUAN OLDER: Sev did this thing . . .

[QUAN *laughs*.]

> Hah. He used to, he would
> Get in my face close.

SEV: QUEEN!

QUAN OLDER: And shake his head side to side.

SEV: QUANNA!

QUAN OLDER: It was so funny to me . . .

SEV: Ah!

QUAN OLDER: He had a big old head!

SEV: You think that's funny cause I got a big
Head. I know why you laughing.

[QUAN *laughs*.]

> Huh. You ain't slick, lil girl. You wait 'til
> You get grown you gone have a son have
> Big head too.

QUAN OLDER: I started thinking right then . . .

[QUAN *stops smiling*.]

SEV: Quan?

QUAN OLDER: Would I ever get grown?

[QUAN *hums*.]

SEV: What's the matter?

QUAN OLDER: It had been two days. And mostly all
There was was sky and water . . . No sign
Of nobody coming.

SEV: It's all right, Quan.

QUAN OLDER: No sign of anyone.

SEV: It's all right.

QUAN OLDER: Not even Jesus.

[QUAN *hums*.]

Just us on that roof. That sun and the heat.

[QUAN *hums.*]

Stinging . . .

[*Lights come up on* MAC, *on the I-10, lying unconscious on the hot asphalt.*]

Beaming down on us . . .
Holding us down.

[MAC *wakes. He tries to lift his head.*]

Wearing us out.

[MAC *opens his mouth, dying of thirst.*]

So hungry . . .

[*He starts to wriggle on his stomach.*]

So thirsty . . .
MAC: Water . . .
QUAN OLDER: Everywhere . . .
MAC: Water . . .
QUAN OLDER: Not enough to drink.

[MAC *can't go on and collapses. Lights fade on* MAC.]

Waiting . . .

[QUAN *hums.*]

SEV [*to* QUAN]: It's gone be all right.
PERE LEON: Everything ain't all right. That water ain't went down
   The none. In fact, it's starting to cook up and
   Make it hard to breath. Make it hard to stay
   Still. Huh.
QUAN OLDER: Heavy breath.
PERE LEON: Nah, this ain't no all-right world. This a troubled world.
   Soon . . . we'll be done with the troubles of the world.
SEV: Pere . . .
PERE LEON: Your old men will dream dreams.
   Your young men will see visions.
QUAN OLDER: It was me who was dreaming . . .
PERE LEON: But I have dreams sad to say look

Something like this here. I can see where the world
Headed and ain't nothing all right or "all good"
About it. Nothing . . .

[PERE LEON *coughs.*]

SEV: Pere, don't get excited.
PERE LEON: It's time to . . . Time to get excited and scared.
    The time coming to a close.
SEV: You just worried, man. Hold on, though. Somebody come for us.
PERE LEON: Who looking for us?
SEV: All this, man, this America, they know we down here.
PERE LEON: That's good, Sev. You got hope. It's in
    The wrong thing. Stop putting your faith in
    Man his hour over. World coming to an end.
    America or no.
SEV: Huh.
PERE LEON: You don't believe . . .
SEV: How come old people always
    Think the world coming to an end?
    When you was my age, you had floods and tornados, hell,
    Didn't y'all have slavery?
PERE LEON: Severance, you know I wasn't no slave.
SEV: I'm saying but the world wasn't coming to an end then.
    Every day was the beginning, right? A day to go do a sit-in
    Or protest the Klan for rights. You wouldn't fought
    For no rights unless there was gone be some day
    To enjoy 'em. Hell, people blowing up little girls in churches,
    Your friends strung on treetops, people who suppose
    To protect you, siccing dogs on you. They shot down
    The president, then blow up half of Asia and still lost the war.
    But nothing about that was the end of the world. Nothing 'bout
    That got you calling out Armageddon. But
    Now you old, tired, and a flood come through and it must
    Be the end. How come 'cause you close to death the world
    Got to be too?
PERE LEON: You see way out of this?
SEV: The sun going down.
PERE LEON: That's right. But can you tell me tomorrow it's gone be all right
    And believe it down in you deep? That's the difference, Sev.

That's the difference. Back then I could assure you tomorrow
Be all right. I ain't so sure today . . .

SEV: I . . .

PERE LEON: I know my Bible. I dedicated my life to church, me and
Your grandmother. I know that in the life after this here
My soul is saved, but I'm looking round at all this, and I'm
Scared. Scared that this what the rapture look like. I'm a saved
Man, and I'm scared. You, hell, you should be near 'bout terrified.

SEV: Don't worry about me.

PERE LEON: What you mean don't worry about you?

SEV: I lie, right? And don't come in when you want me to.
I'm irresponsible, you just worry bout you.

PERE LEON: Look here, boy, now I said some things. I meant
Them but you my . . .

[PERE LEON's *cough wavers.*]

SEV: Gone, Pere, don't argue . . .

PERE LEON: You my family . . .

SEV: You don't even want me to talk to you.

PERE LEON: Boy, we blood! Regardless of the foolishness. It ain't
Up to me to forgive you. I may not be able to, it's the Father
Who is full grace.

SEV: Maybe he ain't got enough grace for me.

PERE LEON [*coughing*]: What you saying, Sev? You don't believe?

SEV: Yeah, I believe. Just be still, Pere.
Don't get up!

PERE LEON: I'm still. Still in the spirit. My body trembling
But my soul on fire.

SEV: Just make sure you don't fall in that water and
Put it out.

PERE LEON: You don't worry bout that. My soul heaven bound, Sev.
You just said it yourself you sin sick. Just like this
World.

[PERE LEON *coughs.*]

SEV: Please . . .

PERE LEON: That's right, please. I'm asking you. You know what
It feel like to be left behind?

SEV: Pere, I'm a be OK.

PERE LEON: You gots to be better than OK! You got to be more than
    All right! I . . . I won't allow it, hear me!
SEV: All right, Pere, calm down.
PERE LEON: This ain't a time to be calm!

[QUAN *hums.*]

SEV: Quan, c'mon, hush.
PERE LEON: Let her hum. "Make a joyful noise unto the
    Lord!"
SEV: Pere, you scaring me!
PERE LEON: Good, boy! Thou shalt know him and fear him . . .
    I got to get you right, Sev!
SEV: Ain't nothing wrong with me.
PERE LEON: In God's eyes, that's right. Nothing wrong with you.
    But you gotta . . . You gotta be clean before you can
    Enter his house! Let me get you right.
SEV: Pere, just lay down. You ain't thinking.
PERE LEON: I ain't! Feeling now!
SEV: You gone slip!
PERE LEON: Slip down and the hands of the angels will guide my feet.
    Order my steps, dear lord! Lead me, guide me . . .
QUAN OLDER: He stumbled.
PERE LEON: Uh . . .
QUAN OLDER: But Sev . . .
SEV: I gotcha!
PERE LEON: Body weak but soul strong. C'mon, Sev, let me take you
    Down to the waters!
QUAN OLDER: They stood there holding each other . . .
SEV: You crazy!
QUAN OLDER: Both trying to save one another!
PERE LEON: No, my mind cloudy but my heart clear . . .
    Let me baptize you here!
SEV: Just sit down, Pere.
PERE LEON: Sit with me, Sev,
    Let me take you to the water!
SEV: Don't worry bout my sins now.

[QUAN *hums.*]

    Hush now.

PERE LEON: Boy, you my son.
   You know I love you? You know that, Sev?
   You sat there told that to Quan, but you know we love
   You? You my son.
   Grand or no, you mine. I won't have you fallin'
   Into iniquity when you can confess it here, Sev.
   [*Coughing*] I wanna see you up there . . .
   [*Coughing*] When we get there in God's heaven! I'll drag
   You if I have to . . .
SEV: OK . . . OK, Pere.
PERE LEON: Come down, Sev.

[QUAN *hums.*]

   That's good, Quan. Hum us a going to the water
   Song.

[QUAN *hums.*]

   Yeah, that's it.
SEV: Please, granddaddy, man. Just . . .
PERE LEON: Shhh! Sev, don't cry.
SEV: You scaring me.
PERE LEON: I'm delivering you. Giving you
   To my Father.

[QUAN *hums.*]

   Mmmm . . .
   Don't cry. Say with me:
   Our Father . . .
SEV: What?
PERE LEON: Our Father . . .
SEV: Our Father . . .
PERE LEON: I come to you humble and weak . . .
SEV: I come to you . . .
PERE LEON: Humble and weak . . .
SEV: Humble and weak.
PERE LEON: I have sinned . . .
SEV: I have sinned.
PERE LEON AND SEV: Against thee.
PERE LEON: Lay down.

SEV: Pere . . .

PERE LEON: Lay down, Sev.

QUAN OLDER: He reached out.

He laid down.

He touched the water.

PERE LEON: As he said to the Father God, John said

To the son of man, it is I who should be

Baptized by thee. But He who was without sin

And born of the Spirit asked him to suffer Him.

And John suffered Him.

QUAN OLDER: He washed my brother with the unclean waters.

PERE LEON [*coughing*]: There you are . . .

SEV: Thank you, granddaddy.

PERE LEON: There you are . . . Sev.

SEV: Just lay down now.

Please. Thank you.

PERE LEON: All right, Sev. You blessed now.

SEV: Rest yourself, Pere. Thank you, man.

PERE LEON: You all I got. You and Quan. Y'all all

I got left in this world. Wasn't gone leave

It behind. Wasn't gone do it.

SEV: I hear you, granddaddy. I hear you . . .

Rest now. Rest.

QUAN OLDER: My grandfather laid down. And Sev held him.

I laid next to him, and he held me tight too.

But I could feel his fingers . . . His fingers losing grip.

[*Lights fade on the rooftop. The audience now hears the sound of a hospital heart monitor beeping urgently, as lights across the stage come up on* MAC *in a hospital bed, with a sheet draped over him.* MAC *has been put under. Writhing, he hears a terrible sawing sound coming from inside him. He panics as* WATER, *at his side, kisses him, trying to seduce him.*]

WATER: Why don't you swallow me? And come inside.

MAC [*faintly*]: Help me breathe, princess, I'm going down.

WATER: CPR.

MAC: It hurts so deep.

WATER: Some storms are too hard, right, baby?

MAC: I'm through?

WATER [*smiling*]: You're gonna be a Mer-Man. Ever been down to Mexico? The water near Tulum?

MAC: Tikrit? My son was there!

WATER: *Turquoise*, we can live in the ruins underwater.

[*She holds up her hand.*]

We got a pact. H-TWO-OH.

[MAC *puts his hand to hers, for the pact.*]

MAC: Body's mostly water, anyway—no difference between you and me, right?

WATER [*coming closer, sexily*]: Salt of the earth.

MAC: I can taste you . . .

WATER: Hummmmm.

MAC: My wife to be . . . ?

WATER: Exactly.

MAC: Linda built me a . . .

WATER: Tomb? She'll be there.

MAC: Where?

WATER: Come see.

MAC: Wait, Linda went to the roof with her mom?

WATER: Shh, Linda went down a drainpipe, marry me now.

[*She holds out her arms, wanting to embrace.*]

You came into the world in a sack of water, you're going out the same way.

[*The sawing sound suddenly stops, and* MAC *starts to come to.*]

MAC: So empty. Where am I?

[*Seeing* WATER, *he frantically pulls at the sheets, repulsed by her.*]

GET THE FUCK AWAY FROM ME, YOU WET SEA HAG. What are you doing? GET AWAY FROM ME NOW!

[*Before he can continue, lights shift and* WATER *turns into a* NURSE, *who holds out her arms trying to calm him down.* MAC's *mind plays tricks on him throughout this next section, and he is never quite sure who she is—*WATER *or the* NURSE. *He is so afraid he is bordering on hysteria—which soon breaks out.*]

NURSE [*totally numb from overwork and what she's seen*]: Mr. MacWeller, please, you're OK—just waking up. You'll be . . . fine.

MAC: You look like a nurse.

NURSE: Why, thank you.

MAC: My son? Need to e-mail him I'm OK.

NURSE [*referring to his file*]: That's why I have these forms—we'll help you to get in touch with your family now . . .

MAC: And I need to call Linda.

NURSE [*nodding*]: We've got some paperwork to do. I'd like to start that process before you leave for Baton Rouge.

[*He is staring at her, now completely paranoid.*]

Not enough beds.

MAC [*trying to understand*]: Thought my leg got cut by a garbage can.

NURSE [*calming him*]: Now, now, you're at Ochsner.

MAC [*looking around fearfully*]: Where'd she go?

NURSE: You see, the anesthesia is wearing off . . . You've been through a lot. You went terminal twice . . .

MAC [*manic*]: She's been following me.

NURSE: Who?

MAC: She doesn't let up, she's *lethal.*

NURSE [*referring to file*]: You were taken by bus from I-10 with a vibrio infection. [*Hiding something*] I'm . . . huh, afraid it has a speedy incubation. [*Showing him the file*] And this man Charlie sent a note with you . . .

MAC: Charlie, with a dead baby?

NURSE: You're on antibiotics. [*Trying to smile to show him it's good news*] You should be able to recover with no problem in Baton Rouge.

MAC [*yelling*]: I'M NOT GOING TO BATON ROUGE!

NURSE: Yes . . . You are.

[*She picks up a glass of water.*]

Drink some water.

MAC: Don't get that near me!

NURSE: Should I call the chaplain?

MAC [*his mind reeling*]: I swam out of my house. *I* GOT AWAY. [*Looking at her*] Did Charlie leave a number?

NURSE [*ignoring him, showing him the file*]: We have some paperwork to do. How about telling me your son's name to get started?

MAC: Francis of Assisi.

NURSE: Is that his full name?

MAC: Francis MacWeller. He's a Marine in Iraq.

[*She writes this down. He is looking at her nametag.*]

No sense of humor, Sandy?

[*She doesn't answer.*]

What's the war news?

NURSE [*still writing, sadly*]: Another suicide bomber in Baghdad. Severe casualties. I think forty people died.

MAC [*losing it*]: I need to talk to Francis! And Linda. [*Bolstering himself*] People like Franny and Linda always pull through!

[NURSE *suddenly takes off her hat, becoming* WATER *again.*]

WATER: Mr. Me-and-Anyone-I-Love-Can-Survive-Because-I-Come-from-the-Jesuits-Who-Have-the-Key-to-God-Himself-and-the-Universe.

MAC [*horrified*]: Get away!

NURSE [*putting her hat back on*]: Are you OK?

[*Beat.*]

MAC: I don't feel very well. [*Wistfully*] I swore to myself I'd never go to Baton Rouge. I never leave New Orleans. [*Feeling a sudden pain under his sheet*] OUCH!!

NURSE: Phantom pain. In two weeks it will be healed, I promise. Do you need something for it?

[MAC *looks under the sheet, becoming upset.*]

MAC: WHAT DID SHE DO WITH MY FUCKING LEG? Tell me!

NURSE: . . . It's been . . . amputated.

MAC: HOW DID THIS HAPPEN?

[*Beat.*]

NURSE: The levees failed . . . They burst . . .

[*He just stares at her.*]

You were unconscious.

[*She reaches for the glass of water.*]

Drink some water. You need to drink plenty.

MAC [*shaking his head*]: I'm afraid of it.

NURSE: Keeps you alive.

[*He refuses to drink.*]

I've been here five days. So many surgeries I can't really keep 'em straight . . .

MAC: So that's how you misplaced my leg.

NURSE [*with some humor*]: Right. [*Apologetically*] We didn't think you were going to make it . . . Mac.

[*Again she offers the glass of water . . . he shakes his head, looking under sheet trying to be strong.*]

MAC: I'm such a sissy, Sandy.

NURSE: Me too.

[*She sags from exhaustion—trying not to show it.* MAC *turns it around.*]

MAC: Looks like you could use a drink. I'm a bartender. What's your favorite cocktail?

NURSE: Oh, wow. I guess, just a beer.

MAC: What kind?

NURSE: Guinness.

MAC: Oh, wow, you don't wimp out. [*Sympathetically*] Come on, Sandy, what *you* got?

NURSE [*getting teary*]: Patients in the ICU—fanning them all day when the power went out, in a hundred-degree heat? Dying . . . like flies. Everyone on TV saying, how could something like this happen in America?

MAC [*confused*]: Where was the president?

NURSE: That is a very good question, Mac.

MAC: Summertime, he's at the ranch . . .

[*She suddenly takes off her hat, becoming* WATER *again.*]

WATER: Time to leave your ranch and go north, cowboy!

[MAC *looks at her horrified, hearing the water sound. He tries to strangle her.*]

MAC: I'M GOING TO KILL YOU.

WATER [*eluding him*]: You better swim!

MAC: Give me back my leg!

WATER: Get over it, wear a prosthetic.

MAC [*outraged*]: HOW DARE YOU!

WATER: Better swim and pray.

MAC: Let me see Franny again!

[WATER *pushes him under.*]

WATER: Hail Mary, full of . . .

MAC [*sputtering*]: Please, I'll wear it.

WATER: BLOOD.

MAC: *Please.* [*Screaming*] Franny!

[*Lights black out on* MAC *and return, after a moment, on the* WOMAN'*s room. She and* LYNCH *are alone now, and she is staring at him—seething. The candles flicker.*]

LYNCH: Just tell me this.

WOMAN [*snaps*]: I got nothin' more to say to you.

LYNCH: Everybody's left now.

WOMAN [*incensed*]: And did you see how they left? Did you see what they was sayin'?

LYNCH: Look, I didn't mean—

WOMAN: You don't KNOW what you're talkin' about. OK? So why don't . . . [*She stops herself*] Like I say, I ain't got nothin' more to say.

[*Beat. She is clearly quite angry.*]

LYNCH: Why hold on to it? Whatever the history, what . . . if it isn't true, it isn't true!

WOMAN: Listen, my uncle was in the Army. And he say he saw a tree come straight out of the ground! Now you got to have some significant pressure for a tree to come up like that. And that only COMES with a bomb.

LYNCH: Still—

WOMAN: Why you keep sayin' that? You understand what I'm tellin' you??? There was people all OVER the Ninth Ward heard that sound. Heard that explosion. People say it was the sound of concrete crackin'. That is not the sound that concrete makes when it cracks. That is the sound—

[*At this, we hear the sound of an explosion. It is muffled, distant, a somewhat ambiguous sound. It could be an explosion. It could also, quite possibly, be something else—a transformer popping perhaps.*]

That is the sound of dynamite.

[*Beat.*]

LYNCH: But say it's not.

WOMAN [*astonished, outraged*]: Say . . . why you talkin' to me like that? "Say it's not." What difference it make to you???

LYNCH: Because if it isn't true . . . I guess the real question is why is it important to say it was a bomb?

WOMAN: Because that's what it was. Now, you can . . . but I'm tellin' you what it was.

LYNCH: But it's described differently by different people. Some people say it sounded like, I don't know, firecrackers.

WOMAN [*raising her voice, irate*]: "Firecrackers!" I didn't hear nobody talkin' about firecrackers. What I heard was people talkin' about that security firm, that "BLACK-water," walkin' up and down these streets like this was EYE-RAQ! This is America! And yet we had people walkin' up and down these streets carrying automatic weapons, and you're gonna talk to me about firecrackers!

LYNCH: I'm just . . .

[*Suddenly the* WOMAN *lets loose. The story that follows is tumbling out of her.*]

WOMAN: Look, here's the story. You want the story? Here's the story. A woman I know lived in a house in the Lower Ninth Ward. And on that morning, that Sunday morning, her husband, a man who works . . . I forget where he works, he says we are leaving town, we are getting out of here. You gather up your family, your mama, your sister, and we are getting out of here. He said this and he went outside to try and turn over their car. They had an old van, he tried to turn it over and it wouldn't start. And this woman is on the phone, she is gathering her people, and she is hearing the sound of that engine not starting. And she is hearing the sound next door of her neighbors doin' the same thing. They too had a van. And they ALSO were trying to get out of town. There was a mandatory EVACUATION order! Our mayor, our wonderful mayor, had finally gotten off his ass and issued this order, and she was listening to see if she was gonna be able to OBEY that order. She didn't know if she would. And then finally it did turn over and they got out of town. She gathered up her mama, her sister, and they *got out of town*. And they made it to Gonzalez. That's about fifty miles outside of town. And that's where their belt broke down. That old van, that van that barely started, it made it fifty miles outside of town and then it broke down. It wouldn't start, wouldn't turn over anymore. But at least they made it OUT. Got a shelter. And they found cots and blankets in that shelter, and they *survived*. The neighbors next door, the folks who also had a car they were trying to start, theirs never did. And they didn't make it out of town. And three of their family, two brothers and a grandmother, they died. And that woman, that friend of mine, she says she thinks about those neighbors *every day.* [*Choking up, voice hoarse*] How those neighbors could have been her—could have been HER family. That's the story. [*Barely contained*] The nearness ... the nearness of death. All around ... [*Crying now*] Needless death. Death caused by ... caused by ...

[*She stops, unable to finish.*]

LYNCH: Caused by what?

WOMAN: Man. It wasn't caused by nature. It was caused by man! [*Long pause.*] Do you see what I'm sayin'?

LYNCH: I do—

WOMAN [*shouting*]: But what!

LYNCH: It doesn't—

WOMAN: Look, I don't have the proof you're asking. OK? If you want proof, I don't have proof. But do I think it was a bomb? Yes. I do ... I'm sorry. I do.

LYNCH: I see. So—

WOMAN [*lightning*]: Let me ask you somethin'. You come from New York, right?

LYNCH: I do, yes.

WOMAN: When you were attacked, when the World Trade Center ... I mean, what did you think about that?

LYNCH: How do you mean?

WOMAN: I mean, did you just take what they told you? Did you just believe what they said?

LYNCH: I—

WOMAN: Those Saudis, for instance. Those Saudis the Bushes flew out ... did ... I mean, what do you think about that?

LYNCH: I don't—

WOMAN: 'Cause I tell you—

LYNCH: But I'll tell you what I DON'T think. [*Now it's* LYNCH *who is angry, enraged really*] I don't think it was Israel. I don't think the Jews were warned. I mean, you bring up the World Trade Center, that's one of the things that was said about that. That the Jews were warned! That the buildings were attacked by the Mossad! [*Sarcastic*] It wasn't Osama who attacked those buildings; it was Israel. That's one of the things that was SAID! [*Beat.*] And I don't believe that. And I believe that believing that, talking about that, saying that story ... [*Taking a moment, before continuing, portentously*] ... causes terrible, terrible harm. [*Beat.*] So no, I don't believe that.

[*She stares at him for a long moment, wounded.*]

WOMAN: Well, I don't believe that either.

LYNCH: But you see . . . I mean, that's the point, isn't it? The way rumors work. You see how dangerous they can be.

WOMAN [*scrambling*]: Look . . . what you're sayin' . . . the one has nothing to do with the other. I didn't say anything about no Jews.

LYNCH: I know.

WOMAN [*getting angrier*]: So why are you saying that?

LYNCH: I'm just—

WOMAN [*aggrieved*]: Why are you SAYING that?

[*Beat.*]

LYNCH: I'm just saying rumors can cause harm. Perhaps they can do good . . . but they can also cause harm. [*Beat.*] And I'm tryin' to show you how.

[*Beat. Then lights go out on* LYNCH *and the* WOMAN. *Lights immediately come up on* MAC *in his wheelchair staring at* LINDA's *wrecked house.*]

MAC [*to himself*]: I can't believe that's Linda's house. Like a bomb hit Gentilly.

[*Suddenly* WATER *appears to* MAC.]

WATER: Yeah, I did a pretty good job, didn't I?!

[*She points at* LINDA's *house.*]

Now say it: "I can see Linda's attic . . ."

MAC: Where she got to with her mom.

WATER: I can see the hole in the attic.

MAC: Where she got to the roof.

WATER: I can see my mark . . .

MAC: The watermark. On the side of her house.

WATER [*firmly*]: You saw Linda's mom's body at the morgue.

MAC: There's the air between the roof and where you were.

WATER: The place where she disappeared. She's dead, Mac.

[*And lights up on* FRANCIS, *who is on leave, wheeling his father closer to the house. Beat.*]

FRANCIS: Dad, we need to talk about Linda . . .

MAC [*trying to distract*]: You caught the baby, Franny!

FRANCIS: I didn't catch any baby, Dad. You keep saying that. There was trouble with some pilgrims at a bridge.

MAC [*gushing*]: You got the medal! Show it to me.

FRANCIS: Everybody gets a ribbon. It's part of serving.

MAC: *You love those people.*

FRANCIS: I love the Shiites?

MAC: You put your life in jeopardy every day, so they can finally have their freedom.

FRANCIS: Bringing up the Shiites to get out of talking about Linda. Jesus!

MAC: No, they believe in Mohammed, Franny. Ha, ha.

FRANCIS: I don't have much time.

MAC: You have bad days, Franny?

[*Beat.*]

FRANCIS [*looking down at his dad with sadness*]: You talking about Linda?

MAC [*facing forward*]: Yes, what do you do? Are there tricks?

[*Beat.*]

FRANCIS: Had a buddy, sergeant, went to this porno site where he'd trade photos of body parts for free porno. He went to the airport road, shot himself.

MAC: That's tough, son. How'd you handle that?

FRANCIS: You gotta turn it around. You taught me that. Saddam is gone. Elections are happening. We can secure that part of the world. People support us. Send us love every day.

MAC: I think about you every minute. The feats you accomplish!

FRANCIS: Look, Linda's boss at the lumberyard says they searched the streets after the water went down. They know she went to her roof with her mom. [*Adding*] They found a fireman in a storm drain, the water came up that fast.

MAC [*becoming upset*]: We didn't see anything there. [*Desperate*] She had clear marks. An appendix scar, my Irish ring. There's no proof she's gone.

FRANCIS: Geez, you are really avoiding the subject.

MAC: Just show me the medal, Franny.

[FRANCIS *takes out a ribbon from his pocket and gives it to his dad.*]

[*Proudly*] I know you. Congressional Medal of Honor. Beautiful.

FRANCIS: It's a ribbon.

[FRANCIS *has picked up a photo and hands it to* MAC, *as* WATER *lurks.*]

MAC [*refusing to take photo*]: All her stuff lying on her porch like a squished cross-section of her life, wrung out to dry. Her chessboard, her books, her DVDs. The shiny trees, lush, old testaments. GONE. She was planning to redo the whole house for me. I was serious about all the meds I was going to start taking. And then the phone went dead.

[*A phone rings.*]

[*Calling out, confused*] Linda?

[FRANCIS *runs to get phone.*]

FRANCIS: That's Uncle Christopher, Dad.

[*Lights out on* MAC. *Lights return to the* WOMAN'*s room, as it was before, the two,* LYNCH *and the* WOMAN *still facing each other;* LYNCH *holds out his hands— exasperated, frustrated.*]

LYNCH [*getting louder*]: But tell me this. How does it end?
WOMAN [*jumping, sharp*]: You know how it ends? This is two days after the hurricane. And a bunch of people were tryin' to leave [*Beat.*] New Orleans. And they went to a bridge in the middle of America. An *American* bridge. This is people leaving toxins in the street—leaving death and filth and dehydration. [*Seething with anger*] And they got met by a line of police officers who turned them away. Who told them there weren't no Superdome in Gretna. Who said, "GET THE FUCK OFF THIS BRIDGE!" and then fired shotguns on 'em to show they meant business. Now you tell me, in a country where such things can happen . . . why shouldn't I believe that other people just LIKE those police officers . . . wouldn't blow up a levee to save their own?
LYNCH: Because this story you're telling . . . this story of the Gretna bridge . . . may not be believed otherwise.
WOMAN [*offended*]: What are you talking about?
LYNCH: I'm saying there are many people in our country who don't want to believe that this kind of thing happens. And when you tell a story that CAN'T be substantiated . . . or worse, can be discredited . . . [*Beat.*] . . . then that story is used to discredit EVERY story—even the true ones. [*Pause.*] And so whatever chance we have . . . of making progress . . . of having justice . . . of saving LIVES . . . [*Long pause.*] . . . is lost. [*Pause.*] That's why you gotta say what is true. And not say what is not.

WOMAN: What I say . . . all that I say . . . every *word* that I say . . . is true.

[*Instantly the lights switch off on the* WOMAN, *and* LYNCH *turns out.*]

LYNCH: And I knew she believed that. That there wasn't a thing I could say . . . not a word . . . that would convince her otherwise. [*Long beat.*] So I went home. [*Longer beat.*] Home with the realization that I still didn't understand . . . and it didn't look like I ever would.

[*Blackout. Lights up on* MAC *staring at* LINDA'S *wrecked house.* LINDA *suddenly walks out of the house.*]

MAC: Linda?

LINDA: No one is as funny as you, where I am.

MAC: Where is that?

LINDA: I grew up inland, remember? Never liked water. I can't swim.

MAC: You saved my life. I couldn't get to you in time.

LINDA [*answering his marriage proposal*]: My answer's "Yes." Wanted to tell ya 'fore time got away . . .

MAC: Thought you were havin' second thoughts.

LINDA: No, I got swept off my feet.

MAC: Make it official, honey.

[*They kiss. She laughs and exits, as lights shift back and* FRANCIS *checks his cell phone, showing* MAC *what had been ringing.*]

FRANCIS: Uncle Christopher's coming to drive you back to his house in Seattle, Dad. They arranged a room for you. They can help you find a new bar to work in *there.*

MAC: You don't abandon a place when it's down, Francis. When you've had a history with a place, you share that history like a marriage. This may seem like a disaster area, but I still see the other place it was. That's more with me than anything. What am I going to do at Christopher's in Seattle? It's always raining.

[*Again* FRANCIS *hands* MAC *the photo. This time* MAC *looks at it.*]

FRANCIS: They say they want to make a mausoleum here for all the unidentified.

MAC [*accepting she's gone*]: For Linda. Right. I'll make my own.

FRANCIS: Livin' in the quarter by yourself?

MAC: Look, Franny, the military understands about Katrina. Stay here and help me rebuild the bar. We'll do it together. They'll give you some time off.

FRANCIS: I got another six-month tour, Dad—I made a commitment. They need me more than ever. I can't stay.

[*Beat.*]

I'm sorry. I can't.

[*Lights fade on* MAC *and* FRANCIS. *Lights go up on rooftop. As before,* SEVERANCE *is holding on to both* PERE LEON *and* QUAN *as the two are singing and humming, respectively, "Soldier in the Army of the Lord."*]

PERE LEON: I'm a soldier . . .
QUAN: In the army of the Lord.
PERE LEON: I'm a soldier.
QUAN: In the army.
PERE LEON: I'm a soldier, Lord.
QUAN: In the army of the Lord.
PERE LEON AND QUAN: Soldier in the army of the Lord.

[PERE LEON *coughs.*]

SEV: Rest, Granddaddy, rest.

[*Blackout on the rooftop. There is the sound of an explosion. It is a huge explosion, louder than anything we have heard before. After a moment, the lights come up on* MAC *starting off toward the sound, devastated.*]

MAC [*repeating softly to himself*]: Boom.

[MAC *is now bartending in the French Quarter. He forces himself to pay attention to a customer—a* POET *who is actually* WATER—*caught midsentence.*]

POET: Like I myself was underwater. I was so depressed. I'd just get up every morning and stare at the sheet of paper. [*Noticing that* MAC *isn't listening*] Mac?

[*Beat.*]

Mac?

MAC [*coming to, a practiced barkeep, but numb*]: Not even the usual *one word*? You average a word a day, right?

POET: It was down to no words. Then I came in here, started writing my epic poem.

[*Beat.*]

This is a damn good Sazerac. No one coats the glass with Herbsaint like you do.

[MAC *stares off in the distance, heartbroken. The* POET *plays bartender.*]

What *you* got, Mac?

[MAC *looks at her for a moment in silence.*]

MAC [*confessing*]: Why are we there? We can't save our own cities, and we try to save theirs?
POET: Right.
MAC [*with difficulty*]: I should have *demanded* that he stay and help me. That he owed it to his old father.
POET: Yes.
MAC: He'd still be alive. Not dead from a roadside bomb. Boom . . .

[*He takes out a medal. A moment passes.*]

In the moment before your last breath and the person who saves you, there's a whole life—I have to look at that, right?
POET: You do.
MAC: Maybe on that road he saved a boy who'll grow up and be president of his country . . . [*With understanding*] Nature. It's *predictable*—it will drown you. But Man. *He* is surprising.

[POET *takes his hand.*]

POET: He is.

[*Beat.*]

MAC: This city is ripe for predators coming in and turning it into something *typical*, and we're going to have to be vigilant. It's not going to be a mausoleum—I can tell you that right now, what we have here is going to be *living*. Make them build Cat 5 levees and none of those coffee places where they call a small "a tall." Survival is the mark of man.

[*He hangs the medal behind the bar.*]

Let me get you another drink.

[*He turns to get the drink.*]

POET: Sounds like you won . . . For now.

[MAC *puts the drink down in front of her.*]

MAC: What *you* got? Wow me with your word, baby.

[*The* POET *reads.*]

POET: Water.

[*Blackout.*]

BECAUSE THEY HAVE
NO WORDS

Tim Maddock and Lotti Louise Pharriss

PRODUCTION HISTORY

Because They Have No Words premiered at the Lounge Theatre in Los Angeles, California, on September 2, 2006, where it won Ovation Awards for Best Ensemble and Best World Premiere Play, an LA Weekly Award for Best Ensemble, and Garland Awards for Best Director (Emilie Beck) and Best Ensemble. The play, again directed by Emilie Beck, was then produced in 2008 at the Piven Theatre Workshop in Evanston, Illinois, where it won a Joseph Jefferson Award for Best Sound Design and was nominated for Best Ensemble. A staged reading of the play was produced in May 2008 at the Acme Comedy Theatre in Los Angeles to benefit In Defense of Animals.

STAGING

The play is written in the style of "story theater." Tim and the other characters not only converse in dialogue with each other, but also narrate directly to the audience. How this is handled is at the discretion of the director. We have only provided a few stage directions for clarification where necessary.

Ideally, future productions should feature an ethnically diverse ensemble of actors to play roles across gender and racial lines, as was the case in the premiere production. Producers may expand the number of actors in the ensemble at their discretion, but a minimum of six is required. A suggested breakdown of roles is as follows:

Tim, played by a white man. A gay male in his late twenties to thirties. One actor plays this part throughout the play and has no other roles.

Actor 1, played by a white woman. White Barista; Bitchy Volunteer; No-Rules Friend; Luna; Utility Guy 1; DeeDee; Captain Deering; Dolly; Computer Nerd; Artemis; Reporter; JoAnn Turnbull; Taco Bell Counter Girl; Shelter Employee.

Actor 2, played by African American or Latina woman. Insurance Adjuster; Celine; Martine; Mandy Honeychurch; Vet; Pet Psychic Nut; Shelly; Evacuee with Cat; White Woman at Taco Bell; Lupe.

Actor 3, played by African American woman. Weather Reporter; Armed Guard 1; Helpful Volunteer; Mikah; Nurse; Animal Control 2; DMAT Woman; Janelle Anderson; Neighbor Woman; Louise; National Guard 2; Momma; Wife; Friend in Line at Taco Bell; Gasper; Bud's Sister; Nancy.

Actor 4, played by white man. Kelly; Jean-Luc; Armed Guard 2; No-Rules Guy; Nice Lady; Angel; Hospital Man; Utility Guy 2; Animal Control 1; Mr. Anderson; Neighbor Man; Bud; National Guard 1; Jerry; Crazy Cat Lady; Cameraman; Sam; Black Man in Line at Taco Bell; François.

Actor 5, played by African American man. Gas Station Attendant; Black Barista; Volunteer Coordinator; Bubba; Hospital Employee; Pete; Jack; Ben Ostenberg; Chalmette Woman; Export; Grandma; Satan's Neighbor; Older Gentleman; Lawyer; Taco Bell Manager; Bud's Sister's Husband.

Most of the actors play the role of an animal at some point during the play. None of these speaks except for Pete (the wolf dog) at the end of the play, and this takes place in Tim's imagination. Our suggestion is for the actors to play these roles as people but perhaps with one characteristic of that animal, rather than as a "caricature" of a cat or dog.

In the premier production, all actors wore a basic "uniform" costume of green army-type pants, white T-shirts, and brown tennis or hiking shoes. Only small costume changes were made to convey individual characters: the addition of a hat, scarf, glasses, or the like.

Set and props were minimal, as all actors were on stage for the entire play. To convey a sense of place in New Orleans after Hurricane Katrina, symbols were spray-painted on the walls and stage floor, like those used to mark houses in the Gulf by the National Guard and other rescue organizations.

To request a disc of production photos, please contact Weirdsmobile Productions: producer@weirdsmobile.net. In accordance with rules set forth by Actors' Equity Association, there is no video copy of the production.

ACT I

SCENE 1—INSTRUCTIONS FROM HQ

ACTOR 1: Disaster response is a hazardous activity and requires a certain kind of person.

ACTOR 5: To be a valuable responder, you must be flexible and willing to do whatever is needed . . .

ACTOR 4: Even if it is not what you thought you would do when you signed on.

ACTOR 3: Life at a disaster site includes heat, humidity, and sun . . .

ACTOR 2: Uncertain accommodations . . .

ACTOR 4: Debris, flooding . . .

ACTOR 3: Uncertain encounters with distressed animals . . .

ACTOR 1: Both domestic and wildlife . . .

ACTOR 2: Sanitation issues . . .

ACTOR 5: And lack of power and communication.

ACTOR 4: Most importantly, you must be a trained professional in animal control, veterinary medicine, or emergency military response to be asked to perform rescues.

ACTOR 3: Untrained volunteers are valuable as well and will be asked to perform administrative tasks and duties associated with keeping animals safe and healthy . . .

ACTOR 5: Including cage cleaning.

ACTOR 2: Our team leaders will make every effort to fit the job to your skills.

ACTOR 1: We will never put you in a situation where you feel unsafe or threaten the safety of the team.

[*Lights shift.*]

TIM: I had wanted to do something at the one-year anniversary of my mom's death to commemorate the kind of selfless person she was . . . and, truth be told, to try to regain my sense of hope that seemed to die with her. Volunteering in New Orleans after Hurricane Katrina would fix this. Revive my sense of hope with people helping people, smile on your brother, love one another, yadah yadah yadah—it's an easy solution. And while it sounded like a great idea in theory, actually calling and giving my name was completely terrifying. I called the Red Cross and the Humane Society and was secretly relieved when they said they were full up for volunteers. A couple of weeks went by, and I pretty much forgot about the whole thing, until I received an e-mail from the Humane Society . . .

ACTOR 1: "Disaster response is a hazardous activity and requires a certain kind of person . . ."

TIM: That's the one. It also contained a list of things I was supposed to bring along on this mission, should I choose to accept it . . .

ACTOR 2: Sleeping bag, long pants, rain poncho.

ACTOR 4: Waterproof work or hiking boots.

TIM: Check.

[ACTORS *begin speaking faster, and* TIM *struggles to keep up.*]

ACTOR 3: Personal first aid kit. Two-week supply of toiletries and medication.

ACTOR 4: Sunblock, hand sanitizer, insect repellant . . .

ACTOR 5: Flashlight with extra batteries, multi-tool kit, canteen . . .

ACTOR 1: Tent, tarp, space blanket . . .

TIM: OK, hold up . . .

ACTOR 2: Filter masks, surgical gloves, goggles . . .

ACTOR 3: Reflective vest, personal flotation device if available . . .

ACTOR 4: Helmet . . .

ACTOR 2: Construction type OK.

ACTOR 5: Water purification system, generator, FRS radio, GPS unit.

TIM: What the hell is a "personal flotation device"? But I thought, OK, those last items are just for animal control officers doing the actual rescues, and I won't have to worry about that if I go.

[ACTORS *cough or whistle guiltily.*]

ACTORS: See you in Louisiana!

SCENE 2—THE JOURNEY TO NEW ORLEANS

TIM: I loaded up my car and left L.A. on Saturday, September twenty-fourth—three and a half weeks after Katrina had hit. I had a lot of anxiety driving that first day by myself—that mixture of fear and excitement, not knowing what I was really heading into. So I was listening to a lot of Tori Amos.

[TIM *sings a portion of a Tori Amos song.*** *See note on copyright page at the beginning of the play. His cell phone rings.*]

TIM: Hey, babes.

KELLY: Hello. How's my LP?

TIM: LP . . .

TIM AND KELLY: Little Prince.

TIM: The French children's story. My mom used to read it to me when I was little. It's about this little man—or, well, child—or man-child, I dunno—who travels to these strange planets and meets these interesting people and animals, including the Fox, which is my favorite part. The Fox has this secret, which is . . .

KELLY: Are you there?

TIM: I'm here, sorry.

KELLY: No, I meant: are you there yet?

TIM: Ha ha. I'm just outside Phoenix. But I've experienced major personal growth already, and I'm ready to come home!

KELLY: No, you have to have adventures and save all the little animals.

TIM: I'm kind of freaking out. I wish you were here.

KELLY: I wish I was there, too. But you'll be fine.

[*Lights shift.*]

TIM: This was the second time in my life that I'd been on a pivotal road trip to New Orleans. The first time was during spring break with a bunch of my fraternity brothers. It was just the guys—we'd banned our girlfriends from tagging along. I know—"girlfriend"—bear with me. New Orleans was the most amazing place I'd ever been to. It was very sensual and alluring, and almost immediately it held sway over me. My first night there, I got up from the bar at Pat O'Brien's, and without saying a word to anyone, I started walking through the French Quarter by myself. I went by an outdoor corner restaurant, and a waiter there locked eyes with me. What? Was my fly down? I stop and stare back, as if to meet his challenge, but I suddenly feel so exposed, so vulnerable. Pure adrenaline is coursing through me, and my head is saying "run"—but I can't.

[*Lights restore.*]

WEATHER REPORTER: "Hurricane Rita is poised to hit the Houston area later today. Evacuations are in effect, and we highly recommend avoiding Interstate 10 if at all possible."

TIM: So I found myself rerouted through Dallas like every other person on the planet. Once I hit Shreveport, Louisiana, and turned south, the chaos of the 10 was replaced by absolute stillness. I stopped in a town called Lafayette . . .

ACTOR 4: Laffy-ETTE.

TIM: Laffy-ETTE. I found a gas station, which was total mayhem.

ACTOR 1: Anybody know where to find a hotel room??

ACTOR 3: I've got two cartons of Pall Malls that I'll trade for a bag of ice!

ACTOR 4: Does anybody have a car-powered cell phone charger?!

ACTOR 2: I do! Do you have a car?

TIM: Are you the only place in town that has gas?

GAS STATION ATTENDANT: Well, today we are. We didn't have any yesterday, and we won't have any tomorrow.

TIM: I arrived at my final destination—Gonzales, Louisiana—at about nine thirty that night. There was a Starbucks right off the freeway.

ACTOR 3: Praise Jesus!

TIM: Every Starbucks in the world looks the same—step inside and you can convince yourself that you're at 26th and Wilshire, Santa Monica.

[INSURANCE ADJUSTER enters, talking loudly on cell phone.]

INSURANCE ADJUSTER: . . . And I told them, I'm not going into the city without a gun. My boss keeps saying it's safe, but I watch Fox News, I know the truth. It's like a goddamn jungle in there now. [To BLACK BARISTA] Yeah, could I get a super-cold tall caramel frappuccino, half-caf, half decaf, with a shot of green tea? [Back into phone] I'm a fucking insurance adjuster, not a Navy Seal! We're talking about properties that were dung piles pre-Katrina. Oh, and they keep asking, "Will we get payment before Christmas?" Sure thing, dickwad—Christmas 2010!

TIM: The town felt deserted, and there were HELP WANTED signs in almost every window. I asked the girl behind the counter, "What's the deal? Where did everyone go?"

WHITE BARISTA: A lot of people left with Katrina.

TIM: But Gonzales wasn't affected that much, was it?

WHITE BARISTA: No, it wasn't. It was more . . . um . . . what came after the storm. Or who . . .

[WHITE BARISTA discreetly nods to BLACK BARISTA next to her.]

TIM: OK . . . Hey, do you know where there's a Target or something like that around here?

WHITE BARISTA: Um, let me think . . .

BLACK BARISTA: There's a Wal-Mart on Burnside Avenue.

WHITE BARISTA: We call it Highway 429.

TIM: How do I get there?

BLACK BARISTA: You go down about half a mile and turn right on Burnside Avenue and just keep going . . .

WHITE BARISTA [*interrupting him sharply*]: Sir?

TIM: Did you say a half mile?

BLACK BARISTA: Yeah, that's right . . .

WHITE BARISTA: SIR!

TIM: Yes??

WHITE BARISTA: I thought you wanted help.

TIM: I did—I do. He was helping me.

WHITE BARISTA: That's just fine. Then you don't need me.

[WHITE BARISTA *walks away.*]

TIM: This place is freaking me out. Do you live here?

BLACK BARISTA: Um, NO.

TIM: Was that like, "No way in hell?!"

BLACK BARISTA: You know that's right! I'm from the city—I had to evacuate from my house in the Upper Ninth and ended up here with my aunt. But a job's a job, you know? Nothin' doin' in the city, that's for sure. Same old, same old, 'cept a lot more people dyin', most of 'em black. But we still ain't seein' Bush or Blanco or Nagin, y'know?

TIM: Are a lot of people disappointed by Nagin?

BLACK BARISTA: Why?

TIM: I don't know, that maybe as a black man he should be doing more . . .

BLACK BARISTA: Nagin ain't black—he's Creole, man! And that's a horse of a different color, if you get my meaning.

TIM: So I got my venti iced coffee and made my way down the street to the Lamar Dixon Exposition Center. At the front gate I was stopped by armed military guards . . .

ARMED GUARD 1: What's your business here?

TIM: I'm a volunteer with animal rescue.

ARMED GUARD 2: OK, follow this road past the FEMA tent and the Red Cross Shelter. That'll take you right to the Barns—you can't miss 'em. Just follow the smell of patchouli.

ARMED GUARD 1: Yeah! If you see a bunch of hippies and rug-munchers, you're in the right place.

[ARMED GUARDS *laugh and high-five.*]

TIM: Um, thanks. So I found it pretty easily, and walked over toward a sign that said . . .

BITCHY VOLUNTEER: VOLUNTEER CHECK-IN HERE.

TIM: Even though it was almost eleven P.M., I was sort of expecting the welcome wagon.

[*Lights shift for "fantasy sequence."*]

Hello! I'm a volunteer, and I'm here to check in!

ACTOR 4: Hi, Tim! I'm your contact person, the one who's been keeping tabs on you and expecting your arrival!

ACTOR 5: How was the drive out? Have any trouble finding us?

ACTOR 2: Let me show you to the volunteer quarters!

ACTOR 3: We'll let you get a good night's sleep then give you the grand tour in the morning!

[*Lights restore, and we return to reality.*]

TIM: Hi, I'm a volunteer, and I'm here to check in.

BITCHY VOLUNTEER: Well, we're all full up. Come back tomorrow.

TIM: What?

BITCHY VOLUNTEER: We're full. I have all the volunteers I need right now. Come back in the morning.

TIM: But they told me to come—I just drove from Los Angeles to be here.

BITCHY VOLUNTEER: OK, so you need to find a place to stay tonight. Come back tomorrow and we'll give you a job.

TIM: But I came all this way, and I brought my sleeping bag, a tarp, food, gloves, rain poncho, a canteen, and the broomstick of the fucking Wicked Witch of the West! And now she's telling me to take a hike??

BITCHY VOLUNTEER: And be sure to wear long pants tomorrow—you can't work here without long pants.

[HELPFUL VOLUNTEER *steps in.*]

HELPFUL VOLUNTEER: I just got here today, too. Let me give you the rundown.

BITCHY VOLUNTEER: And wear close-toed shoes!

[BITCHY VOLUNTEER *exits.*]

TIM: I was wearing close-toed shoes that I was contemplating sticking up her ass. And between those and the long pants, I was burning up. Even that late at night, the heat and humidity were unbearable. I was desperate for a shower.

HELPFUL VOLUNTEER: Oh, those are on the other side of the Expo Center—you pretty much have to drive to them. And there's only two of them for all the guys. They're also covered in black mold. You did bring flip-flops, right?

TIM: Flip-flops . . . No, I did not bring flip-flops, because flip-flops were not on the list!

HELPFUL VOLUNTEER: There's 300 cots in the FEMA tent—if you can find an open one, grab it. There's a meeting for all volunteers who are going into the city at five thirty in the morning. They'll give you a map with addresses where owners left animals, where we have permission to break in and rescue their pets.

TIM: Oh, I'm not trained for that.

HELPFUL VOLUNTEER: None of us is. As long as you go in with someone who's been into the city one time before, you're fine.

[*Other* VOLUNTEERS *begin to gather.*]

TIM: But I thought I was just gonna be walking dogs and cleaning cages.

ACTOR 2: Animals are dying out there! They've been almost four weeks without food or water, time is running out, and you're just going to sit here and clean cages??

TIM: But I don't think they'll let me . . .

ACTOR 4: Who's "they"? Man, who do you think is watching you? Did you fill out anything when you got here—contact sheet, emergency numbers, anything?

TIM: No . . .

ACTOR 5: Then do you really think anybody's going to stop you?

ACTOR 3: Do you think anybody even knows you're here?

SCENE 3—THE FIRST MORNING

[*The* ACTORS *present a picture of barely controlled chaos.* MIKAH *and another* VOLUNTEER COORDINATOR *are leading the meeting.*]

MIKAH: OK, everybody line up over here to get maps!

VOLUNTEER COORDINATOR: For those of you not going into the city, please see me for another assignment!

MIKAH: The city is broken up into eighteen sections! You and your partner will be given a list of addresses and a map of sections where there are still animals needing to be rescued!

VOLUNTEER COORDINATOR: We need people at Intake and Export, as well as inside the barns! Please see me if you are not going into the city!

NO-RULES GUY: Hey, y'all—could I say something?! PLEASE DO NOT LABEL ANIMALS AS AGGRESSIVE! If the animal is a fear-biter, then you are just dooming it to DEATH!

CELINE: Yeah! And could I say something?! Pay attention, everybody! PLEASE DO NOT BREAK THINGS IN PEOPLE'S HOMES THAT DON'T NEED TO BE BROKEN! Like, don't break down a door if there's a perfectly good window to break right next to it!

NO-RULES FRIEND: Could I say something? I feel totally helpless in this situation, and if I can just get you to listen to me, and get this one thing regulated, I think I can get through one more day without LOSING MY SHIT, OK?! Thank you.

TIM: Uh . . . Is there anybody here who has been into the city who doesn't have a partner?

NO-RULES GUY: I don't need one today, but I will tomorrow!

NO-RULES FRIEND: Yeah, I'm leaving after today, and you're going in with him tomorrow!

NO-RULES GUY: And just so you know—I break all the rules! I stay past curfew, I stay till I've rescued every damn animal I can get my hands on, man!

TIM: Great. IS THERE ANYBODY HERE WHO DOES NOT HAVE A PARTNER?

CELINE: I need a partner, but we're taking your car.

TIM: Thus began the process of loading up my 4Runner for my first trip into the city with this white Canadian woman . . . Let's call her "Celine."

CELINE: It's like a military operation.

TIM: I wanted to put a tarp down in the back . . .

CELINE: No tarp, it takes up too much space.

TIM: OK . . . So I packed in the cages, dog and cat carriers, dog and cat food . . .

CELINE: Power bars and two cases of Dasani water bottles . . .

TIM: Gloves, masks, and alcohol disinfectant spray.

CELINE: All right, do you have your credentials?

TIM: My what?

CELINE: Your credentials that identify you as a volunteer, that get you into the city. Come on, you're holding us up!

TIM: I asked the volunteer coordinator how I might obtain these mystery credentials.

VOLUNTEER COORDINATOR: Sure, let me see your driver's license.

TIM: Basically, he taped my license to a piece of letterhead from the Office of Homeland Security and the City of New Orleans . . .

VOLUNTEER COORDINATOR: "This authorizes the below to travel inside the City of New Orleans for animal rescue and response effort," signed Mayor Ray Nagin and Colonel Terry Ebert . . .

TIM: . . . photocopied it, and handed back my license with this bullshit piece of paper that would now supposedly serve as my official "credentials."

VOLUNTEER COORDINATOR: Heck of a job, Brownie!

CELINE: It was almost ten A.M. by the time we finally drove out of Lamar Dixon.

TIM: We were assigned to Section B, St. Bernard Parish, just east of the city proper in an area called Chalmette. St. Bernard Parish was one of the areas that was easily fifteen feet under water. The water had receded by that time, and this was the first week that the residents were allowed back into their neighborhood.

CELINE: This is good—I bet nobody's been here yet. Lots of animals. Everyone wants to go rescue in the damn French Quarter. Have you seen it yet? It looked fine to me.

TIM: I don't think I'm going to make it this trip—I'd like to remember it the way it was.

[*Lights shift.*]

JEAN-LUC: It's really dark, but don't be afraid.

TIM: The waiter . . .

JEAN-LUC: Jean-Luc.

TIM: Jean-Luc had led me to a bar called Lafitte's, which seemed to be all guys . . . and that was OK. There was that feeling of fear mingled with excitement, of a spirit inside me being unleashed . . . and the knowledge that there was no turning back from this moment.

[*Lights restore.*]

CELINE: Driving into New Orleans, you could start to see the first real signs of physical damage.

TIM: It went from, OK, the Wendy's sign has been blown out, to, wow, that entire apartment building has been destroyed.

CELINE: Roofs missing, entire wings of buildings sheared off, high-rises with every glass window in them gone.

TIM: There were boats everywhere—in the middle of people's yards, in the middle of the road. One that was sitting halfway on the freeway had the following message scrawled on it:

BUBBA: "Please don't tow my boat. Bubba."

TIM: You saw anything that could float strewn about: bathtubs on tops of houses, cars on top of refrigerators—everything buried in mud.

CELINE: Some things you had to look twice at to even know what you were looking at, like a mounted moose head lodged in a window frame.

TIM: There were military and police roadblocks at almost every exit on the 10 to keep nonresidents from driving into the city—luckily we had our "credentials."

CELINE: Our maps were horrible . . . [*To* TIM, *off his questioning look*] There are hardly any street names! [*Back to audience*] . . . and we ended up in the wrong neighborhood.

TIM: Our vehicle had ANIMAL RESCUE written on it in that "just married" ink, which seemed to draw people to us.

NICE LADY: Hey, are y'all lost?

CELINE: Yeah, we're trying to get to Chalmette.

NICE LADY: Well, you're nowhere near it—this here's Metarie. But here, sugar, take my map and follow me. It's a lovely neighborhood, Chalmette.

TIM: So we followed the lady back onto the interstate, and as we came over the bridge into Chalmette, the first thing we noticed was the stench . . .

CELINE: Like a punch in the gut . . .

TIM: Like sulfur, like raw sewage and decay punctuated with thousands of rotten eggs.

CELINE: Oh my God, I think I'm gonna be sick.

TIM: Out the window! Chalmette was a complete and utter wasteland. I was trying to imagine the lovely neighborhood the woman was talking about, but all I saw was a trash heap . . .

CELINE: . . . Like a slum someone had dumped manure all over.

TIM: I quickly realized why Celine didn't have a partner. Besides being bossy as hell, she couldn't read a map to save her fuckin' life. And some stuff came up over the course of the day, like . . .

CELINE: I hate people.

TIM: And . . .

CELINE: The penis is the root of all evil.

TIM: And . . .

CELINE: I own fourteen cats.

TIM: And she didn't seem to care as much about the dogs on our list. It would be like . . .

CELINE: Well, the dog's not here—let's go.

TIM: But for cats we were there for, like, two hours, climbing up under box springs. Not that I have anything against cats, but . . .

CELINE: You're a dog person.

TIM: Yeah, and I'm saying we should look for them all the same. Anyway, we were heading down this street where we had two addresses on our list, numbers 211 and 219. One was a cat and one was a dog . . .

CELINE: I'll take the cat.

TIM: Right, I'll take the dog. I stepped out of the car—I was wearing tennis shoes like these—and sank ankle-deep in what can only be described as shit.

CELINE: C'mon, get the lead out!

TIM: I found 211 pretty quickly while she was wandering up and down the street.

CELINE: 219 isn't . . . The addresses going up the street . . . The one next to yours is 227. It goes 211 then 227!

TIM: I looked on the other side of 211, and it was 223. So it went 223, 211, 227. Who's the Cousin Jim Bob that addressed this street??

CELINE: And then we realized: 211 had been knocked completely off its foundation during the storm, traveled up the street, and knocked 225 back behind it.

TIM: Having taken this journey, 211 was barely standing.

CELINE: It was creaking as we were touching it.

TIM: All right, I'll knock in a window and see if anything answers my call, but there's no way I'm going into that structure.

CELINE: We don't have a sledgehammer! They told us we should get a sledgehammer or a crowbar before we left, and you neglected to do so! How are we going to break in??

TIM: Mind you, we're standing in a yard whose appearance would rival any swap meet. On one hand, you feel so weird breaking into people's houses, even though everything's trashed. On the other hand . . . I fulfilled a childhood fantasy, picked up a basketball, and whammed it through the window.

CELINE: But nothing answered our call. We left a lot of open bags of food and pans full of fresh water. Hey, look, ANIMALS INSIDE.

TIM: Let me check the list . . .

CELINE: No, let's go!

TIM: I wasn't going to say no, but Celine goes charging into this apartment, ready to get those animals—or at least the cats. She zoomed right past a parakeet in its cage and a frustrated and starving kitten, its eyes glued on the bird.

CELINE: It was an adorable gray tabby kitten, wide-eyed and very thin. It immediately jumped down and wedged itself behind the refrigerator.

TIM: After much contortion, I somehow managed to get the cat out and into a carrier.

CELINE: We looked around and couldn't find any other animals . . .

TIM: But we walked out of there with a cat and a bird, feeling pretty damn triumphant.

CELINE: Until we noticed that almost every house had a BEWARE OF DOG sign hanging in a window or on the front gate.

[*Lights shift.*]

TIM: Our next stop was a hospital, the Chalmette Medical Center, and by far the most unnerving two and a half hours of my life.

HOSPITAL MAN: A man had gone in with his dog to try to rescue his grandfather on his way out of town, but he got trapped by the floodwaters. And when the National Guard came, they forced him to leave the dog on the second floor of the hospital.

CELINE: Somebody had spray-painted DOG with an arrow pointing up to that floor on one of the pillars outside of the hospital.

TIM: So we decided to go in and look. Which meant leaving my car unattended and running in the middle of the city, so that the air could stay on for the animals we'd already rescued.

CELINE: The hospital was completely destroyed. One wing of it was knocked away, just gone, and most of the windows were blown out.

[TIM *and* CELINE *enter hospital.*]

TIM: There were no windows in the main corridor, so it was very dark. I had a flashlight, but it sucked.

CELINE: The floors were slick as ice underneath a foot of sludge and standing water.

TIM: The ceiling had completely caved in in places, and its panels were like waterlogged bombs that dropped without warning.

CELINE: There were loose wires hanging down and across. You couldn't see more than two feet in front of you. We got to the end of the first corridor and made a left . . .

[*Lights shift to nearly pitch black.*]

TIM: . . . and then we didn't even have the light from the doorway behind us.

CELINE: No way, I can't do this. I'll wait with the car.

TIM: Which of course in my mind I'm like, You dog hater! If it was a cat, you'd fucking slog through this with me! I felt my way through a few more hallways, gripping my St. Francis medallion, channeling Shelley Winters in *The Poseidon Adventure*. I found a stairwell and was able to climb up to the second floor, where thankfully there was more light. It was like time had just stopped in every one of the patient rooms, like the people had just evaporated. There were names on the doors, but just handwritten notes that said . . .

ACTOR 1: "Bill in this room."

ACTOR 4: "Joe."

TIM: There was a urine sample still in the container next to one of the beds, food lying out, a pack of cigarettes . . . I don't know any smokers who would leave without their cigarettes. And I pretty quickly realized that they weren't just from the patients, that people had been living in there after the hurricane. So now I'm expecting to see desperate drug addicts rummaging around at any minute. I had seen the news before I left, and according to it, they were everywhere! In one room I found this message scrawled on a mirror . . .

HOSPITAL EMPLOYEE: "Dear Boss, I hope you enjoyed your vacation while you left us here to die."

TIM: In several rooms I found traces of where the dog had been, but there were hundreds of rooms in this place.

[CELINE *reappears, startling* TIM.]

CELINE: I have persevered and found a way up another outside stairwell.

TIM: OK, I take back the dog-hater thought bubble. Suddenly a flashlight beam started coming down the hallway from the opposite direction. It was totally fight-or-flight mode, like, "I can make it! She might die, but I can make it!" The potential serial killer turned a corner . . .

NURSE: Hi.

TIM AND CELINE: Hi.

NURSE: I just came by to look at my work station—I'm a nurse. I lost everything in my home, but I had a few pictures of my family on the corkboard above my desk, and I just wanted to see if they were still here.

CELINE: You shouldn't be in here by yourself—it isn't safe!

TIM: What happened here? What does that message on the mirror mean?

NURSE: Our boss went on vacation and told us that if we didn't come in for work the night of Katrina, we were all fired. There were some permanent elderly care residents, and we hadn't evacuated any of them until that night . . . so it was a major disaster.

TIM: We never found the dog. Back outside, the car was still there. Where were all those crazed looters I had seen on CNN?

NURSE: Not to say there aren't any, but my looter sightings have been about as frequent as my George Bush sightings. Even so, some folks are coming back now, so you best be careful if ya plan on driving back to . . . Where y'all from?

TIM: L.A.

CELINE: Banff!

NURSE: And you came all this way to help? And here we thought we'd been forgotten. It's almost enough to give me hope that things are gonna be all right.

[NURSE *exits.*]

CELINE: This whole thing is so traumatizing. We can't even understand at this point what it's all about, what effect this will forever have on our lives!

TIM: Uh-huh.

CELINE: Emotionally this will reverberate through every future action we take, and every life we touch along the way.

TIM: Uh-huh.

CELINE: You know, after this is all over, you have to come to Canada.

TIM: Oh, uh . . .

CELINE: I'm going to have a decompression therapy gathering at my home for volunteers. You really need that, Tim.

[UTILITY GUYS *enter.*]

UTILITY GUY 1: Hey, y'all. We saw the sign on your car there.

UTILITY GUY 2: This big dog over here—we think it's part wolf—it come up on us while we was eating. We tried to feed it, but it's too scared to get close enough.

UTILITY GUY 1: No, man—you're afraid of the Big Bad Wolf!

[PETE *enters.*]

TIM: I saw this enormous, beautiful animal standing in the road.

CELINE: It was definitely part wolf . . .

TIM: . . . and the other half looked to be Malamute. Like most of the animals we saw, it was nearly skin and bones.

UTILITY GUY 2: He ain't got no tags, but maybe y'all can help him find his home?

CELINE: There's no way. We can't take this dog.

TIM: What are you talking about?

CELINE: It won't fit in any of our carriers! Even our large dog carrier, it's too big.

TIM: I'm not leaving this dog here without trying to get it.

CELINE: It's not just a dog—it's part wolf! So even if we get it back, it'll probably be put down. And, I cannot bring an aggressive animal in when I'm already in trouble!

TIM: So she spills out this whole story . . .

CELINE: When Hurricane Rita was moving in, there was a federal mandate to evacuate the city and stay out until after the storm. Well, a bunch of us thought it would be the perfect time to do some liberating at the zoo. I fucking hate zoos, they're all like goddamn Guantanamo for animals! Anyway, we got caught trying to free a couple of baby hippos. Now I'm on their shit list.

TIM: Now you may be wondering, as I was at that point, why they didn't ask Celine to leave after that incident . . .

ACTOR 4: Who's "they"? Man, who do you think is watching you?

TIM: I poured out some food, and the wolf dog came right to it and started eating.

CELINE: Then I tried getting the leash on him while he was eating. It's usually a bad sign if animals are extremely food-protective.

TIM: He took the leash right away. I threw open the back of the 4Runner . . . Here, puppy dog!

CELINE: Tim, we are not doing this!

TIM: He tried to jump in but was too weak, so I led him back farther to where he could make a run at it. He made it in and lay down—he was exhausted. Then Celine started messing with his leash to tie him down. She went out of his line of vision, and he snapped at her.

CELINE: Oh, that's it! That's it, he's an aggressive animal!

TIM: Listen to me! You can't label this dog aggressive, or it's a death sentence!

CELINE: He's wild—he tried to bite me!

TIM: He didn't try very hard!

CELINE: What do you know of wolves? I am Canadian—I know wolves! Do you have wolves in Los Angeles??

TIM: He was just saying, "Back the hell up!" He didn't get through two hurricanes by being stupid!

CELINE: So we didn't tie him down.

TIM: I win.

CELINE: We have to hurry and get back to Lamar Dixon—there's a six P.M. curfew imposed in the city.

TIM: Which was extremely unfortunate, because it was so hot that animals didn't start coming out until around five thirty. Driving out of the city, we went from quiet desolation to a bad Disney cartoon, with animals popping out of every nook and cranny.

CELINE: Keep moving—I can't be late!

TIM: What are you so antsy about??

CELINE: That dog could sever our heads while we're sitting here driving!

TIM: Whatever. Maybe I was naive, but he was so weak. He had this weird, persistent cough, which I could only assume was from all the toxic sludge he was exposed to, or heartworm. Between the cough and his low weight, being part wolf and the fact that Celine was going to blab that he was aggressive the second we got back, I didn't think he stood a chance.

CELINE: By the way, your wolf just crapped in the back. And you don't have a tarp down.

SCENE 4—NIGHTS AT LAMAR DIXON

ACTOR 3: Evenings at Lamar Dixon were more chaotic than the mornings.

ACTOR 5: There was a long line at Intake of volunteers waiting to check their animal rescues in.

ACTOR 2: Some people were too impatient or lazy to fill out the paperwork . . .

ACTOR 4: Making sure pets were never reunited with their owners.

ACTOR 2: Smart people would try to find a piece of mail from the house where they'd found an animal, identifying the owner.

ACTOR 1: Occasionally a "critical case" would be rushed through to see one of the few vets they had available, like this one dog being carried in on a sheet that was just breathing bones.

TIM: There were certain people I'd see all the time there, like the group of animal control officers from Riverside County that I'd sit and smoke with outside the FEMA tent.

ANIMAL CONTROL 1: Look, bro, untrained civs shouldn't be out there. I understand that time is running out, but they're sending inexperienced people into a disaster zone, where, dude, anything can happen.

ANIMAL CONTROL 2: I'm sorry, bro, but he's right. We're overwhelmed, and we've got the equipment and training to handle this. You're not prepared at all. Like, are you gonna crawl under a house after a pregnant pit?

TIM: People would invariably be gathered in pairs or small groups, sharing their stories, like everybody just desperately needed to unload.

ACTOR 1: The air conditioning failed in one of the Export semis, and the entire truckload of dogs died!

ACTOR 2: Someone needs to be held accountable for all this!

ACTOR 1: Right, but who the hell is in charge?? HSUS? LA SPCA? Nobody knows!

ACTOR 5: Most of these animals were never even fixed. Girl, I haven't seen this many balls since Fire Island in '81!

ACTOR 2: The state vet is saying people can permanently adopt these animals on October 15th. That's in two weeks! It's not enough time for residents to find their animals!

[ACTOR 1 *sobs audibly.*]

TIM: And it wasn't shocking at all to find people just sobbing. You weren't like, Oh, so-and-so's crying—should I find out what's wrong?

ACTOR 3: No, because everyone's crying—and you know what's wrong.

TIM: Then there were the people who'd get shit-faced drunk every night.

ACTOR 4: Dude . . . This one night about ten of us flipped the hatch on one of the tanker trucks that supplies water to the porta-potties and went "swimming" in there . . . !

TIM: That was sort of a thinning-the-herd moment waiting to happen. There were the love-the-earth people . . .

ACTOR 3: Hello?!

ACTOR 5: Aerosol can??

ACTOR 1: Binaca—it's just Binaca!

TIM: And then there were the crazy animal people, the ones who . . .

NO-RULES GUY: Didn't follow the rules!

TIM: Right . . . and also didn't care for the residents who'd lost their pets. There were people who stole animals they'd rescued and decided they could care for them better than the owners. I quickly developed my own nightly routine. It consisted of amping up on caffeine at Starbucks and calling Kelly.

KELLY: John Roberts is the new head of the Supreme Court.

TIM: Wow.

KELLY: "Wow," that surprises you?

TIM: No. "Wow," a week ago that would have filled me with fear and anger, but it almost seems unimportant now.

KELLY: Well, you're dealing with a lot right now. How was today?

TIM: The good part is we saved a wolf dog . . .

KELLY: You know this story. What you don't know is how these nightly calls would end with a grown man sobbing uncontrollably to me. And how I hated not being there, not being able to hold him and make it all right. But even if I were there, some things just can't be fixed. I could listen, but I couldn't really understand. It was like his mom's death all over again. I couldn't possibly know all that was behind that sadness. It's so mysterious, the land of tears.

SCENE 5—THE STORY OF XENA

TIM: I met Xena's family when they came to Lamar Dixon to find their cat . . . and dog.

JACK: We evacuated to a hotel in Texas—that was the closest thing we could find. It was me, my wife DeeDee, my sister-in-law Martine, our daughter who has Down syndrome, and our Chihuahua Xena.

MARTINE: Xena was actually our mother's dog . . .

DEEDEE: Mama passed away from cancer a week after the hurricane, and so we took Xena after that.

TIM: I'm sorry.

JACK: Anyway, we couldn't leave Xena alone in the hotel room, so we brought her with us in the car when we came to find our cat, who had been in our house during Katrina.

DEEDEE: So, Jack and Martine went into the barns to look for the cat, and my daughter and I waited outside with Xena. Well, my daughter fainted from the heat and needed help right away, so we was taken over to the Red Cross by some military guy. And when we got there, the Red Cross people told us that the dog couldn't come into that compound. So this woman, I think she was a vet, she offered to walk Xena back over here to Jack and Martine, while they were looking for the cat.

MARTINE: But no one ever came to us with Xena . . .

DEEDEE: . . . and we ain't seen the dog since.

TIM: So this is bad—the dog was lost at Lamar Dixon and had been MIA for almost two weeks at this point. It was so absurd, so incomprehensible, that I'd been walking through barns with them for half an hour before I understood what they'd been saying: Their dog was lost by us, on our watch.

DEEDEE: See, Jack and Martine met up with us at the car, and I was so upset telling them what happened to our daughter, we were in the car for ten minutes driving before we even realized that we didn't have Xena.

MARTINE: So we turned around and came back, but we had to wait in the line again for three hours, and we couldn't find her.

JACK: It was late, and we had to get our daughter outta that heat and into bed. So I drove back on my own the next day from Texas, and still no sign of her. Then Rita hit, and I couldn't get back here for over a week. I guess this is our third time here, lookin' through the barns for her.

TIM: So I got all the information about what happened and descriptions of all the people involved. Listen, this could take all day. You could stay and wait, but I think it'd be better if you let me try to track these people down, and you can call me on my cell for updates. [*Recognizing they are still not convinced*] I'm going to make you a promise that I will not stop looking for Xena until I can tell you what happened or where she is.

MARTINE: Thank you.

[JACK, DEEDEE, *and* MARTINE *exit.*]

TIM: No one I talked to at Lamar Dixon had heard anything, no one had seen the dog, and there was no trace of her in the animal database. The next day I decided to follow up on the physical description of the military guy who drove them to the Red Cross. Walking over there, I passed a group of DMAT women . . .

DMAT WOMAN: DMAT. Disaster Medical Assistance Team.

TIM: Excuse me? This is going to sound a little ridiculous . . . And I told them the whole story, describing the guy who drove DeeDee and her daughter in the military vehicle.

DMAT WOMAN: You've perfectly described my boss, Captain Deering. I've got his phone number, hold on.

TIM: She calls him on her cell and puts me on with him. So I tell him the whole story . . .

CAPTAIN DEERING: I remember the entire incident. The woman who took the dog is a nurse, not a vet. Mandy Honeychurch, from Minnesota. Here's her phone number.

TIM: So I called Mandy Honeychurch in Minnesota . . .

MANDY HONEYCHURCH: Yes, I remember it perfectly. I couldn't find anyone named Jack, so I handed the dog off to an LSU volunteer named Ben Ostenberg. Here's his phone number.

TIM: This is almost ridiculous at this point, because my experience had been that people barely knew each other's first names, let alone their phone numbers, and then suddenly it's like "The Telephone Hour" in *Bye, Bye Birdie*. So I called Ben Ostenberg . . .

BEN OSTENBERG: Sure, I remember—I even took her picture, I can e-mail it to you. But I left the dog with Janelle Anderson, who was the manager of Barn One. Here's her phone number in Georgia.

TIM: So I called Janelle Anderson and left her a frantic voice mail. I didn't hear back from her that day, so I tried her again the next morning. Her husband picked up.

MR. ANDERSON: I'll get her for you. Can I tell her who's calling?

TIM: So I gave him my name and told him the whole story.

MR. ANDERSON: OK, Tim—just a minute.

[TIM *waits a moment.*]

Oh, I'm sorry, Tim—she must have just left for work. Can I have her call you back?

TIM: Yes, please tell her to call me right away. It's very important that she calls me back today.

MR. ANDERSON: Sure thing, Tim—she'll get right back to you.

SCENE 6—DAY TWO, WITH "THE DOG LADY OF DALLAS"

TIM: The second morning I headed over to the five-thirty meeting, with a wee bit of pride that I was now "experienced," having been in the city once before. If I could just avoid that one . . .

NO-RULES GUY: Just so you know, I break all the rules!

TIM: That guy. But luckily this woman stepped up to me . . .

DOLLY: Hi. Do you need a partner?

TIM: Do you have a car?

DOLLY: Yes, I do.

TIM: Sold! I'm Tim.

DOLLY: Hi, I'm the Dog Lady of Dallas! I learned everything I know from watching Animal Planet. I've even been on the morning news. And I'm a respiratory therapist, but I mainly do that for humans.

TIM: That made me a little nervous . . . But at least she was a dog person. That first day I spent with the Dog Lady—let's call her Dolly, for short—was not very successful.

DOLLY: We only rescued one cat, and the darn thing bit me. As we were bringing it out, the neighbors next door waved us over.

NEIGHBOR MAN: Hey!

DOLLY: Hi! Do y'all know this cat?

NEIGHBOR WOMAN: Sure, that's Mrs. Danvers. Mr. Charles will be so happy to know she's alive.

NEIGHBOR MAN: Hey, I have a question for you . . . Would you mind taking a look in my house for my cat?

TIM: Have you been inside the house at all?

NEIGHBOR MAN: Well, I've been in the den. But I left our cat in the bedroom, and I just can't make myself go in there. My momma told me I have to, and I really can't do it. Would you mind doing it for me?

TIM: Uh, sure. What's the cat's name?

NEIGHBOR MAN: Spiral. He's black and real big.

DOLLY: All right, hon. We're gonna go in there and look for Spiral, OK?

[*Lights shift.*]

TIM: It was amazing to me that any animals survived, let alone got rescued, under such hopeless conditions.

DOLLY: But you put your mask and your gloves on, brace yourself, and go into the house to look for an animal that may or may not still be there, or alive.

TIM: Sometimes the houses had already been broken into by the National Guard, which probably—hopefully—saved a lot of animals.

DOLLY: You'd see these X's spray-painted on the outside of the house. Within each of the four sections of the X were these symbols.

TIM: I could only focus on the number in the bottom quadrant, which told you how many bodies had been pulled out of the house.

[TIM *and* DOLLY *enter the house.*]

DOLLY: There's no electricity, so most times you can't see going in . . .

TIM: And the air, even with a mask, was unbreathable. The window frames were too bloated and warped to ever open again . . .

DOLLY: So sometimes we'd break a window, just to get some light and fresh air in there. Or fresh*er* air. Most of the houses were one story, which didn't bode well for the animals.

TIM: Like I said, Chalmette had been completely under water. The recipe for disaster inside these houses seemed to be . . .

ACTOR 5: Fill one-third with mud, the other two-thirds with water, and then shake the hell out of it. Seal it up and bake for thirty days at 105 degrees.

NEIGHBOR WOMAN: The stench, the black mold, the toxic muck covering everything were almost unbearable.

TIM: I almost left a shoe behind every time I took a step.

DOLLY: The ceilings were falling in, the floors were giving way.

NEIGHBOR MAN: Furniture was in the wrong room, or it had gone right through walls.

NEIGHBOR WOMAN: Every single thing that you owned was in the wrong place . . .

NEIGHBOR MAN: The family china, lamps, Christmas decorations . . .

NEIGHBOR WOMAN: Wedding photos . . .

ACTOR 2: Silverware, Monopoly game . . .

ACTOR 5: Ironing board, your computer . . .

ACTOR 2: Refrigerator magnets . . .

NEIGHBOR WOMAN: Your children's artwork . . .

NEIGHBOR MAN: All gone. Just thrown into the middle of the room.

DOLLY: And that was why it was so bizarre when you saw something that actually stayed on the wall, or one item in the room that was totally clean and identifiable.

TIM: These people had all those Simpsons figurines, like Chief Wiggam and Principal Skinner and everybody, still in the boxes. My kind of people. They had all floated, and as the water receded, the cardboard melded to the wall. And so you had these Simpsons action figures just arbitrarily stuck to the wall, looking perfect, while everything else was complete carnage. There was no rhyme or reason to any of it.

DOLLY: So you go into these homes that have been turned upside down, and you look for an animal that may or may not still be there, or alive . . .

TIM: And you try not to think about how hopeless that task seems.

DOLLY: You see the watermark about four inches from the ceiling . . .

[DOLLY *and* TIM *take a moment to shine their flashlights on the watermark.*]

TIM: And my first reaction always was, this animal is dead. There's no way it could have survived a flood of that magnitude. And with all the furniture bouncing around, where would it even go?

NEIGHBOR MAN: That's our bedroom. We'll just wait out here.

DOLLY: The room was completely turned upside down. Katrina had deconstructed the furniture, and everything had settled at knee level, as if a trash compactor had compressed the room's contents.

TIM: There were zero telltale signs that the cat made it through the flood—no footprints, droppings, nothing.

NEIGHBOR MAN: If you find him, and he's, you know . . . just say "not good."

TIM: And part of me was like, Please, God, don't let me find this cat's body with this man right here. I'm not a therapist, I don't know how to help.

DOLLY: Dag gummit, look—back there in the closet.

TIM: Dolly was shining her flashlight on some matted black fur in the back of the closet. I reached in with a gloved hand . . . It was a pair of fucking slippers!

DOLLY: Come on.

TIM: I'm really sorry, sir—we couldn't find anything.

NEIGHBOR WOMAN: That's all right—Spiral will be back! Everything's gonna be just fine!

DOLLY: I wish there was more we could do to help.

NEIGHBOR MAN: You know, it's fine. I'm alive, my wife's alive, most of my family's alive . . .

TIM: MOST of his family's alive?

NEIGHBOR MAN: Do you think DVDs are OK to take?

TIM: Yeah, I think they are. So he's left with his *Star Wars: Episode One* DVD, and the only thing I had to give him: a bottle of Purell hand sanitizer.

DOLLY: The rest of the day was no better.

TIM: It was pretty much a long parade of finding dead animals in various states of decomposition. It was obvious some animals had been feeding on the remains of others to stay alive.

DOLLY: Then there was the ferret.

TIM: I had chased a cat into the attic of this one house, where there was a huge hole cut into the wall.

DOLLY: The hole led out onto the roof, and there were ropes out there, so they must have literally chainsawed their way into the house to air-vac those people out of there.

TIM: The room was full of toys.

DOLLY: This is the kid's playroom.

TIM: There were several dead rabbits in cages and a ferret. He was just skin and bones, and most of his hair had fallen out.

DOLLY: He moved!

TIM: When I touched him, his entire body convulsed.

DOLLY: I had a clean pillowcase, so we wrapped him in that. He needs electrolytes. We had some Gatorade—Tim managed to open his mouth and rub his throat, and he got about two good gulps in him.

TIM: We've gotta get him to the triage thing, that emergency vet thing in the park!

DOLLY: OK, we'll take him, but I need you not to expect too much. You need to know that this animal is not going to make it, that he is in the dying process. He's got adrenal failure, and his little organs are shutting down.

TIM: So in the car, I just held him and talked to him . . . [*To the ferret*] It's OK, you're OK now. I'm sorry we took so long. [*Resuming with narration*] . . . And he died before we even turned down the next street.

DOLLY: You know, we aren't supposed to take their bodies with us. We really ought to go back and put him in his cage.

TIM: I can't do it. I just need for them to believe he made it. They'll find his cage with the door open and believe that he made it out alive.

DOLLY: You're right. Let's find someplace nice to bury him.

TIM: But there was no sacred space, and I couldn't bring myself to leave him out where some other animal could eat him. So we turned over a trash can and dumped the water out, and laid him inside of it, wrapped in his sheet.

SCENE 7—LUNA, GASPER, AND ANGEL

DOLLY: A woman pulled up next to us . . .

CHALMETTE WOMAN: Hey, y'all! Do you folks know anything about the animals that were pulled out of an apartment building over on Jackson?

TIM: Yeah, a gray tabby and a bird—I'm actually the person who took them.

CHALMETTE WOMAN: Oh, my golly! My folks know the people who live there, their name's Hazzard. You know, like the Dukes!

DOLLY: Oh, I love that show!

CHALMETTE WOMAN: Bud and Lupe's their name. My folks might know how to contact them. I know they stayed in that apartment during the flood, but I don't know where they're at now.

TIM: I'll give you my cell phone number. If your parents talk to them or have any information, please have them call me, and I'll help them track down their pets.

CHALMETTE WOMAN: Oh, swell! Say, did you get that other cat—the black one?

TIM: Great. We had no idea there was another cat, because they weren't on our list—we had just seen the spray-painted sign that said ANIMALS INSIDE. So in a panic Dolly and I drove over there. Celine and I had painted . . .

CELINE: REMOVED ONE CAT, ONE BIRD.

TIM: . . . on the side of the building.

DOLLY: And now someone else had painted right next to it . . .

ACTOR 3: REMOVED ONE CAT.

TIM: So while it was good that all three had been rescued, they were now split up, and I had no idea where to begin looking for the black cat. Besides the volunteers at Lamar Dixon, there were several other groups rescuing in the city, so the cat could be anywhere at this point. When I got back to Lamar Dixon that night, I was lucky enough to find the gray tabby I'd pulled out. I put notes all over his cage saying that I'd found the owner, so the cat should not be sent away. For the black cat, I checked with the computer people to see if any other cats went through Intake from that address, or under the owner's name—Hazzard.

COMPUTER NERD: Nothing.

TIM: A couple of days later, I heard from Bud Hazzard, the owner. He had gotten my number from that woman I met in the city.

BUD: Well, we're in San Diego now, but even if we never see them again, Lupe will be so happy to know they're OK. The bird's name is Angel, the gray cat you found is called Luna, and the small black one is Gasper. We named him that 'cause he was sick and gasping for breath when we found him.

TIM: Even though the computer said Gasper wasn't at Lamar Dixon, I decided to look through the barns anyway. Sure as shit, there he was. I took his forms over to the computer people.

COMPUTER NERD: Intake paperwork for this one was erroneously filled out. For the owner's name, they wrote the first names of the two owners, Bud Lupe. And their last name appeared on the subsequent line, after the street address: Two West Jackson Hazzard—thus explaining why I couldn't find him in the computer. Computers don't make mistakes—people make mistakes.

TIM: I was on a roll, so I ran over to check on the gray tabby, Luna—

EXPORT: He's gone.

TIM: Where the hell did this cat go?! I asked Export to see if he was one of the thousands of animals being shipped to shelters all over the country.

EXPORT: Yeah. The cat that's gone . . .

TIM: Luna.

EXPORT: . . . looks like it went to the Dixon Correctional Institute in Baton Rouge.

TIM: The cat is in prison?

EXPORT: Yep, that's one bad kitty. The parakeet . . .

TIM: Angel.

EXPORT: . . . is at a bird vet—it's in very good hands, so great news for you. And this other feller . . .

TIM: Gasper.

EXPORT: He's slated to fly to New Jersey tonight.

[*All* ACTORS *give a yell of panic and frustration.*]

TIM: Obviously notes on cages don't do a damn thing, so how am I going to stop Gasper from being sent to the opposite end of the country from where he needs to go?? I found Mikah, who was fairly high up in the chain of command, and told her the whole story . . . So, I talked to the guy at Export, and he said you have the authority to keep this cat from being shipped.

MIKAH: Um, I don't know that I do? Are you sure that I do?

TIM: Well, that's what I keep hearing . . .

MIKAH: OK.

TIM: So she wrote a big, red note:

MIKAH: "DO NOT SHIP THIS CAT."

TIM: With her signature . . .

MIKAH: . . . and attached it to Gasper's cage.

TIM: Thank you so much!

MIKAH: No problem. I just don't know if it's gonna do anything.

TIM: Yeah. Well, I have one more favor to ask you . . .

MIKAH: Uh-huh . . .

TIM: I want to take these three animals when I leave and drive them to the owners in San Diego.

MIKAH: Uh-huh. Listen, Tim—I need to know that you want these people to get their pets back, that you're not some crazy animal person.

TIM: Mikah, I promise you I'm being sincere. Then, in my best closing argument, I pulled out a photo of my beasty sheepdog, Bailey. I could never have two cats in the same house with her.

MIKAH: Well, let's get the owner on the phone and see what he says.

TIM: So she calls Bud, not entirely sure she wasn't just calling some friend of mine back in California . . .

MIKAH: Bud, would you mind faxing us copies of vet bills or some other paperwork that proves these animals are yours?

BUD: Darlin', I hate to break it to you—vet bills weren't the first things we grabbed when we went running for our lives.

MIKAH: Tim, I am going to take a leap of faith here, that you are not a crazy animal abductor.

TIM: Let me just say I did seriously consider kidnapping Gasper. Other people had gotten away with it, why couldn't I? But I knew I couldn't do it—I had to hope that being upfront and honest would pay off. So she signed off on the paperwork, which I ran back to the Export guy . . .

EXPORT: All right, under my authority, I will move the black cat into my RV for tonight so he doesn't get shipped.

TIM: Which is kind of funny, since he's the one in charge of shipping.

EXPORT: But Tim, neither my authority . . .

MIKAH: Nor mine!

EXPORT: . . . is enough to get Casper . . .

TIM: Gasper.

EXPORT: . . . past the armed guards at the gate. You need a licensed, brick-and-mortar, 501[C] 3 animal shelter . . . or a vet.

TIM: Fine. So I got the number for the Dixon Correctional Facility in Baton Rouge, and I tried to convince the vet there to come down and pick up Gasper the next day.

VET: So the cat you have down there and this one I have are from the same home?

TIM: Yes, sir.

VET: Don't call me sir, I'm not that old. Well, as a bonded pair they should stay together. Yup, I'll come down tomorrow and pick up this Gaspar.

TIM: Gasp-ER.

VET: Tomay-to, tomah-to. I'll see you tomorrow.

TIM: Then I tracked down the info on the bird vet, who was also in Baton Rouge—so all three animals would now be in one city for me to pick up on my way out of town. I was sure that I had just organized the mother of all Katrina pet reunions.

SCENE 8—CRASH COURSE IN ANIMAL WELFARE

ACTOR 1: We volunteers are here because the animals have no words!

ACTOR 4: They need us to advocate on their behalf!

ACTOR 2: United, we can do anything!

ACTOR 5: We can do what the government won't!

[LOUISE enters.]

LOUISE: Hi, I'm Louise. I'm trying to find my two pit bulls, Salt 'n' Peppa.

ACTOR 4: Well, Louise, we're here to help! What do they look like?

ACTOR 5: Look at her! We're here to help, all right—help the animals!

ACTOR 2: Yeah, I'm sure "Salt and Pepper" really miss being a part of the dog-fighting circuit!

ACTOR 4: You can't say things like that! Just because there are so many pits doesn't mean they were ALL used for dog fighting.

ACTOR 1: Most of the ones here weren't. The dogs used for fighting would have been euthanized by now in everyone's best interest.

ACTOR 2: What? That's not in the dogs' best interest! NO-KILL SHELTERS ONLY!

ACTOR 5: Why should we give dogs back to someone who would abandon them? I'd NEVER leave my dog behind!

ACTOR 2: Yeah! No return to sender, and NO KILL!

ACTOR 1: No, you're not listening to me. Sometimes euthanasia is the only humane thing!

ACTOR 4: What the hell are you talking about?? Murder is never humane—!

LOUISE [cutting them off]: Just stop! This is my third time here, and I got to tell you—I have heard it all! I swear I am gonna lose my weave if I hear one more lecture about heartworm, about spay and neuter, about dog fighting, and about how my gold tooth means I can't care for my own dogs. Do not sashay in here and tell me that I don't love my girls. Shame on you! Now y'all came here to help, and don't get me wrong—we are so eternally grateful for your help. God bless you for coming to help. But why don't you do just that? Don't come in here lookin' to teach, preach, and beseech! Could you please keep your little agenda out of my state when it's already on its last breath?! This is not the time! I may not be educated like you, and I may not look like you—praise Jesus!—but that does not make me some gang-bangin', drive-by-shootin', Olde-English-800-drinkin', Kool-menthol-smokin' dog fighter! How dare you come to my home and judge me! YOU DON'T KNOW ME!!

[Lights shift.]

When we were airlifted out by the Coast Guard, they wouldn't let my dogs on the helicopter.

ACTOR 2: We'd been through so many hurricanes, but it was never like this. I thought I would just be gone for a few days. I didn't know it was gonna be a whole month.

LOUISE: We'd been on that roof for thirty-six hours without food or water. I have a baby and a disabled aunt to look after.

ACTOR 4: I tried to stay—I wanted to stay. But the National Guard officer said he'd shoot my dog if I didn't leave him behind and evacuate with them.

ACTOR 5: We were on vacation when Katrina hit and couldn't get back in the city. Our petsitter left them behind when she evacuated. By the time we got back to the house, the door was broken in, and they were gone.

ACTOR 1: We had eleven people in one car, and one of them was deathly allergic to cats. Everyone else said I couldn't bring him—I was overruled, and they put my cat out the window. They just dropped him right out the window.

LOUISE: I promised them, "I'll be back for you."

[*Lights shift, and the sounds of rain falling and distant thunder begin. The* ACTORS *morph into other characters as* TIM *looks on. Meanwhile, the sounds of the storm build along with the* ACTORS' *emotional intensity throughout the scene.*]

DEEDEE: Tibideaux? Tibby? Where are you, Tibby?

JACK: Here, kitty, kitty . . .

MARTINE: Jack, we have to go . . . Jack?

JACK: We'll be right there, Martine.

DEEDEE: Tibby? Come on out, baby, please?

[DEEDEE *continues to look for and call to the cat throughout the scene.*]

MARTINE: We don't have time for this. It's gettin' bad out there already.

JACK: Just let us get the cat and we're out the door.

MARTINE: The cat will be fine! Mama and Xena are sittin' out there waitin' for us.

JACK: I know, I know! Here, Tibby . . .

MARTINE: Mama is in no condition to . . . We got to get her someplace she can rest, Jack!

DEEDEE: Please, you're scaring him! Tibby . . . ?

MARTINE: JACK!

JACK: Stop yelling at me and help us find the damn cat!

MARTINE: Do you know how bad the traffic is out there? We're gonna sit stock still for two hours at this rate!

JACK: Martine, help us or shut up!

MARTINE: Don't you talk to me that way, Jack! I'll leave with Mama if you don't stop this!

JACK: Then go! We'll be right behind you.

MARTINE: If we get separated . . . Jack, I can't care for Mama by myself! Please!

[*The other two* ACTORS *brush past* TIM *and enter the scene.*]

NATIONAL GUARD 1: Folks, National Guard. You need to evacuate these premises immediately.

JACK: What the hell are you doin' in my house?!

NATIONAL GUARD 2: Sir, you and your family need to leave here ASAP.

JACK: We're just gonna grab our cat and then we'll go . . .

NATIONAL GUARD 2: Sir, there's no time for that. You need to leave this house right NOW.

MARTINE: Jack, we have to go! Come on!

JACK: Just give me a minute!

NATIONAL GUARD 2: There is a category five storm moving in, sir! Do you know how many more homes we have to hit?!

MARTINE: Jack, PLEASE!

JACK: I know, I know!

[*Overlapping with these last few lines,* DEEDEE *is still frantically searching for the cat.*]

NATIONAL GUARD 1: Ma'am, we have an order for you to evacuate.

[DEEDEE *ignores him.*]

NATIONAL GUARD 1: Ma'am? Ma'am!

[*He reaches for her to pull her up.* JACK *sees this and explodes.*]

JACK: DON'T YOU TOUCH MY WIFE!

NATIONAL GUARD 2: We're just doing our job, sir.

NATIONAL GUARD 1: Then you need to get her. Now!

[JACK *reluctantly pulls* DEEDEE *up.*]

JACK: DeeDee, baby, we have to go . . .

DEEDEE: No, no, I just need to find Tibby . . .

MARTINE: DeeDee, come on! Mama needs us!

NATIONAL GUARD 2: We don't have time for this!

NATIONAL GUARD 1: Move out NOW! Let's go!

JACK: I'm sorry, baby . . . We got to!

NATIONAL GUARD 1: Pick her up, sir, or I will!

DEEDEE: NO, NO!!

[JACK *picks up* DEEDEE *and forcibly carries her offstage, as she wails.* MARTINE *and* NATIONAL GUARD OFFICERS *follow quickly behind. Sounds of the storm begin to swell, and* TIM *exits. Lights slowly fade to black, as sounds of the storm grow louder and louder.*]

ACT II

SCENE 1—THE XENA PLOT THICKENS

TIM: Flash forward. We'll come back to New Orleans in a minute, but this story went on long after I got home. I didn't find Xena the Chihuahua before I left Lamar Dixon. My one real lead was Janelle Anderson . . .

MR. ANDERSON: Sure thing, Tim, she'll get back to you.

TIM: But unfortunately . . .

JANELLE: I never did.

TIM: Two months after I'd gotten back from New Orleans, I'd still gotten nowhere with finding her. I'd searched through hundreds of Katrina dogs on petfinder.com. I had a couple hundred pages of lists of shelters to call, and the lists contained about four thousand animals. I'd sent e-mails to scores of shelters, foundations, volunteers, and animal rights organizations, and in return I received dozens and dozens of e-mails a day from compassionate strangers who wanted to help.

ACTOR 1: Is this Xena?

TIM: No, but thank you!

ACTOR 5: What about any of these I found on petharbor.com?

TIM: No, no, and no. But thank you!

ACTOR 2: There's a Chihuahua on the front of *People* magazine. Is it Xena?

TIM: That's Paris Hilton's dog. But thank you! As the story spread, people posted it on websites, blogs, and discussion boards. They also posted my phone number.

PET PSYCHIC NUT: I've been working with a pet psychic in Quebec City, and she's given me a lot of great information. First off, she can tell you whether or not your dog is still in this world or . . . in the beyond. Which is really good to know. But she can also see through the animal's eyes and give you clues. Like, the first time we talked, she let me know that my cat was up a tree and was scared. But then the next time we talked, she said that my baby was feeling more confident and wasn't ready to come home just yet. The cat was feeling very proud of herself—which is just like my cat! I hadn't told her what her personality was like or anything—she just knew that, you know?

TIM: So she can communicate with the cat?

PET PSYCHIC NUT: Yes, she can!

TIM: Well, then can you ask her to have the cat look at a street sign?

PET PSYCHIC NUT: No, it doesn't work like that! She can't control the cat, she just gets this very valuable insight into the cat's mind . . . all for only ninety dollars!

TIM: Oh, I see. Next!

ACTOR 1: I'm helping a guy find ten shih tzus. Do you think he's running a dog fighting ring?

ACTOR 5: All you have to do is say the St. Anthony Prayer: "St. Anthony, St. Anthony, please come down! Xena is lost, and she's got to be found!"

ACTOR 4: I've been doing my genealogy, and I think I might be related to Xena's family. Can you find out if they have a great-uncle Buford by marriage who lives in Slidell?

TIM: NO! I can't! This promise is going to kill me. I tried calling Janelle Anderson one last time, from a different number she might not recognize on caller ID. She answered.

JANELLE: I'm so sorry I didn't call you back. You know, I just couldn't deal when I got your message. I was so emotional after I left that place, and I had to not think about it anymore. But yes, I remember that dog very clearly. I had been checking up on her. She spent time in Barn Six with the evacuees' animals, but I know she ended up in Barn Five, and then I never saw her again.

TIM: So I'd tracked down thirteen volunteers from Barn Five, and not one of them ever saw Xena. Ended up in Barn Five, my ass. All I knew of Barn Six was that it was used to house the pets of evacuees staying in the Red Cross facility at Lamar Dixon. It was a total Hail Mary, but I called the Red Cross to see if they knew who managed Barn Six. I mean, an organization that was actually organized—dare I hope?

ACTOR 4: Oh sure, the person you want is named Artemis. Here's her number in Fargo.

TIM: I'd picked up the scent again! So I called this "Artemis" . . .

ARTEMIS: I remember it perfectly . . . There were two women. They were very generic and bland, possibly lesbians. When I saw them, I remember my exact thought in detail was, All the women in those barns are clones of one another. They're all middle-aged and white with brown hair . . . Janet Renos! They're all Janet Renos! Anyway, they came every day and took care of that sweet little doggie with a face only a mother could love. Well, a really ugly mother—ha ha! After about three days, it was the day Rita came, they came back and said, "We found a home for her!" And they took her. One's name was . . . I think . . . Julie? Jen . . . ?

TIM: Janelle?

ARTEMIS: I'm not entirely sure that's it. But doggie found a home! Hooray for doggie! Anyhoo, if I can help you any more, just let me know. My e-mail is smellybutt@hellokitty.com.

SCENE 2—SECOND TIME OUT WITH DOLLY

TIM: Back at Lamar Dixon on day three, I was just going to volunteer to clean cages. Whenever I walked through the barns, I always made a pass by the wolf dog in the aggressive section. He had a slight furrow in his brow, and he seemed so lonely. Then he saw me. He stood and began wagging his tail—he knew me! I wasn't allowed to go in there, but I couldn't just walk away and leave him alone again. Oh God, I really was going to be that guy who . . .

NO-RULES GUY: Doesn't follow the rules!

TIM: I looked around and quickly ducked into his den . . .

[*Lights shift.*]

MOMMA: Oh look, Jean-Luc's back with another one!

JEAN-LUC: Momma, this is Tim. He's visiting for spring break.

MOMMA: Hi, Tim. Get on in here, we don't bite!

GRANDMA: I do!

JEAN-LUC: Oh Lord, now she's gonna take her dentures out and chase us around . . . You're making him nervous! Be nice!

MOMMA: We're only funning with you, Tim. Welcome. You can call me Yvette or Momma, whatever you're most comfortable with.

TIM: It's nice to meet you.

GRANDMA: Huh? What?

MOMMA: Jean-Luc's dragged home another stray, Ma. This is Tim.

GRANDMA: RIM??

MOMMA: TIM! Supper's almost on, we'll drag up another chair. It's andouille sausage and beans.

JEAN-LUC: Tim, how do you feel about sausage?

MOMMA: Jean-Luc, you're terrible! And you said Grandma was making him nervous . . .

TIM: And just that quickly I was welcomed into their home and became a member of the family. Jean-Luc, his gay twin brother François and his lover, their mom and grandmother, all living under the same roof. And something changed. I'd always tried to deny this part of me, the different part. The part I knew some people saw as frightening or predatory. I was not like the rest of our species, and now I knew it. And what if that's OK?

[*Lights restore.*]

I knew—looking at that wolf dog—that I had to go into the city again. Because even if I could bring back just one more, ya know? Besides, Dolly's car had broken down, and if I didn't take her, she'd also have to stay behind.

DOLLY: On the drive in we were makin' with the chit chat, as usual.

TIM: I was being pretty cautious about opening up. But little bits of information were starting to come out here and there, like, I'm the youngest of six, with one girl in the family . . .

DOLLY: Hey, I'm the youngest of six, with one boy in the family!

TIM: So yeah, weird things in common. But would she be just as tickled to discover our mutual love for Dolly Parton and Cher?

DOLLY: We decided to hoof it door-to-door in Chalmette, since the lists were turning out to be completely unreliable, and rescue volunteers were hitting the same houses twice.

TIM: Residents were trickling back into the city at this point, and you could get better information directly from them.

DOLLY: We had stopped to try to pick up this scrappy black cat we saw, but it wasn't having anything to do with us.

[SATAN'S NEIGHBOR *enters.*]

SATAN'S NEIGHBOR: Hey.

DOLLY: Hey! Do you know that cat?

SATAN'S NEIGHBOR: Yup. That cat's awful. That cat likes to get into my boat and make its mess in there. That's Miss Dorothy's cat, but you'll never catch it. That cat hates people. That cat only likes Miss Dodo.

TIM: Do you know the cat's name?

SATAN'S NEIGHBOR: Honey! What's that cat's name?

WIFE: SATAN!

SATAN'S NEIGHBOR: Yup—SATAN. Better just leave that cat alone. It's mean enough, it'll survive just fine till Dodo gets back. Sure hope Dodo's all right. Ain't seen her since the gymnasium.

DOLLY: What's that?

SATAN'S NEIGHBOR: Oh, we went by boat over to Andrew Jackson, the high school off Judge Perez, pickin' up people and dogs as we went. Yup, every dog we passed swimmin' at us, I didn't have the heart to kick 'em out, so we'd scoop 'em up and put 'em in the boat with us. We had us maybe ten dogs by the time we got over there.

DOLLY: Wait . . . Where are all those dogs now?

SATAN'S NEIGHBOR: Oh, we left 'em in the high school when we evacuated. They wouldn't let us take 'em, but the schools were s'posed to be safe places to leave animals behind. The sheriff promised everybody that the police'd take care of 'em.

TIM: But we'd heard stories about dogs being used for "target practice" by cops in and around St. Bernard high schools.

DOLLY: At least one sheriff's officer was caught on video by a *Dallas Morning News* reporter, shooting two dogs.

SATAN'S NEIGHBOR: Andrew Jackson is clean. I checked it out this morning, and there were no dogs—dead or alive. But if you wanna check it out, the folks across the street got a beagle I ain't seen since we got back.

[*Lights shift.*]

DOLLY: Certain houses just stuck with you.

TIM: I still see this one over and over . . . There was a large portrait of a beagle puppy hanging in the entrance hall. On the shelf below there were trophies it had won in dog shows, and you could just tell how important this pet was to them.

DOLLY: We saw its little prints all over the place.

ACTOR 2: You could almost track its movement in that house after the storm.

ACTOR 5: You could feel its desperation as it scratched its way into the lower kitchen cupboards, even getting into the cleaning supplies.

ACTOR 3: And the claw marks on the master bedroom door.

ACTOR 4: You see what lengths an animal will go to, trying to find anything to stay alive.

TIM: It got harder and harder the longer I was in there to look under things. Because on one hand, you want to find the dog. On the other hand, you don't want to find the dog. You have to tell yourself . . . You make stuff up. I convinced myself that they had paid somebody to come in and take that dog out.

ACTOR 5: These people obviously loved this dog so much—this dog was the centerpiece of their house—so they wouldn't have just left it here. Right?

DOLLY: We never did find the beagle puppy.

TIM: There was one room in that house that was blocked off with a child safety gate. It had steps leading down into pitch blackness. I've been in that house, and I've stood at that gate a hundred times in my dreams. Sometimes I'm looking for the puppy, sometimes it's my dog, sometimes it's Kelly. Most of the time, it's my mom. And I stare into that blackness, and I call out, but nothing ever answers. And as hard as I try, I can't make myself cross over into that unknown.

[*Lights shift.*]

ACTOR 4: There's this dog right up there, it's just walking down the street. We tried calling to it, but it wouldn't come to us.

[SHELLY *enters.*]

TIM: Sure enough, we saw this cute black Lab that was not in good shape. You could count her ribs from twenty yards away.

DOLLY: Many of the dogs that were on the loose had started forming packs, but this girl was on her own.

TIM: She was drinking from sewage-filled water blanketed with an oily film.

DOLLY: When she saw us, she took off running. I'll follow her down that way, and you go around the front side of those houses!

TIM: So I ran around to try to head her off.

DOLLY: Tim! I've got the dog cornered!

TIM: What followed was an hour of amazing animal behavior.

DOLLY: I'd walk up to the dog just until she was about to run, and then I'd immediately turn my back on her. As soon as I did that, she'd start sneaking back up on me, getting closer every time. Soon she was close enough to get a whiff of my hands, so I started putting pieces of beef jerky in 'em that the dog would eat—it was a game of trust-building.

TIM: Then Dolly put her arm through a loop in the leash, hoping to slide the leash over the dog's head when she went for the jerky. But the dog was onto her again.

DOLLY: Stop! Sit!

TIM: The dog's first impulse was to follow her commands, but then she sort of woke up, like, Wait, you're not my owner—see ya!

DOLLY: And after all that, she took off again, going through a hole in the fence. Dammit!

TIM: So I ran around the fence to try to block her from the other side, and I found myself face to face with her, both of us unsure of what to do next.

DOLLY: Tim! Chase the dog back through! I rigged the leash around the hole so when the dog came running through, I just zinged it. And she didn't try to fight or bite or nothing—she just seemed glad it was finally over. That's right, sweetie, it's gonna be OK now. Hey, let's call her "Shelly," 'cause we're in Chalmette!

TIM: Dolly, you tamed her! It's like the scene with the Fox, before you learn his secret!

DOLLY: Mama always told me secrets don't make friends.

TIM: No, the Fox's secret, from *The Little Prince*. To tame something means to "establish ties," just like you did with Shelly.

DOLLY: Oh, that's beautiful. I remember when being tamed felt like a good thing, like back when I was a real hellcat and met my husband . . .

TIM: Dolly and I talked all the way back to Lamar Dixon, and everything came out. I told her I was gay and that Kelly is actually [*lower register to indicate male*] "Kelly."

DOLLY: Tim, I have to come out of the closet about something, too . . . I used to be a stripper. This was years ago, and I used to work under the name "Candy Cane." I had this bit in my act where I wore this Mrs. Claus microminiskirt with candy canes hanging off it, and when customers tipped me they could rip one off with their teeth.

TIM: Rowr!

DOLLY: I made a killing in tips with that act! But I have to tell you that tinsel does not feel good down in the nether region. Anyway, there was another dancer in town who'd been around for a long time—and was a little past her prime, if you get my meaning—and she went by "Peppermint Patty."

TIM: Was she a lesbian?

DOLLY: Yep.

TIM: Oh.

DOLLY: Anyway, she was mad as a wet hen because she did a similar bit with those little Starlight mints that she glued on her pasties, so she went around telling anybody who'd listen that I was stealing her act. Then she kept trying to raise the stakes, which only resulted in a terrible accident involving a mistletoe thong and a flaming Christmas pudding.

TIM: Oh. [*Getting it*] Oooh!

DOLLY: I tell you, Moses wasn't the only one who saw a burnin' bush! I got out of it while I still had my youth and my looks intact. And, well . . . Now I'm married and things are just . . . different. Oh, Tim, I haven't been able to talk about all this in so long! I've tried, but people just, well . . . they don't get it. So ya take those parts of you and ya tuck 'em away. Lately I just feel like there's more of me tucked away than out and about.

TIM: I take a little snapshot of the moment: I am in New Orleans, I've rescued animals after a major hurricane, and I'm stuck in traffic with a woman I ıet thirty-six hours ago, sharing the private details of our lives. But some-ıow, it all seems sort of right.

SCENE 3—LAMAR DIXON POLITICS AND THE REUNIONS

TIM: Day four!

MIKAH: Listen, everyone! As of today we're changing from a rescue to a recovery mission!

BITCHY VOLUNTEER: Excuse me, but what the hell does that mean?!

MIKAH: It means only bring critical cases in from here on out! If they have lacerations, severe dehydration, or if they're emaciated, they're critical—bring that dog or cat in!

VOLUNTEER COORDINATOR: To me, a critical animal is any animal that could walk into the street and be hit by a car!

TIM: Huh??

MIKAH: Listen, a couple of weeks ago we were bringing hundreds of animals in from the city every day! Now it's only a handful at best!

VOLUNTEER COORDINATOR: There are rumors that Lamar Dixon is kicking us out and closing this facility!

ACTORS: Boo!

MIKAH: Look, we're trying everything—

VOLUNTEER COORDINATOR: That will not happen! If I have to, I will find another place, and we will move this entire operation there before I let this just stop!

ACTORS: Hooray!

VOLUNTEER COORDINATOR: People are saying that animals are being stolen from these premises! But I'm here to say we all know that's not true!

TIM: We do?

VOLUNTEER COORDINATOR: So let's all work together to squash those rumors whenever you hear them!

MIKAH: Thanks, everybody—have a good day out there!

ACTOR 2: Hi, do you have a partner? Have you been into the city yet?

VOLUNTEER COORDINATOR: Hell no, and I don't plan to. I'm not that stupid.

TIM: Oh, you don't have to be trained. I went into the city on my first day—

VOLUNTEER COORDINATOR: I am trained, man. But look at me—a black man crawlin' through somebody's window, and you think anybody's gonna believe I'm in there to look for Fluffy?? That sounds like a good way to get my black ass shot!

TIM: That was the first day I decided not to go into the city. Dolly had left the night before, and I really didn't feel like breaking in a new partner. So that day I volunteered to lead residents through the barns to look for their animals. This job took some people skills . . .

[BITCHY VOLUNTEER *yells at the* EVACUEES *waiting to be led through the barns.*]

BITCHY VOLUNTEER: Hey, you're in my way here!

TIM: . . . which were in short supply.

BITCHY VOLUNTEER: Line up against that wall—all the way against the wall!

TIM: Luckily, other people were much more competent, like Mikah.

JERRY: Excuse me, miss? I'm next! My paperwork is on the bottom of that box. I've been waiting an hour and a half in this heat, and you're taking forms from the top of the pile, from the people who just got here!

MIKAH: OK, what's your name, sir?

JERRY: Jerry!

MIKAH: OK, Jerry—I understand. I was wrong—you are next. Let me get a volunteer to lead you through, and meanwhile I'm gonna rework our system here, OK?

[MIKAH *beckons* BITCHY VOLUNTEER *to help* JERRY.]

TIM: Most people who went through the barns came out empty-handed . . .

JACK: No sign of Xena.

MIKAH: But then one family found all of their pets . . . A dog, a lizard, two snakes, and a bird!

TIM: It was like spinning a roulette wheel.

CRAZY CAT LADY: HELLO?! I'm looking for thirteen cats!

TIM: Right. Can you give me detailed descriptions of each one?

CRAZY CAT LADY: Yes. I actually had seventeen cats. Eight disappeared, one came back, five were found in the house, and there was a note on the outside that thirteen were taken out.

TIM: Wait . . . what??

CRAZY CAT LADY: Let me repeat, and you listen this time! Beulah was left behind, but Samantha and Morticia were not. Boo Radley was found in the house, but Josephine and Napoleon are still missing . . .

[TIM *quickly pushes her off on* BITCHY VOLUNTEER *and intercepts* EVACUEE WITH CAT.]

TIM: Hey, you found your cat! How happy are you?

EVACUEE WITH CAT: Well, I found her, but my dog died. When I got back home, I found him there. And I just can't let it go. I just can't stop asking myself, What if I had left more food? What if I had filled the bathtub up, rather than just leaving bowls of water around? I mean, I didn't know it was gonna be a whole month before I could get back.

[*A* REPORTER *and* CAMERAMAN *who have been hanging around push* TIM *out of the way to shove a microphone in the* EVACUEE'*s face.*]

REPORTER: Miss, can I speak to you for a brief moment? How did you feel when you found your dog dead in your home?
EVACUEE WITH CAT: Well . . . It was pretty horrible.
REPORTER: Take us back to that horrible moment . . .

[*They exit.*]

TIM: By the end of the day, I was wiped out from so much disappointment and so few happy reunions. One of the last people I led through the barns was an older black man who had been there the day before looking for his cat.
OLDER GENTLEMAN: She's white and has a wandering eye to go with her oddball personality . . . Maybe you've seen her?
TIM: Hope springs eternal, so Mikah and I took him through again. He was very shy and would barely step into the stalls to look.
MIKAH: Get in here! There are lots of cats to look at, so come on and take a good look at every one of them!
TIM: But he didn't—he sped through as though he'd know that cat at a glance. We were rapidly running out of cats to show him.

[OLDER GENTLEMAN *bends to glance at a cat then starts to walk away—then turns back and points toward one of the cages.*]

OLDER GENTLEMAN: That's my cat.
TIM: He pointed to a dark gray cat.
MIKAH: Sir, I thought you said she was white?
OLDER GENTLEMAN: She is.

[MIKAH *and* TIM *exchange a look.*]

MIKAH: She is?
TIM: Mikah and I leaned in for a closer look at the gray cat. And then we saw it—the cat's crazy Marty Feldman eye!

OLDER GENTLEMAN: I probably walked right past her yesterday—I was looking for her to be white, but Katrina dyed her like new lamb's wool. Would it be possible to hold her?

MIKAH: Well, of course it would! Are you kidding?

[*All* ACTORS *gather round the happy reunion.* TIM *notices* MIKAH *audibly wheezing.*]

TIM: It's OK . . . This is one of the happy ones.

MIKAH: It's not that . . .

TIM: Then what?

MIKAH: I'm allergic to cats.

SCENE 4—XENA: THE REVEAL

TIM: Flash forward again to after I got home to L.A. I felt certain that Janelle Anderson had been lying to me about Xena. I had gotten my hands on a picture of Janelle and e-mailed it to Artemis, but she couldn't say one way or the other if she was the culprit.

ARTEMIS: All those women are clones of one another . . . Janet Renos!

TIM: Still, my hunch was that Janelle and an unknown accomplice had stolen Xena out of Lamar Dixon. Just before Christmas, I was referred to a guy named Sam, who'd volunteered with Janelle in Louisiana. My hope was that they were close enough that he could elicit the truth from Janelle.

SAM: Well, I didn't know Janelle that well. We volunteered in Barn One together for about four days. I wouldn't have thought she'd steal a dog, but it certainly sounds like subterfuge. How do you want to do this?

TIM: First, I have a question for YOU . . . Ethically, are you up for a little deception and one major bluff?

SAM: You're scary, Tim. Mikah told me you're one of those crazy animal people! OK, tell me the plan, and I'll call Janelle.

[JANELLE *steps forward.*]

JANELLE: Oh, it's been good catching up, Sam!

SAM: Well, I also wanted to ask you about one other thing. I'm helping this volunteer named Tim try to find a Chihuahua named Xena. You've heard about this, right?

JANELLE: Oh, uh-huh.

SAM: Well, the family is desperate for some word on the dog. They can't take her back, but because she was their mom's—who died, you know—they're wracked with guilt. They just want to know that they didn't leave their mom's dog to die.

JANELLE: Right . . . Well, I'm not sure what I—

SAM: And their poor little girl . . . Did you know she's got the Down syndrome? Just tragic. Well, she can't sleep at night anymore, she's just so worried about Xena.

JANELLE: Oh, lord . . .

SAM: Anyway, can you remember anything that might help this family find some peace? Anything at all?

JANELLE: Hmm . . . I don't really recall . . .

SAM: Well, that's OK. We'll just have to wait until Artemis identifies the thieves.

JANELLE: What's that?

SAM: Yeah, this Red Cross volunteer named Artemis saw who took the dog, and she's looking at pictures Tim is sending her of volunteers. Once she points out the thieves, then it'll become a whole legal thing with lawsuits and criminal charges being brought by the animal rescue organization.

JANELLE: Artemis, huh? I had forgotten all about her. Wow. Anyway, Sam, like I told Tim, the last time I saw Xena, she was in Barn Six. I was looking after her every day with another volunteer friend. I might know how to find her and see if she knows anything about this.

SAM: I thought you told Tim she ended up in Barn Five?

JANELLE: No, no—he must have misunderstood. But I'll see if I can reach my friend . . . or try to find her number, I mean . . . OK?

SAM: Hey, Tim. I heard from Janelle's accomplice. Her name's JoAnn, and . . . are you ready? She has Xena.

[JOANN *steps forward.*]

JOANN: I do have a dog I saved at Lamar Dixon who looks VERY MUCH like the dog in the photo you e-mailed Janelle. IF she's the same dog, the family that abandoned her should know that she's living with an older relative of mine who loves the dog very much. The dog has experienced snow for the first time, goes by the name Katie Ann, and looks adorable in her new winter sweaters.

SAM: The family wants their dog back.

JOANN: Screw you! This dog is happy now, and she isn't going anywhere! And I never said the dog I took was Xena.

[LAWYER *steps forward.*]

LAWYER: Ms. Turnbull, allow me to introduce myself. Chas Traggert, attorney-at-law. We don't really care if it's the same dog. You've admitted that you stole a dog from Lamar Dixon. We'll take THAT dog.

JOANN: No, please listen! I didn't know anything about dead mothers and retarded kids. I did know that someone left this dog, and they never came back for her. I knew that when I took her to my vet in Massachusetts, she had an infected tooth and a severe case of heartworm. It's supposed to be ANIMAL welfare. Anyway, she wasn't even their dog—the dog's owner is dead. Please tell me you're not going to pursue this—that you have a heart?

LAWYER: The law has no heart, Ms. Turnbull. It deals in facts. The fact is that you stole property. Allow me to feign compassion while expediting this process . . . We'll reimburse you the expense of the veterinary bills, and we'll give you a waiver of responsibility when you hand over the property.

JOANN: This is wrong. Have you thought about that? What if you're wrong?

SCENE 5—TACO BELL

TIM: By day six at Lamar Dixon, I was emotionally and physically exhausted and way over the dehydration . . .

ACTOR 4: Sunburn . . .

ACTOR 2: Heat rash . . .

ACTOR 4: And feet with blisters on top, bottom, and in between my toes.

TIM: I went into Gonzales looking for comfort food and found a Taco Bell— just what the doctor ordered. Inside there were two black people waiting for food, a white woman whom I recognized from Lamar Dixon, and me. Behind the counter is this white girl who's running the register and assembling all the orders . . .

COUNTER GIRL: That'll be right up, hon.

TIM: . . . and a tall black guy in the back who's making the food. So we all go through the line.

[Long pause.]

And after about fifteen minutes, no food had come out.

MAN IN LINE: What, they got FEMA running the Taco Bell?

TIM: Another ten minutes go by, and everyone is getting really restless.

FRIEND IN LINE: It'd a' been faster to go to Taco Bell in Houston.

TIM: Finally an order of food comes up.

COUNTER GIRL: Here you go, ma'am.

[COUNTER GIRL *indicates* WHITE WOMAN.]

WHITE WOMAN: Wait, I didn't order this burrito. And where's my cheesy potatoes?

COUNTER GIRL: I'm sorry, let me get that for you.

TIM: Another five minutes go by before any more food comes out.

[COUNTER GIRL *motions to* TIM.]

COUNTER GIRL: Here you go, sir.

MAN IN LINE: Wait a minute—we ordered before him and her! Where is our food at?!

COUNTER GIRL: I gave you your food, sir.

MAN IN LINE: No, you didn't! This shouldn't be that hard!

COUNTER GIRL: Well, sir, they come out in order, so if they're getting their food, you must have gotten yours.

FRIEND IN LINE: OK, do you speak motherfucking English?! WE DID NOT GET OUR FOOD!

COUNTER GIRL: It's OK, hon—let me see your receipts.

TIM: So she disappears into the back to talk to the guy cooking food, for another five minutes or more.

MAN IN LINE: HELLOOOOOOO?! We're still here! Where the hell is our food?!

TIM: Yeah, WHAT'S GOING ON?!

COUNTER GIRL: We don't know what happened, but there's been some kind of confusion. But sir, the manager is gonna come out and take care of this.

MAN IN LINE: Well, the confusion seems to be that you wanna help everybody who came in here after us—and I know exactly what that's about!

COUNTER GIRL: Look, hon, we are trying to sort this out, and I'm not supposed to talk to anybody until the manager comes out!

TIM: It dawned on me that the guy making the food was also the manager. Why the hell isn't he coming out?? He's right there—I can see him sour creaming with the caulking gun!

MAN IN LINE: Look, we paid for that food, and we want it right now!

COUNTER GIRL: I'm sorry, sir, but I think we gave you the food, or else you need to prove that we didn't. Where's your receipt?

TIM: Uh-oh.

MAN IN LINE: WE GAVE YOU THE MUTHAFUCKIN' RECEIPTS! THIS IS BULLSHIT!

FRIEND IN LINE: YEAH, THE HELL WITH THIS! I JUST EARNED ME A FREE SODA, BITCH!

MAN IN LINE: YOU DON'T WANT US IN YOUR FUCKIN' RED-NECK TOWN?! WELL, WE DON'T WANT TO BE HERE EITHER!!

[TIM *locks eyes with* COUNTER GIRL.]

TIM: OK, listen! LOOK AT ME! Go back to the kitchen, and get them whatever they said they paid for.

COUNTER GIRL: But I don't . . . They don't . . .

TIM: Don't move. Sir, what are you still missing?

MAN IN LINE: WHAT?!

TIM: What are you still missing?

FRIEND IN LINE: A number five, a number six, and a cheese quesadilla!

TIM: Go and assemble a number five, a number six, and a cheese quesadilla. That's all.

COUNTER GIRL: But I don't . . .

TIM: It doesn't matter at this point, just get it!

[COUNTER GIRL *quickly assembles food then puts the bag tentatively on the counter for* MAN IN LINE.]

COUNTER GIRL: Sir?

TIM: And everyone calmed down and left. Well, not before . . .

[MAN IN LINE *yells at* MANAGER *in the back.*]

MAN IN LINE: And you back there, man—you were back there doin' nothin'! Thanks for helpin' a brother out.

TIM: My order? Totally wrong—but I didn't care. I sat down and ate it, looking for sanctuary in my Cheesy Gordita Crunch.

WHITE WOMAN: I just wanted to say, you handled that really well. I was just trying to pretend it wasn't happening.

[TIM *approaches the counter.* COUNTER GIRL *is now hiding in the back, near tears, but the* MANAGER *has emerged.*]

MANAGER: Can I help you, sir?

TIM: No, actually I wanted to see if I could talk to that girl for a minute.

MANAGER: Well, I can help you—I'm the manager.

TIM: Now he's the manager. No, I actually want to talk to her—I want to apologize to her.

[MANAGER *laughs in* TIM's *face and walks away.*]

New people were coming in and starting to line up . . .

[COUNTER GIRL *reluctantly comes back out to the front, muttering to herself.*]

COUNTER GIRL: I cannot take this.

TIM: Miss?

COUNTER GIRL: Look, I'm doing the best I can! I'm working two jobs, sixteen hours a day, and I'm not even on the clock anymore!

TIM: I just wanted to say that I thought you handled that really well. You know, you kept your calm even with everything that was going on. And I just wanted to say I'm sorry I yelled at you.

[COUNTER GIRL *ignores him and starts helping next customer in line.*]

TIM: I started to wonder who I would become if everything around me was turned upside down. If my routine, my safety and security, were all taken away . . .

MAN IN LINE: Would you become aggressive, to have your basic needs met?

MANAGER: Would you lay low in the brush till the danger passed?

COUNTER GIRL: Or would you bite back out of fear?

SCENE 6—THE JOURNEY HOME

TIM: Day nine, my last morning at Lamar Dixon, I woke to find half the cots permanently vacated. Mikah was crying hysterically—some bureaucratic screwup had landed in her lap.

MIKAH: All anyone sees is what went wrong! And plenty has, but it's a disaster site! How many thousands of animals are alive because of our organizations and the money we spent?!

TIM: I think everyone's just frustrated and feeling helpless.

MIKAH: Yeah? Well, fuck them!

TIM: I checked on my wolf dog. Luckily the behaviorist had taken a liking to him after observing him for a few days and had reserved a spot for him at a sanctuary for wolf dogs in North Carolina called Full Moon Farm. And while it broke my heart to say good-bye, I just had to hope for the best.

MIKAH: Operations at Lamar Dixon were closing down in the next couple of days . . .

TIM: So I decided it was time to go. I packed up the 4Runner, headed out to Baton Rouge, and picked up the parakeet from the bird vet and the two cats from prison. On the trip to San Diego, I became quite taken with my constant companions, especially Gasper—the grumpy old man who wasn't even a year old. He was the first cat to tame this dog lover's heart.

BUD: You must be Tim!

TIM: The big reunion was taking place at Bud's sister's house.

BUD: Hey, buddy, come on up and meet everyone!

TIM: But the animals . . .

BUD: Hey, where'yat, kitties! That's all right, they'll be fine in the car for a few minutes. Come on up, we'll get you a cold drink and let you settle down for a minute.

TIM: I was introduced to Bud's sister and her husband, and Lupe.

LUPE: Hola, Tim.

TIM: So the vet says your babies are in good shape . . .

BUD: You saw our place, right? Take a look at these.

[*He hands* TIM *some photos.*]

We stayed after the flood, for about four days. We're on the second floor, but the water came right up to the edge of our balcony. We stayed as long as we could with what we had. I went out in a boat at one point, trying to help rescue people off roofs and things. But with food and water running out, it was becoming an every-man-for-himself situation. People would ride by in boats, with guns—clearly not nice people. And then there was this one woman, a crack addict or something, who crawled out of the floodwater onto our balcony one morning. She was batshit crazy, smashing everything and threatening to kill us if we didn't hand over what food we had left. I had to throw her back in the water. She kept trying to climb back up, all the while screaming about cutting us open and eating us if she had to. You know, you can't imagine. Part of you knows, I could be killing this person by doing this. But we had to look out for ourselves, right?

LUPE: We did not know what was happening in the rest of the world. We had no radio, no TV . . . No idea why no one was coming to help us.

BUD: Oh, there'd be these city officials coming by in boats, waving at you and telling you on their bullhorn, "Everything is fine! Stay calm!" And we'd be yelling back, "We ain't got no food or water! Can you bring us something??" And they wouldn't even acknowledge what we were saying—they'd just make their public relations rounds and disappear.

[TIM *notices* LUPE *getting more and more anxious.*]

TIM: Hey, I'm sorry—do you want to see the animals?

LUPE: Yes, please!

TIM: And she was out of her chair and at my car in a nanosecond. It was obvious that these were really her pets.

LUPE: Oh, Gasper! Luna! I was certain to never see them again. Bud, he can never understand why my niños mean so much to me. But he work all day, and I spend the day with these boys. The man who save us during the flood, he tell us the government will not let us bring them. I do not understand this. I am so confused, and the man with the boat is waiting. Bud, he tell me the animals will be OK. And for many weeks I was so angry at Bud and, I am ashamed to say, angry at God. I had lost my faith. It hurt so bad to close that door and walk away from them. I promise them I would come back for them . . . but I don't. But I should have known that God had everything planned—how when everything is lost with no hope at all, God so easily fixes. It is two blessings at once, to have back my family and also my faith.

SCENE 7—WOLF DOG AND JEAN-LUC FOLLOW-UP

TIM: A few weeks after I got home, I was paid a visit by Nancy, the woman who runs Full Moon Farm Wolf Dog Sanctuary. She'd driven cross-country to save a pair of wolf dog pups. I liked her immediately.

NANCY: Your Katrina fella? His name's Pete. See, the night before I drove down to Louisiana to pick him up, I had this dream—and I sleep so heavy that they call me the Log, because when I lie down, that's it. But that night, I sat bolt upright in bed after having the clearest dream of my life, that that dog had spoken to me and said, "My name is Pete, and I'm waiting for you." And when I saw him, it was love at first sight—just like that. We didn't have any vacancies for another wolf dog, but I had lost my best house dog the month before, and part of me thinks he let go to make room for Pete.

TIM: Did you ever hear from an owner?

NANCY: Nope, but he was somebody's dog for sure. He eats right off a fork. I been givin' him beef and rice to get weight back on him. He should weigh over a hundred pounds, and he only weighed sixty-four when he got here. Oh, he's spoiled rotten now. He'll never get adopted—most of these guys don't. Some people just should not have wolf dogs. 'Course, they're usually the same people that shouldn't have Chia Pets, but still. Pete has a home here now, and we'll take good care of him. Everyone feels displaced at some point in their life. The lucky ones, like Pete, find another place to belong and get to start again.

[*Lights shift.*]

FRANCOIS: Hello?

TIM: Hi, is Jean-Luc there?

FRANCOIS: Who's calling, please?

TIM: Um, my name is Tim. I'm a friend of Jean-Luc's from about fifteen years ago. I was on spring break in New Orleans and met him and stayed . . .

FRANCOIS: Oh, hey, Tim!

TIM: Jean-Luc?

FRANCOIS: No, this is François, his twin.

TIM: Oh, hi!

FRANCOIS: Can I help you?

TIM: Well, I was just calling to see how he is. I was in New Orleans after Katrina, and, well, you know how hard it's been to find anyone with no phones. Your mom's old number isn't in service, and I found this number for the same last name on the Internet and thought I'd try it.

FRANCOIS: Well, aren't you the super sleuth? I'm afraid I have no good news for you. Jean-Luc is gone.

TIM: Gone? Like . . . what do you mean, "gone"?

FRANCOIS: I mean, he's not here right now. He's gone to buy more cat food for the army of strays we're feeding. We've got cats crawling out of our asses these days.

TIM: So everyone is OK?

FRANCOIS: OK is a relative term. My mom's house in Gretna was destroyed. Jean-Luc's place in the city, too. So now Jean-Luc, me, and my lover, our mom and grandmother, are all living under the same roof . . . mine.

SCENE 8—XENA, THE END

TIM: For six months after I got home, Xena consumed my thoughts, and during that time I must have played out every possible ending to her adventure. There's the one where . . .

JOANN: I was so selfish! I'm getting on a plane right now to bring Xena home. Oh, and make sure Tim is there for the big reunion!

TIM: There's the one where . . .

JOANN: It's just you and me now, Katie Ann! We have to forget our old lives—no more husband, home, job . . . JoAnn and Katie Ann Turnbull are gone. From now on, we're Thelma and Louise!

TIM: And there's my personal favorite: I fly to JoAnn's house in Massachusetts, and while they're on their evening walk, I forcibly take Xena from her. The speech I deliver varies, but my favorite is, "NOW YOU KNOW HOW IT FEELS, BITCH!" There were about five thousand possible endings for this story, and I'd thought of them all . . . Except this one. The lawyer had set a deadline . . .

LAWYER: DeeDee? Chas Traggert calling. In order to move forward and reclaim your property, I need to hear back from you no later than April second.

TIM: A week went by after that deadline, and there was no word from the family. I had a phone number for their sister, Martine . . . I spoke to the lawyer, and he says you all haven't called yet. I'm just trying to see what's going on.

MARTINE: Tim, you really should talk to DeeDee about this.

TIM: I've tried, but she's not answering. I know things are still crazy there, but we have to stay on top—

MARTINE: I want Xena back so badly, but we absolutely can't take her with my shepherds—they'd kill the poor thing within a day. And DeeDee can't pull it back together since losing her house and Mama. See, the night of the storm, Jack and DeeDee got separated from Mama and me. They ended up in Texas, and we were in Mississippi. After a week, they called a hospital and found us. Mama told them to drive careful, and she'd be here waiting for them. She died before they could get there. We all knew Mama's time was coming, but this wasn't how it was supposed to be. Katrina took more than you can know. Mama was everything to DeeDee—do you know what I mean?

TIM: Yes, I do.

MARTINE: I know she feels so guilty about losing Xena, and since then we've been afraid to get our hopes up that we'll ever get her back. Just because some lawyer says to, doesn't mean she'll give our dog back. And I think DeeDee's afraid that every time she looks at Xena she'll be reminded of Mama. Xena was there, on Mama's lap, when she died—but DeeDee didn't make it in time.

TIM: OK, so . . . Bottom line, what are we going to do?

MARTINE: Oh, Tim, I can't believe I'm about to say this, but . . . I think we should leave her be.

TIM: OK. I'll let the lawyer know.

MARTINE: At least we know Xena is alive. I'm sure she's loved, and that's a relief. Hey, Tim? I remember when we very first met you what you said. I just wanted to say on behalf of them and me, thank you for keeping your promise. We lost a lot, and that meant something.

SCENE 9—LUNA AND GASPER UPDATE

TIM: I hadn't talked to Bud for several months, and after a couple of last-minute cancellations, we arranged to meet up in San Diego.

BUD: Well, we still don't have a place. But work is starting to come in, and we're trying to save money. Thing is, every time we're almost on our feet, the FEMA checks either stop or go to the wrong address, or you name it. I don't like taking handouts, but come on—give me a fair shot!

TIM: Would you let me help you out a little?

BUD: Not a chance.

TIM: This place looks great. Are you all renting?

BUD: Here? No, I don't live here. I just put in some copper plumbing for them.

TIM: Oh, I'm sorry. I thought you said we were meeting at your place . . .

BUD: Well . . . These days Casa Bud is a 1988 Chevy panel van. It doubles as my office.

TIM: Is Lupe living with you?

BUD: No, she's at her sister's with Angel. Lupe and I aren't married, so Sis wants nothing to do with me or the cats. Blood is thicker than water, I guess . . .

TIM: So Luna and Gasper are in the van? It would be great to see them.

BUD: Well . . . Oh man, Tim, I was really hoping I wouldn't have to tell you this . . . They ran away.

TIM: Wait, what do you mean, they ran away?

BUD: I'm so sorry, Tim. I'm just so sorry. I had to leave the windows down for them so they'd get some air, and I guess I left them down too far, and they squeezed out. The kicker is, I was just gearin' up to call you, ya know? Lupe thinks I let them go on purpose.

[*Lights down on* BUD.]

TIM: After seeing Bud, I went to the San Diego shelter to try and track Luna and Gasper through the microchips that were implanted at Lamar Dixon.

SHELTER EMPLOYEE: The gray tabby . . . Luna? Yeah, he was here for a few days and was adopted out to a really great guy. And the black domestic shorthair . . . Jasper?

TIM: Gasper.

SHELTER EMPLOYEE: I got nothin'. Sorry.

TIM: I followed up with three trips to San Diego, putting up fliers everywhere with Gasper's photo . . . but nothing. So I just wait. And I hope that he'll turn up. If you see him, don't let me go on being so sad. Send word immediately that he's come back . . .

[KELLY *enters.*]

TIM: I should have called him back in January when that FEMA deadline came. I thought about it, and then I didn't.

KELLY: LP . . . stop. It's just like the book says: "You risk tears if you let yourself be tamed."

TIM: I'm fine.

KELLY: Liar. You have to let this go now. You can't save everyone.

TIM: I couldn't even save a fucking cat! And that bitch takes Xena, and just to throw salt in the wound, names her Katie Ann?!

KELLY: OK . . . Remember when you asked me to tell you if you started becoming a crazy animal pers—

TIM: I'm not! It was never about the dog—I never met the dog! I met that family, and I saw the hopeless looks on their faces. And I knew that look: "Somebody—anybody—help us!" I didn't do this to be a hero—I just wanted to make my mom proud. This was supposed to fix everything.

KELLY: You know what I'm going to say: Some things . . .

TIM AND KELLY: . . . can't be fixed.

KELLY: Listen, I have to go to Raleigh next week for business. I want you to come with me. I looked it up, and it's about four hours from there to Nancy's place. We can drive over and see your wolf dog.

TIM: We don't have money for that . . .

KELLY: It's not about the money, and you know it. We're going—end of discussion.

SCENE 10—PETE

NANCY: Do you need me to draw you a map?

TIM: Nancy greeted us next to her truck, which had a RAISED BY WOLVES bumper sticker on the back.

KELLY: Nancy was not exactly your typical Red-Stater.

NANCY: Don't even get me started on most of the folks around here. There's a lot of these real prude 'n' pious types, and I love to piss in their Cheerios every chance I get!

TIM: Right away she took us to see Pete.

NANCY: He recognizes you, see!

TIM: I don't know if that's true, but it was so good to see him looking healthy and happy.

KELLY: Nancy gave us the tour and introduced us to the rest of the wolf dogs.

NANCY: Don't get too close to that one—she was hit with a tire iron. Take your hat off around him—he was beaten by a redneck who wore a baseball cap.

TIM: And I thought, how does she deal with this every day, when each one of these animals is coming from such a horrible situation?

KELLY: Then she put us to work for most of the day feeding dogs, scooping poop, putting up tarps—but we loved it.

TIM: There was a moment when I thought, I could do this forever and be happy.

NANCY: You boys are hard workers. My son's gay, and I've got nothin' against it except that he's a big ol' drama queen. He's always saying I love these dogs more than my own kids.

TIM: Then we got back to Pete.

NANCY: I finally did hear from his owner, and man, did he love that dog. Pete's thirteen, which is gettin' way up there for a wolf dog. He was origi-nally named Maicoh, which is the Navajo word for wolf—but he doesn't respond to that name at all. He is a male aggressive, ripped up a rottweiler when he was younger. He had a mate and two pups when Katrina hit, and they were all left in the backyard during that storm. No one's seen the female or pups since.

TIM: Just thinking of Pete, I was so grateful for the Nancies of the world, protecting the defenseless, the illegals, the mixed species, the out—

NANCY: First of all, they're not mixed species. They're the same species, just so ya know.

TIM: Oh ... sorry.

NANCY: And they're only illegal, pardon the expression, because of idiots and assholes. Wolves, by nature, are timid and afraid. Dogs are the aggressive ones. No one should be afraid of a wolf—they're afraid of you. Little Red Riding Hood was a fuckin' idiot! We're spaying and neutering the wrong species, if you ask me. I dunno, Tim ... I guess I'm always just fighting for the underdog. But if not me, who?

KELLY: We'd better get on the road—we have a four-hour drive back to Raleigh.

TIM: OK, I just want to say good-bye to Pete first.

[KELLY *exits, but* NANCY *lingers behind.*]

NANCY: How you doing?

TIM: Fine.

NANCY: Uh-huh, sure you are. Look, I know how disappointing that business with the Chihuahua and the two cats was for you. I relate. Disappointment is part of my job description, but the one four-letter word I don't use is quit. If nothing else, just by showing up down there, you gave everyone you met a little hope. Hell, you gave me hope.

[NANCY *starts to walk away.*]

Which sure beats a kick in the ass.

[NANCY *exits.* TIM *approaches* PETE.]

TIM: Hey there . . .

[*They sit in silence for a moment.*]

PETE: I feel like I should say something.

TIM: You don't have to.

PETE: You want me to tell you I remember you.

TIM: Yes.

PETE: Did you come all this way to see me?

TIM: Yes. I did it because of the Fox's secret: you become responsible forever for what you've tamed.

PETE: People have forgotten this truth, but you mustn't forget it.

TIM: I won't, I promise.

PETE: You know I can't really talk, right?

TIM: I know.

PETE: Tim, do you know what I'd say if I could talk?

TIM: You'd say you're sorry you pooped in my car?

PETE: I couldn't help it. I was so sick.

TIM: I know.

PETE: I'd say thank you.

TIM: You're welcome.

THE TRASH BAG TOURIST

Samuel Brett Williams

PRODUCTION HISTORY

The Trash Bag Tourist was first developed at the Mason Gross School of the Arts (Rutgers University, New Brunswick, New Jersey). The play premiered in August 2006 at the New Orleans Arts Center, where it was produced by the New Orleans Theatre Experiment (directed by Michole Biancosino).

CHARACTERS

Dorothy, sixty, moves with a walker
Molly, thirty
Chuck, African American, forty

TIME

October 2005

PLACE

Arkadelphia, Arkansas. A dilapidated trailer.

SCENE 1

[*Night. Lights rise on* DOROTHY *in an oversized floral muumuu, sitting on the sofa, watching television.*]

NED PERMY [*from the television*]: The count is six down, the amount two hundred and twenty dollars, I'm Ned Permy, and it's time to go *Dialing for Dollars!*

[DOROTHY *removes a telephone from her muumuu and sets it down beside her. She claps excitedly.*]

I am now dialing the number of one lucky Arkansan.

[*Beat.*]

And there's the first ring.
DOROTHY: Dang it to heck.

[DOROTHY *huffs. She puts the telephone back in her muumuu, removes a remote control from her muumuu, turns the television off, puts the remote control back in her muumuu, begins eating Sam's Choice double mint fudge ice cream with a spork. A few seconds pass. Noises are heard offstage.* MOLLY—*wearing a clown outfit and carrying a Wal-Mart bag—enters through the front door. Exhausted, she drops the bag to the ground and plops down in a lawn chair.*]

DOROTHY: Tired?
MOLLY: I'm a fuckin' rodeo clown. What do you think?
DOROTHY [*concerned*]: Ya ain't hurt, is ya? Didn't break your legs or nothin'?
MOLLY [*agitated*]: Lemme check, Mamma.

[MOLLY *raises her left leg.*]

One.

[MOLLY *raises her right leg.*]

Motherfuckin' two.

[*Beat.*]

Na, I didn't break my legs or nothin'. Thanks for askin', though.

DOROTHY: You can quit if ya want, Molly. Go back to cuttin' meat at the Piggly Wiggly.

MOLLY: I ain't never goin' back there. Too many people from high school. Used to call me a pilla' head.

DOROTHY: Those people wuz just jealous.

MOLLY [*looking around the trailer*]: Of what?

[DOROTHY *has no answer for this, so she eats more ice cream. Beat.*]

DOROTHY: Ya wanna order a cheesy crust pizza?

MOLLY: You haven't even finished your goddamn ice cream, and you sure as shit know I gotta keep my weight down for my tryout. Why ya gotta tempt me like that, Mamma?

DOROTHY: Stop your dreamin', Baby Girl. You're too old. You had a window of opportunity, but unfortunately your ass wuz too fat to fit through it.

[DOROTHY *goes back to eating, then stops.*]

And you're a woman.

[DOROTHY *goes back to eating, then stops.*]

And you know how I feel 'bout that tour. Bad enough you're workin' the local rodeo.

[MOLLY *begins taking off her shoes, slowly, laboriously.*]

DOROTHY [*looking at* MOLLY's *Wal-Mart bag*]: Did ya get my Icy Hot?

MOLLY: No, but I did get to wait in line for over an hour, 'cuz of all them trash bag tourists. I mean, don't get me wrong, I'm sorry Katrina took all their houses, and I'm glad Brother Eric is bein' hospitable by openin' up Arkadelphia to 'em, but I don't need the hassle of maneuverin' around 'em all at Wal-Mart when I'm just tryin' to buy my Tampax after a long day of rodeoing, ya know what I mean?

DOROTHY [*still eating ice cream matter-of-factly*]: Tyler from next door said that all the trash bag tourists have done since they got here is steal cars and rape little boys.

MOLLY: I would expect Tyler to be nicer—what on account of him bein' gay and all.

DOROTHY: Why, I've never heard such a thing. Tyler gay? You know damn well what Brother Eric would do if he thought there were homosexuals livin' in this town.

[DOROTHY *finishes her ice cream and throws the container on the floor.* MOLLY *looks up.*]

MOLLY: You best be pickin' that up, Mamma. 'Fore I rip your wrinkled titties off.

DOROTHY: It's not mine.

MOLLY: If you ain't been eatin' that Sam's Choice double mint fudge, then why you got a spork in your hand?

[DOROTHY *throws the spork down.*]

DOROTHY: I don't remember.

MOLLY: Good, that means you have the Alzheimer's, so now I can finally call the hospice to come and kill ya. Put *me* outta *my* misery.

[*Beat.*]

DOROTHY: Maybe it wuz mine.

[MOLLY *stares at* DOROTHY. DOROTHY *gets the picture. Moaning, she rises and hobbles over to the ice cream container. She picks it up then hobbles back to the couch and places the container on the table.* MOLLY *removes a bottle of malt liquor from the Wal-Mart bag. She opens it and begins taking swigs straight from the bottle for the rest of the scene.*]

I used to be a debutante, ya know.

MOLLY: Ya done told me that a thousand times too many, Mamma.

DOROTHY: Pilla' head.

MOLLY: You know what that means? I used to ask people at Piggly Wiggly, but they would just roll their eyes and laugh at me. The day we broke up, Davy told me what it meant. A pillow head is a girl who's so ugly that when you fuck her, you have to put a pillowcase over her head.

[*Beat.*]

DOROTHY: I always hated Davy.

MOLLY: He wuz at the rodeo tonight. With some girl from Burger King. She wuz wearin' a paper crown.

DOROTHY: Whore.

MOLLY: Definitely.

DOROTHY: Pay him no 'tention, Molly. You're so much better than him it hurts. Goin' 'round cheatin' on you—just like I said he would. I hate him. Hate him so bad I wanna cut his ding-a-ling off.

MOLLY [*touched*]: You'd do that for me, Mamma?

DOROTHY: I'd do anythin' to protect my Baby Girl.

[MOLLY *reopens her Wal-Mart bag. She removes a container of Icy Hot and throws it to* DOROTHY.]

My Icy Hot.

[DOROTHY *opens the container and immediately begins rubbing Icy Hot all over her body.*]

MOLLY: Ya know, Mamma, I wuz thinkin' at Wal-Mart today—when I wuz waitin' in line—what if . . . well . . . I tried to help one of them trash bag tourists?

DOROTHY: Have you done lost your mind, Baby Girl? I told ya 'bout the little boys, and I didn't even mention how smelly they are.

MOLLY: Your Icy Hot don't smell like roses, and I still haven't thrown you out yet.

DOROTHY: Couldn't collect my social, then. I know why you keep me around. It ain't got nothin' to do with love and everythin' to do with five hundred dollars a month.

MOLLY: Once I join the tour, I ain't gonna need none of your social.

DOROTHY: Wind up just like your daddy. If he'd a gone to work at the Piggly Wiggly, then—

MOLLY: Daddy ain't got nothin' to do with this, and you don't know shit bout the Piggly Wiggly, so shut the fuck up.

DOROTHY: I know it paid better than—

MOLLY: I'd go in there in my white apron and cut meat for hours, Mamma. Never glancin' up to look at no one—never so much as sayin' a word. The mind drifts when you're slicin' pig intestines—it drifts to places far away from Arkansas . . . it drifts to places where no one knows me . . . where I can just . . . be . . . without people starin' or talkin' or hatin'. I wuz the best butcher they had, 'cuz I detached myself from my meat—I detached myself from . . . you.

[*Beat.*]

I'm gonna get outta here. You mark my words, Mamma. I'm gonna join the tour, and I'm gonna get out.

[*Blackout.*]

SCENE 2

[*The next day. Lights rise on the empty living room.* CHUCK *enters. He is carrying a trash bag.* MOLLY *enters behind him. She has another Wal-Mart bag and is once again dressed like a clown.*]

CHUCK: Accusin' me of takin' that knife. You hadn't stopped us—we woulda come to blows. I ain't gonna take a step back for that man—he can't treat me like trash.

DOROTHY [*from her bedroom*]: Molly! Molly, is that you?

MOLLY [*yelling back to* DOROTHY]: No, it ain't me.

CHUCK: Who's that?

MOLLY: Dorothy, my mamma. Don't mind her none. She's old and crazy. You can put your trash bag down now. Make yourself comfortable.

CHUCK: Four days I been holdin' this—all through my eatin', sleepin', and movin'. If I had been with a woman at the gymnasium, then I would've had one hand on a booby and the other on this here trash bag.

MOLLY: I ain't gonna steal nothin'.

CHUCK: Don't suppose ya will, but . . . I wanna keep it just the same. It's all I got left. I lose this and there ain't nothin' to prove I exist.

DOROTHY [*from her bedroom*]: Who's there?

MOLLY [*yelling back to* DOROTHY]: A burglar—now go back to bed, ya old hag! [*To* CHUCK] Wanna sit?

[CHUCK *nods and sits on the couch with his trash bag.* MOLLY, *still holding her brown paper bag, sits beside him.*]

Why'd Mr. Mack think you stole his knife?

CHUCK: I went in that man's store lookin' for a job. He said he wuzn't hirin', so I decided to glance around. 'Fore I leave, he stops me and says he wants to look in my trash bag. I tell him, "Let me go to your house and look in your underwear drawer." He wuz none too kin to that idea, Miss . . . uh . . . what'd she say your name wuz again?

MOLLY: Molly.

CHUCK: Chuck.

[*They shake hands awkwardly.*]

DOROTHY [*from her bedroom*]: Molly, I need my Icy Hot.

MOLLY [*yelling back to* DOROTHY]: I got you some last night! Use that! [*To* CHUCK] What she needs is my boot up her ass.

CHUCK: No need to be talkin' 'bout your mother that way. Mothers are the only people who can truly love. No one should put a boot—or anythin', really—in a mother's ass.

MOLLY: Your mother must not be alive no more.

CHUCK: Never met my mamma. She died birthin' me.

[MOLLY *produces a bottle of malt liquor from the Wal-Mart bag. She opens it, swigs, and passes it to* CHUCK.]

Mighty hospitable of ya.

MOLLY: Church looked crazy when I drove by it today.

CHUCK: Crowded. Not much food. Hot like July. Smelled of sport. Reminded me of a locker room. Wuz a high school janitor once. That's what it smelled like—a giant football locker room.

MOLLY: Brother Eric seems to be doin' a lot.

CHUCK: I ain't never seen a man so excited 'bout tragedy in my whole life. Tellin' people to go here—tellin' people to go there. He don't care 'bout Katrina victims—he cares 'bout news cameras. Told me to wash his truck for three dollars—like I'm a bum or somethin'.

DOROTHY [*from her bedroom*]: I'm all out of the Icy Hot, Molly. I used it today.

MOLLY: If you used an entire container of Icy Hot in one day, then you don't deserve no more, ya smelly bitch!

[CHUCK *gives her a look.* MOLLY *feels bad.*]

[*Yelling at* DOROTHY] Ya ain't that smelly, Mamma.

[CHUCK *nods in approval.* MOLLY *opens her Wal-Mart bag and removes a box of cookies. She tosses them to* CHUCK.]

CHUCK: Really?

[MOLLY *nods.* CHUCK *devours the cookies.*]

CHUCK [*eating*]: Can I ask you a personal question, Molly?

MOLLY: I suppose.

CHUCK: Why're you dressed like that?

MOLLY: Ya ain't never been to a rodeo?

CHUCK: There's a lotta places I ain't never been.

MOLLY [*proudly*]: I'm a rodeo clown.

CHUCK: Meanin'?

MOLLY: Meanin' I distract the bulls. Keep 'em from sitting on riders and stuff.

CHUCK: Ever been hurt?

MOLLY: Everyone works a rodeo is always hurt. Ya just don't wanna get injured—that means you can't do it no more. Bull got his horns in my barrel once and cracked my nose. Iced it 'tween rides. Next day—I didn't have ta wear no clown paint. My eyes wuz as black as a farmer's mornin' coffee.

CHUCK: Ya like the rodeo that much, huh?

MOLLY: When I'm out there, and the rider's been bucked, I can feel everyone's eyes—in a good way. They're watchin' with hope—hope that I'm gonna keep the bull from getting' the rider . . . hope that I'm gonna keep the bull from gettin' me. That bull—he's death—and I'm dancin' with him. I can smell his sweat, and he can smell mine. We respect each other.

[*Beat.*]

[*Pointing to the bookshelf*] That belt—it's got real gold in it. Most valuable thing I own. Arkadelphia Rodeo Association gave it to me for my "heroism in the line of fire."

[MOLLY *gets up, grabs the belt, and shows it to* CHUCK.]

It actually has Brandon Smith's name on it, but a bull tore off his face 'fore they could give it to him, so they gave it to me instead.

CHUCK: Congratulations?

MOLLY: Tomorrow I got a tryout for the PRCA Tour. It goes all across the South. If they pick me up as a professional rodeo clown, then I'll be rich. We're talkin' like four hundred dollars a week. Plus vacation.

[*Beat.*]

Mamma wants me to quit the rodeo and go back to the Piggly Wiggly, though. She thinks it's too dangerous, 'cuz . . .

[*Beat.*]

She just don't wanna be alone.

CHUCK: If you go back to Piggly Wiggly, then how ya gonna be a famous rodeo star?

[MOLLY *smiles. Silence. They share a moment.* CHUCK *removes brochures from his trash bag. He hands them to* MOLLY.]

That's the Merv Moore School of Wrestlin'. I've always wanted to go there. It costs fifteen hundred dollars. That's where the Rock wuz trained. Once I get my government check and my FEMA trailer, I'm gonna go.

MOLLY: Ya think you're too old?

CHUCK: Nope. Not even close. As soon as you let your dreams expire, that's when ya die. I know. I've seen it happen.

MOLLY: Well, why haven't ya gone to school sooner, then?

CHUCK: I wuz barely makin' 'nough for food and shelter 'fore the storm hit.

MOLLY: What wuz it like? The storm, that is.

CHUCK: Water pushed the walls outta shotgun shacks. Dropped roofs. Took everythin' away. Nobody made it. People survived. But they ain't the same people.

[*Beat.*]

Don't wanna talk 'bout it, really.

DOROTHY [*screaming from her bedroom*]: I'm calling the police if you don't tell me who's in my house!

MOLLY: I'll be right back.

[MOLLY *gets up and heads for* DOROTHY's *bedroom.*]

CHUCK: Be nice, now.

MOLLY: Oh, I will. I promise. [*As she exits*] Mamma, if you don't go to sleep right now, then I'm gonna take off my boot and use it to beat ya brain dead!

[MOLLY *exits.* CHUCK *stays seated for a nervous second or two. Finally, he gets up and looks around—all the while still clinging to his trash bag. He touches the championship belt, looks under the sofa, and even inspects an empty pizza box. The whole time he is glancing back to the bedroom for* MOLLY. *Eventually, he returns to the malt liquor and drinks, while standing up.* MOLLY *reenters and stares at him.*]

[*Worried and hurt*] Ya leavin'? Where ya going? Why ya wanna leave me so soon?

CHUCK: Ah, I ain't goin' nowhere, Molly. Just stretchin' my legs. If I'm welcome, I'd like to stay a few days. In a week I get a FEMA trailer. I ain't goin' back to the church gymnasium—so if I could just stay a week, that would be—

MOLLY: You can stay as long as you want.

CHUCK [*smiling*]: Mighty hospitable of ya.

[*Silence. Another moment.*]

MOLLY: Ya wanna see my room? I got my own refrigerator. Might have some leftover cheesy crust pizza—that is, if Mamma ain't gone snoopin' again.

CHUCK: I'd like that. I'd like that a lot.

[CHUCK *approaches* MOLLY, *slowly.*]

MOLLY [*nervous rambling*]: Cheesy crust pizza is my favorite kind in the whole world. I dip it in French dressin'. Most people dip it in—

[CHUCK *kisses* MOLLY. MOLLY *pulls away.*]

CHUCK: I'm sorry, I thought—

MOLLY: Davy. My last . . . did things to me . . . things I ain't gonna let no man do again.

CHUCK: Ya want me to stab him?

MOLLY: No. I just . . . I gotta be able to trust you. That's all.

[CHUCK *opens his trash bag and removes a scarf. He hands it to* MOLLY.]

What's this?

CHUCK: I found it at the gymnasium. Wuz gonna take it to the pawn shop and ask for 'bout three dollars. But I been thinkin' maybe . . . well . . . you might be worth more than three dollars.

[MOLLY *is touched. They kiss.* CHUCK *releases his trash bag. It drops to the ground. They continue kissing.* DOROTHY *enters and gasps.* CHUCK *and* MOLLY *turn to her, holding each other. Blackout.*]

SCENE 3

[*The next day. Lights rise on* DOROTHY *sitting on the couch. She has a knife in her hand.* CHUCK's *trash bag is on the table in front of her.* CHUCK *enters, wearing only jeans.*]

CHUCK: Whadda ya think you're doin'?

[*Startled,* DOROTHY *points the knife at* CHUCK.]

DOROTHY: Why are you still here?

[CHUCK *walks toward her.*]

CHUCK: Molly said I could stay till I get my FEMA trailer. Now, put that knife down.

DOROTHY [*while still waving the knife*]: Did ya fuck her?

CHUCK: That's none of your business.

DOROTHY: Did ya give it to her good? Flush her cheeks? Make her brow sweat? Touch her down there?

CHUCK: Gimme my fuckin' knife back 'fore someone gets hurt.

DOROTHY: You threatenin' me, boy?

CHUCK: I ain't no boy, and you're the one with the knife.

DOROTHY: I'm callin' the police on ya.

CHUCK: For what?

DOROTHY: Fuckin' my daughter.

[*Beat.*]

And stealin'.

[CHUCK *grabs* DOROTHY *and wrestles the knife away from her. He puts it to her throat. He pulls it back.*]

CHUCK: Don't feel too pleasin'—does it?

DOROTHY: You stole that. I know you did.

CHUCK: Don't go thinkin' you know my business—'cuz you don't know nothin' near my business.

DOROTHY: I know I can hear everythin' from my room, and I heard ya tell Molly you didn't steal a knife from Mr. Mack, but now ya got a nice big one in your trash bag—a nice big one with a price tag on it . . . a price tag from Mr. Mack's store.

CHUCK [*looking around*]: Ya got my sheath, too?

[DOROTHY *holds the sheath out for* CHUCK. CHUCK *reaches for it.* DOROTHY *slaps him.*]

What the—

[DOROTHY *slaps* CHUCK *again.*]

Listen here, you—

[DOROTHY *slaps* CHUCK *again.* CHUCK *grabs the sheath and slips his knife into it. He puts the knife in his trash bag.*]

Don't ever fuckin' touch me again. Ya stupid bitch. You're outta your goddamn mind.

[DOROTHY *huffs.*]

DOROTHY: Molly's gonna be none too pleased 'bout that knife—I can tell ya that right now, mister . . . but . . . maybe . . . I could be inclined not to say anythin'.

[*Still angry, but now somewhat interested,* CHUCK *looks at* DOROTHY. DOROTHY *smiles seductively.* CHUCK *almost vomits.*]

CHUCK: Oh, hell no.

DOROTHY: You best not be gettin' comfy, then, 'cuz Molly don't like liars. She's been down that road and back. A couple times. When she finds out what you done, then she's gonna throw your black ass outta here.

CHUCK [*seriously*]: No need to be gettin' racial, Dorothy.

[DOROTHY *huffs. A long, awkward silence.*]

DOROTHY [*finally*]: Molly has AIDS.

CHUCK: No, she don't.

DOROTHY: How do you know? I'm her mamma. I should know, and I do know. She's got a lot of AIDS—all over her.

CHUCK: I don't believe you.

DOROTHY: Shut up. It's true. Now, I reckon it's time you left. I'm tired of your face.

[CHUCK *stares at her. He is not happy.* DOROTHY *removes a remote control from her muumuu. She turns on the television.*]

NED PERMY [*from the television*]: What's up, Arkansas? The count is four down, the amount two hundred and sixty dollars, I'm Ned Permy, and it's time to go *Dialing for Dollars!*

[DOROTHY *can't help but clap excitedly.*]

CHUCK: Ned Permy ain't never gonna call Arkadelphia—he only calls big Arkansas cities, like Lonoke or—

DOROTHY: They got *Dialing for Dollars* in Louisiana?

NED PERMY [*from the television*]: I am now dialing the number of one lucky Arkansan.

DOROTHY: I wuzn't joshin' 'bout the police. I'm gonna call 'em and tell 'em 'bout that knife. You're a Bayou bum, so you don't know 'bout Arkadelphia jails, but they ain't too hospitable ta people like you.

CHUCK: What do you mean—people like me?

NED PERMY [*from the television*]: And there's the first ring.
DOROTHY: Dang it to heck.

[DOROTHY *turns the television off.* CHUCK *reaches for the remote control.* DOROTHY *puts it back in her muumuu.*]

You best be leavin' without sayin' good-bye to Molly. I heard ya fillin' her head fulla lies last night—'bout her being a rodeo star and whatnot. She ain't never gonna make the tour 'cuz she's too old and too fat. She needs to know that. 'Sides, rodeo . . . it . . . takes people. Now the food industry, on the other hand—
CHUCK: She don't wanna go back to the Piggly Wiggly—she told me—
DOROTHY: I don't care what she told you. This is my trailer, and it's my social that feeds us every month. And Molly ain't never gonna leave me—ya hear?

[CHUCK *says nothing.*]

I said—did ya hear?

[CHUCK *remains silent.*]

Did ya hear, Negro?
CHUCK [*seriously*]: Twice. You've been warned twice now.

[DOROTHY *removes a container of Icy Hot and puts some on her finger. She reaches for her mouth.*]

I don't think you should put Icy Hot—

[DOROTHY *puts it in her mouth.*]

Jesus, woman. That's disgustin'.
DOROTHY: Whadda you know 'bout Icy Hot? Whadda you know 'bout anythin'? I wuz a debutante. What wuz you?
CHUCK: I've been alotta things—a farmer, a janitor, a burger flipper, a—
DOROTHY: My granddaddy wuz a farmer.
CHUCK: My daddy wuz till some fellas came and destroyed his crops.
DOROTHY: Why would somebody come and destroy your crops?
CHUCK: Nobody wants to see a black man succeed.
DOROTHY: That ain't true.
CHUCK: When I wuz nine some white men came in the middle of the night. Killed our cows, put herbicides in our crops, and set our barn on fire. I came out in my pajamas and watched it burn. Smoke filled the air like death, and

Daddy didn't say nothin'. We moved to another city, and the only job my daddy could get wuz flippin' burgers. Daddy and I didn't talk much after that—my mamma wuz dead, so we had a real quiet house. I dropped outta school at fourteen to flip burgers alongside my daddy. He passed away a few years later. If we hadn't lost that farm, he'd still be alive today. I know it. White people trampled his soul. Killed it. They ain't gonna get mine.

[*Long silence.*]

DOROTHY: Where'd ya flip burgers?
CHUCK: Burger Barn.
DOROTHY: I like the Burger Barn a great deal.
CHUCK: Yeah, it's purty—
DOROTHY: The Double Decker Bacon Cheeseburger. That's what I get.
CHUCK: I'm more partial to the Crispy Chicken Deluxe. Sometimes they put too much mayonnaise on it, though. When I worked there—'fore they shut my store down—I never put too much mayonnaise on sandwiches. I wuz sensitive to that.
DOROTHY: Too much mayonnaise will ruin a sandwich.

[*Beat.*]

CHUCK: Dorothy?
DOROTHY: Yeah.
CHUCK: Are ya still gonna call the police on me?
DOROTHY: You bet your black ass I am.

[*Angry,* CHUCK *gets up, grabs his trash bag, and goes to the bedroom.* DOROTHY *smiles.* CHUCK *reenters and takes* DOROTHY's *Icy Hot. He then runs back to the bedroom.*]

Hey! Hey, get back here, you—

[MOLLY, *wearing the scarf* CHUCK *gave her and once again dressed like a clown, enters, excited.*]

[*Immediately*] Molly! Molly, your colored boy is worse than Davy!
MOLLY: What?

[CHUCK, *now fully dressed, enters with his trash bag in hand. Silence. Awkward.*]

Where ya goin'?
CHUCK: Don't feel welcome no more.
MOLLY [*hurt*]: Just like that?

CHUCK: Just like that.

DOROTHY: Good-bye.

CHUCK: Don't know where I'm gonna go. Still got a week till my FEMA trailer comes. Might sleep in a tent display at Wal-Mart. One thing's for sure—I ain't goin' back to the church.

[CHUCK *goes to the front door and opens it.*]

MOLLY: Chuck, wait!

[CHUCK *stops, turns around, and looks at* MOLLY.]

DOROTHY: Ask him where your championship belt is.

CHUCK: What're you talkin' about?

DOROTHY: That means he stole it.

CHUCK [*to* MOLLY]: You know how I told you to love your mamma? Well, I wuz wrong. She's a crazy old bitch.

DOROTHY: You stole Mr. Mack's knife!

CHUCK: I needed that knife for protection. I got in a fight with Brother Eric 'bout washin' his truck. He kicked me outta the church gymnasium. I didn't know where I wuz gonna have to stay till my FEMA trailer came. I wuz scared and depressed and . . . well, then I met you, Molly, and I knew that if I could just lay down beside ya, then nothin' would be too troublin' no more.

MOLLY [*hurt*]: So you really did lie to me?

CHUCK: I'm sorry. I didn't know if I could trust you.

MOLLY: Now I can't trust you.

[*Silence.*]

DOROTHY: He's a thief and a liar, and he don't love you.

MOLLY [*not angry, just sad*]: Why ya do this to me, Mamma? It's like ya enjoy givin' me hurt. Mammas shouldn't do that—Mammas should just love.

[*Silence.* DOROTHY *says nothing.* CHUCK *puts his head down and goes to leave once more.*]

CHUCK: I guess I'm goin' to Wal-Mart now. It's OK. Last time I wuz there, they had a real nice family-sized tent with a sleepin' bag and bug zapper and everythin'.

MOLLY: Wait.

[CHUCK *turns around.*]

THE TRASH BAG TOURIST ✺ 193

DOROTHY: No, don't wait. Keep goin', ya fuck face.

MOLLY: Show me everythin' that's in your trash bag, and ya can stay.

[CHUCK *looks at his trash bag. He thinks.*]

CHUCK: I can't do that. It's all I got left that's . . . that's mine.

MOLLY: Wal-Mart'll kick you out so fast. They might not even let you shop in there.

[*Silence.* CHUCK *thinks about this.*]

CHUCK [*sadly, almost to himself*]: I don't got nowhere else to go.

DOROTHY: He won't do it 'cuz he's got your belt in there. Let him go, Molly. 'Fore he tries to rape us both.

CHUCK [*to* DOROTHY]: Woman, are you insane? A blind, backwards boy with no teeth wouldn't touch you out of loneliness and you're sayin' rape?

[DOROTHY *huffs.* CHUCK *turns back to* MOLLY.]

Molly, I ain't got nothin' of yours. I swear.

MOLLY: Prove it.

CHUCK: You don't trust me?

MOLLY: That belt . . . it's important. It's a sign that I got some talent at some-thin'. It's about the only thing in Arkadelphia that don't make me sad.

[*Silence.* CHUCK *takes his trash bag over to the table and opens it, slowly. This is embarrassing, hard, emotional. He removes some shirts, underwear, socks, and a small card. He places the card in his pocket.*]

CHUCK: That's my Pizza Hut discount card. I got a free pizza comin'. We can share it.

MOLLY: Keep goin'.

[CHUCK *looks to* MOLLY. MOLLY *nods.* CHUCK *glares at* DOROTHY. *He removes the knife and drops it on the table. Silence. He holds his trash bag upside down, showing that it is empty, then tosses it aside.*]

CHUCK [*to* MOLLY]: You've seen all of me now.

[CHUCK *looks down.*]

MOLLY: Is there anythin' else you wanna tell me?

[CHUCK *goes to say something then stops.*]

I can't take no more lyin'. I've done told ya how I feel 'bout that.

CHUCK: There is one more thing.

[DOROTHY *huffs.* CHUCK *stares at her.*]

> I don't love cheesy crust pizza as much as I said I did. I think it's OK. I like thin and crispy crust more.

MOLLY: Did you mean what you said—last night—when we wuz in bed?

CHUCK: Every single word.

MOLLY: You really don't think I'm too ugly?

CHUCK: I don't think you're very ugly at all, Molly.

[CHUCK *and* MOLLY *walk toward each other.*]

DOROTHY: I think I'm gonna throw up all over myself.

[CHUCK *and* MOLLY *kiss.*]

> And I'll have you know a blind, backwards boy with no teeth would touch me out of loneliness. He'd do it, and he wouldn't hate it none at all. I wuz a debutante.

[DOROTHY, *disgusted, rises and begins to leave the room. The championship belt falls out of her muumuu. It crashes on the floor.* CHUCK *and* MOLLY *look at it. Silence.*]

MOLLY [*finally*]: Guess what, Mamma? I had my tryout today, and the PRCA Tour picked me up as a professional rodeo clown. I'm joinin' it in Houston next month, and if Chuck wants—he's comin' with me. But you ain't. You're stayin' here. To die. Alone.

[DOROTHY *is speechless. Blackout.*]

SCENE 4

[*A week later. Lights rise on* CHUCK, *wearing Fruit of the Loom underwear and sitting on the couch with his legs propped up on the table. He has a bottle of malt liquor in one hand and the remote control in the other. He is watching wrestling.* DOROTHY *hobbles into the room. She makes her way to a chair, sits down arduously, and removes an empty container of Icy Hot. She begins trying to rub some out.* CHUCK *puts the remote control in his underwear.*]

CHUCK: I ain't never seen a woman loves Icy Hot more than you. Ya been scrapin' that container dry for a week now. There ain't no more left.

DOROTHY: I hurt.

CHUCK: We all do, Dorothy. Get over it.

DOROTHY: Could ya . . . maybe get me some more at Wal-Mart? Please?

CHUCK: We don't got no more money left for the month. Your social can barely support two people—much less three. And Molly don't make shit. Don't worry, though—as soon as my FEMA trailer gets here—

DOROTHY: My FEMA trailer this, my FEMA trailer that. It wuz supposed to be here last week—where is it, Chuck?

CHUCK: Church said there's some complications.

DOROTHY: The only complications are you and all the other trash bag tourists. Tyler from next door said you people have made the grocery store too crowded, slowed down our school system, and pissed all over everythin' we've given ya. Everyone wants Arkadelphia back the way it wuz. I heard that Brother Eric's even 'bout to lose his temper.

CHUCK: Brother Eric's the reason the trailers ain't here yet. If that asshole were in charge of a two-car parade, then one car would disappear and the other would explode into flames. Then he'd say it wuz all God's will.

DOROTHY: At least he's not a thief.

CHUCK: Ya know damn well I took that knife back and humbled myself to Mr. Mack.

DOROTHY: 'Cuz you wuz scared I wuz gonna call the cops.

CHUCK [*threatening*]: Look, Dorothy, I don't wanna fight no more, all right? I'm just gonna watch my wrestlin' videos, and you're gonna be quiet for once in your stupid fuckin' life.

DOROTHY: My life ain't stupid. Yours is.

CHUCK: I'm watchin' wrestlin', woman!

DOROTHY: That's all you ever do!

CHUCK: I done told ya already—I'm goin' ta wrestlin' school. Molly inspired me. Supports me even. So, if you don't mind, I'm studyin' right now.

DOROTHY: You don't have to study for wrestlin' school—ya just hit people.

CHUCK: That's like sayin' Michael Jordan just put a ball in a hoop, or Beethoven just put paint on a canvas.

[*Silence.*]

DOROTHY: *Dialin' for Dollars* is comin' on in a minute.

CHUCK: That's nice to know.

[CHUCK *continues watching wrestling.* DOROTHY, *frustrated, throws her Icy Hot container on the floor. She huffs.*]

DOROTHY [*almost in tears*]: Look at me. I used to be a—

CHUCK: I know, I know—a debutante—ya used to be a fuckin' debutante. Congratulations, Dorothy.

DOROTHY: I wuz my mamma's only child. She cleaned houses for rich folks all her life. Only thing she wanted wuz for me to be a debutante.

CHUCK [*pointing to the television*]: Shaun Michaels is tuning up the band— he's 'bout to give Bret "The Hitman" Hart some sweet chin music.

DOROTHY: She cleaned houses for a month and didn't charge nothin'—just to get the committee to let me go to one dance. I wuz thirty-two.

CHUCK [*still with the television*]: Here comes the sharpshooter!

DOROTHY: My mamma made my dress by hand. I felt like a princess. None of the other girls would talk to me, but I didn't care—'cuz that wuz the only time I've ever looked in a mirror and not been sad at all. Nate wuz waitin' tables that night. He came up to me and said I wuz his. He wuz right. I ain't never seen a man more handsome. We married and moved into this trailer twenty-nine years ago.

[DOROTHY *breaks down crying.*]

CHUCK [*looking at the television*]: He wuz Molly's father?

DOROTHY: He wuz till he left us both for the rodeo. Drew a bull one day that . . . that couldn't be ridden.

[*Silence.* CHUCK *looks at* DOROTHY. *He picks up a fast-food napkin off the floor and tries to hand it to* DOROTHY. *She reaches out and . . . grabs the remote control out of* CHUCK'S *underwear. She turns on* Dialing for Dollars.]

CHUCK: Hey! What the fuck you think you're doing?

DOROTHY: It's my television and my remote control!

[CHUCK *grabs the remote control back.*]

CHUCK: Not no more it ain't!

NED PERMY [*from the television*]: Hello, Arkansans! The count is seven down and three hundred dollars, I'm Ned Permy, and it's time to go *Dialing for Dollars*!

CHUCK: Three hundred dollars?

DOROTHY: It's been a long time since anyone's won anythin' in Arkansas.

CHUCK: Well, now, three hundred dollars is kind of exciting.

DOROTHY: I always think I'm gonna win.

NED PERMY [*from the television*]: I have one lucky telephone number in my hand, and I am now dialing . . .

CHUCK: Well, that's a shame—maybe tomorrow.

[CHUCK *turns off the television.*]

DOROTHY: It takes a second to ring!
CHUCK: Listen, Dorothy, I done told ya Ned Permy don't call small—

[*The telephone rings.* CHUCK *and* DOROTHY *look to the bookshelf, speechless.*]

DOROTHY: Oh, my God! Oh, my God! Oh, my God! We're rich! We're rich!
CHUCK: Hot damn!

[CHUCK *dashes to the bookshelf and answers the telephone.*]

DOROTHY: Tell Ned Permy I love him! I watch him every day! [*Looking up to the heavens*] Thank you, God! I never thought you wuz listenin', but now I—
CHUCK [*into the telephone quickly*]: Four up, and three hundred dollars!

[*Beat.*]

What? Yeah, she lives here. This is—it don't matter who this is.
DOROTHY: Don't be rude to Ned Permy.
CHUCK [*to* DOROTHY]: Shut up, bitch. [*Into the telephone*] Calm down, calm down. Not you. The other bitch.

[*Beat.*]

What? Huh? How? When? Is she—yeah, I can get there. I mean, I gotta get my shoes, but—is ... is she gonna ... gonna make it? I understand. OK. All right. I'm comin' right now.

[CHUCK *hangs up the telephone.*]

DOROTHY: What happened? What's going on?
CHUCK: A bull sat on Molly. I gotta go.

[CHUCK *rushes to the bedroom.*]

DOROTHY [*yelling to the bedroom*]: Is she gonna be OK? Take me with you. Please.

[CHUCK *enters with shoes on but still no pants.*]

Tell her ... tell her ...

[CHUCK *exits.*]

I love her.

[*Silence.* DOROTHY *sits alone in the trailer, worried about her daughter, trying not to cry. The telephone rings. She makes her way to the bookshelf as fast as possible.*]

DOROTHY [*out of breath*]: Molly? Ned Permy? Hello?

[*Beat.*]

Oh. Hello, Brother Eric. Did ya hear? Molly broke her legs. A bull sat on her.

[*Beat.*]

Well, prayers don't mean much in my trailer, but that's a nice gesture.

[*Beat.*]

I got a question for ya, Brother Eric. Do you think God has a ding-a-ling? 'Cuz, ya know, I think I'd be more inclined to believe in Him if He didn't. Have a ding-a-ling, that is.

[*Beat.*]

Hello? Brother Eric? Are ya still there?

[*Beat.*]

Yeah, we got one staying here. Yeah, Chuck—ya know him? I don't know his last name. He's been here two weeks—waitin' on his FEMA trailer. He can't talk right now 'cuz he just ran to the hospital in his underwear.

[*Beat.*]

Oh really? You don't say. That's interesting, Brother Eric. That's very interestin'. No, no . . . keep going. I wanna hear all of this . . .

[*As* DOROTHY *listens to* BROTHER ERIC, *a huge smile comes across her face. Blackout.*]

SCENE 5

[*Later that night. Lights rise on* DOROTHY, *sitting in a lawn chair.* MOLLY *enters in a wheelchair with two broken legs.* CHUCK *is pushing her. He still doesn't have pants.*]

DOROTHY: How's my Baby Girl?

[MOLLY *is silent, deeply depressed.*]

CHUCK: She ain't said nothin' since I picked her up.

[CHUCK *rolls* MOLLY *over to the couch.*]

[*To* MOLLY] I got some liquor left.

[CHUCK *picks the liquor up off the table and holds it out.* MOLLY *grabs the bottle and begins chugging it.*]

Don't you worry none, Molly. I'll turn us on some wrestlin' and then order a cheesy crust pizza. How 'bout that?

DOROTHY [*to* CHUCK]: I know somethin' 'bout you, mister.

CHUCK: Pipe down, bitch. I don't got no time for your nonsense.

[CHUCK *sits on the couch and turns on wrestling.*]

[*To* MOLLY] I think you're takin' this too hard, Molly. Your legs'll heal.

MOLLY: That bull didn't just sit on my legs. He sat on my dreams too.

CHUCK: Listen, you can rejoin the tour just as soon as—

MOLLY: When that bull sat on me—nobody rushed to help. I wuz stuck. Couldn't move. I could see, though. I saw a daddy nudge his little boy. They pointed and laughed.

[*Beat.*]

I wuz wrong. Rodeo don't respect me. It just laughs like everyone else.

[*Long silence.* CHUCK *gets the Pizza Hut discount card out of his blue jeans, which are now hanging over the edge of the sofa.*]

CHUCK [*finally*]: What do you want on your cheesy crust pizza? I'll get ya anythin' you want. Up to three toppings. Or a specialty. That's what my card says.

MOLLY: Stuck under that bull . . . in front of all those people I know from school and Piggly Wiggly and church . . . it wuz . . . it wuz worse than the time Davy . . . gave me to his friends.

[*Another long silence.* CHUCK *puts the card on the table.*]

CHUCK [*finally*]: Molly, listen to me, baby—when I get my FEMA trailer and my money, then we're gonna get outta here—just you and me. I'm gonna go to wrestlin' school and take care of you for a change. You won't have to do nothin' that brings ya hurt or sadness no more. Your mamma won't be around to hassle us, so we can just . . . be . . . together . . . forever . . . livin' the American Dream.

DOROTHY: Chuck ain't a flood victim.

[*Silence.*]

MOLLY: What?

[CHUCK *says nothing.*]

DOROTHY: His name ain't Chuck either—accordin' to his Pizza Hut discount card—it's Marvin Jones. Brother Eric said some people been fakin', so the church checked social security numbers, and Chuck—or rather, Marvin—ain't legit. Brother Eric took it upon himself to call everyone and warn 'em 'bout the scam.

[*Beat.*]

MOLLY: Did ya lie to me . . . again . . . Marvin?
DOROTHY [*to* CHUCK]: I think ya best be goin' now.

[CHUCK *looks to* MOLLY. *She says nothing.*]

CHUCK: I didn't mean ta deceive ya much, Molly—I really didn't. I wuz livin' in Lonoke—in a dump smaller than a shotgun shack—I wuz workin' at the Burger Barn, and they got shut down, and no place else'd hire a forty-year-old black man with no education. I lost my house and—
DOROTHY: Don't believe anythin' he says—he's a liar.
CHUCK: It's true—it all is—on my mother's grave it is. I wuz usin' the Best Buy bathroom to clean up one day, and I saw Katrina on the news and heard Arkadelphia wuz helpin'—givin' food and shelter—and no one ain't never helped me 'fore, so I came here, and I . . . I'm sorry, Molly—I am. I wanted ta tell ya, but . . . but I wuz scared . . . I just couldn't get nothin' to work out . . . till you come into my life.

[*Silence.* MOLLY *looks away from* CHUCK.]

DOROTHY: Here, I already packed your luggage. Don't say I never did nothin' for ya.

[DOROTHY *throws the trash bag on the floor.*]

CHUCK: Molly . . . Molly . . . I believed in ya.

[*Silence.*]

DOROTHY: *Dialing for Dollars* is comin' on, Molly. Turn that wrestling shit off.

CHUCK [*to* MOLLY]: I meant it when I said I didn't think you wuz too ugly, and you're worth three dollars, and—

DOROTHY: Listen up, Negro. She don't want you here no more. Nobody in this town does. The time for bein' hospitable is over. So get the fuck outta my trailer. Now.

[CHUCK *rises and puts his pants on, slowly. He then gets his trash bag and begins to leave.* DOROTHY *grabs the remote control off the table and turns on* Dialing for Dollars.]

NED PERMY [*from the television*]: Hello, Arkansas. The count is six down, and the amount is three hundred and twenty dollars!

CHUCK: I don't got nowhere else to go. Can I just stay one more night? Look, if I wuz ta find a job ... somewhere close ... maybe ... to where I could make some money ... could I then ... maybe ... just ... please ... maybe ...

NED PERMY: I have the number of one lucky Arkansan in my hand, and I am now dialing!

CHUCK: Dorothy, what if I wuz to get you some Icy Hot? I could go down to the Wal-Mart and pick some up real quick. If I did, could I—

NED PERMY: And there's the first ring!

[*The telephone rings.* MOLLY, DOROTHY, *and* CHUCK *are all shocked. They look to the table.* DOROTHY *picks the telephone up and answers it.*]

DOROTHY: Hello?

NED PERMY [*from the television*]: This is Ned Permy, and I'm *Dialing for Dollars.* Do you know the count and the amount?

DOROTHY: Six up, three hundred and twenty dollars!

NED PERMY: No, I'm sorry, ma'am. It's six *down.* But don't worry, there are no losers in *Dialing for Dollars*—I will make sure we send you a twelve-pack of Diet Mr. Pibb—thanks for playing, and better luck next time!

[DOROTHY *hangs up the telephone. No one knows what to say. Finally,* DOROTHY *turns to* CHUCK.]

DOROTHY: That wuz your fault, you goddamn piece of trash. I couldn't concentrate 'cuz of all your jabberin'. If you don't leave right now, I'm callin' the motherfuckin' police—and we both know you don't want that, 'cuz Arkadelphia's kindness has been all used up, and there ain't no tellin' what they might do.

[*Silence.*]

CHUCK: Thank ya for lettin' me stay these last two weeks, Molly . . . I appreciate it . . . it wuz real nice . . . I ain't never been treated so nice.

[CHUCK *opens the front door and looks to* MOLLY *one last time. He walks out.* MOLLY *then looks to the empty doorway. A few seconds pass.*]

DOROTHY: I warned ya 'bout pickin' up bums. But you don't listen to your poor, old, gray-headed mother, now do ya? What do I know? I wuz just a debutante.

[MOLLY *looks to* DOROTHY *and then back to the open door.*]

MOLLY: CHUCK! I MEAN, MARVIN! WHATEVER, JUST WAIT! DON'T GO! PLEASE, DON'T LEAVE ME! NOT HERE! NOT WITH HER! NOT LIKE THIS! I FORGIVE YOU! I LOVE YOU! I'M SORRY! I'M SO SORRY! PLEASE COME BACK! PLEASE! PLEASE! PLEASE!

[*Silence.* MOLLY *stares at the empty doorway.*]

DOROTHY: He's gone, and he ain't never comin' back.

[DOROTHY *gets up, walks to the front door, slams it, and locks it. She goes back to the couch and sits down.*]

Still wanna order a cheesy crust pizza?

[MOLLY *says nothing.*]

We got a little money left. Could maybe even get buffalo wings. 'Fore long you'll be healthy enough to go back to the Piggly Wiggly anyway. And if not, we can just sell your belt.

[DOROTHY *picks up the Pizza Hut discount card and looks at it.*]

That figures. His Pizza Hut discount card is expired.

[DOROTHY *wads the discount card up and throws it on the ground.* MOLLY *stares at it.*]

MOLLY: Someone'll help him . . . don't ya think?
DOROTHY: Don't nobody care 'bout that nigger. At least not no more. His time's done come and gone.

[DOROTHY *removes the Icy Hot from her muumuu. Lights slowly fade to black with* MOLLY *staring at the discount card and* DOROTHY *trying to rub a little more out of the empty container.*]

KATRINA: THE K WORD

Lisa S. Brenner and Suzanne M. Trauth

PRODUCTION HISTORY

Katrina: The K Word premiered at Montclair State University in 2007 (directed by Suzanne Trauth with the assistance of Lisa Brenner). Since then it has received staged readings and productions on college campuses in thirteen states and Washington, D.C. (www.katrinathekword.com). At the invitation of artistic director John Pietrowski, of Playwrights Theatre of New Jersey, *Katrina: The K Word* was included in a festival of plays about Hurricane Katrina in 2008.

STAGING

The style of *Katrina: The K Word* is presentational—these characters tell their stories directly to the audience, except when they are engaged in a scene with another character. When not on stage, some actors might sit in the first row of house seats or in chairs outlining the playing area stage right and left; occasionally they will say a line of dialogue from these seats. In the original production, the space the actors inhabited was open and clear until part 3, when the levees broke.

The initial production used a set design that included a huge wall that moved and crashed to suggest the levees collapsing. A fourteen-by-twenty-four-foot wall constructed of parallel two-by-fours that resembled the studs of a gutted house was covered with personal and household items, many of which are mentioned in the play. When it tilted forward at the beginning of part 3, the objects fell off and smashed onto the stage floor. Some items actually broke and had to be replaced repeatedly. The wall served as the visual focal

**SPECIAL NOTE ON SONGS AND RECORDINGS
For performance of copyrighted songs, arrangements, or recordings mentioned in the play, the permission of the copyright owner(s) must be obtained. Other songs, arrangements, or recordings may be substituted provided permission from the copyright owner(s) of such songs, arrangements, or recordings is obtained; or songs, arrangements, or recordings in the public domain may be substituted.

point of the play—once the wall fell, clearing it of props, actors could walk through the open studs and climb on them. A much simpler design, supported by lights and sound, could have a similar impact.

The "X" drawn on a wall surface in part 5 was a symbol used by the National Guard and other rescuers to mark houses affected by Hurricane Katrina. It indicated date searched, who completed the search, and results of the search.

Every actor plays several characters. Twelve are primary characters whose stories are told throughout the play; others simply pop in to help someone else tell a story. Though costume pieces and props help to delineate these "pop-in" characters, acting choices may provide the clearest differentiation. The play will benefit from a smooth, swiftly flowing shift from one scene to the next, preserving the relentless nature of the story.

Ideally, productions and readings should feature an ethnically diverse cast of actors. There is some flexibility in casting that would allow for adjustments along racial lines; however, the authors' intention is to have a balanced cast in terms of race and gender.

CHARACTERS

Ted, white man
Joe, white man
Vivie, African American woman
Brianna, African American woman
James, African American man
Desiree, white woman
Cory, white man
Darryl, African American man
Faith, white woman
Gabe, African American man
Shakira, African American woman
Rachel, white woman

PROLOGUE

[*AT RISE: As audience enters, a jazz band plays. Characters walk in, greet each other, set up chairs, and mingle with the audience, welcoming the tourists to New Orleans. After the band plays its last song, the characters formally introduce themselves.*]

TED: I been here all my life. All my life. Fishing industry's all right. I should know, I'm a chef. Soft-shelled crabs. Ever had that? You eat one of them, it's the best thing you ever ate in your life.

JOE: If you want really good New Orleans cooking, go to Mother's. It's on Poydras, four blocks west of Canal. It's oyster po'boys, uh, shrimp po'boys, that kind of stuff. I like the roast beef special. I shouldn't eat the grease, but man, they just slobber it on. Beans and rice on Mondays.

ENSEMBLE: Muffulettas, beignets, jambalaya, gumbo, étouffé, andouille sausage, crawfish, shrimp creole, café au lait, pralines, dirty rice, bread pudding.

VIVIE: I'm a fourth-generation New Orleanian. The French Quarter's cool, isn't it? High and dry. Yes. High and dry.

BRIANNA: Gentilly, New Orleans. Born, raised, educated. I have a master's in public health. New Orleans is . . . I don't know, so full of character that there are always interesting things going on.

JAMES: Yeah, I work for the National Parks Service. And what we do here is put on jazz concerts every day.

DESIREE: My grandparents moved here in the fifties. That's why we're not locals, we haven't been here long enough. I love the way it smells. I love the architecture. I love that people live together here, and everybody knows how to say, How you doing, baby? Doesn't matter if you're black, white, or brown. [*To the others*] Hey, m'babies!

ENSEMBLE: Hey, m'baby!

BRIANNA: Growing up, it always struck me as odd that the rest of the world didn't have a Mardi Gras parade. It's nice to live in a place where there's always a celebration.

[*The band plays.*]

ENSEMBLE: Mardi Gras balls, Mardi Gras Indians, masks, beads, lots of beads, Jackson Avenue, parading up St. Charles Ave., police cars with lights flashing, the King and Queen of Zulu, second line parades.

CORY: My family is from Baton Rouge. If you're that close to New Orleans and not coming down here and being a part of it . . . if you're a musician . . . I think that's silly. Hard to be that close to the flame without wanting to get closer.

DARRYL: I'm an engineer and supervisor for sewage and water works by day, a professional, and by night this is what I do.

[*He indicates instrument.*]

I make people forget about all of that shit. When they hear us, they forget about that and enjoy a moment in time.

CORY: What really brought me down here was partying . . .

[*Music plays.*]

CORY AND DARRYL: Louie Armstrong, The Meters, Preservation Hall Jazz Band, Dr. John, the Neville Brothers, Wynton Marsalis, Fats Domino, Pete Fountain, Terence Blanchard.

[*They high-five.*]

FAITH: I met my husband working nights as a nurse at Charity Hospital in the emergency room. He's a paramedic. My husband was born and raised in New Orleans. And, um, he actually went to school in Brooklyn, and did some college in New Jersey, and then moved back to New Orleans. I've always been here.

GABE: I am not a native of New Orleans . . . I've been here six years now . . . coordinating emergency management for the utility company.

SHAKIRA: I lived in the Ninth Ward, across the canal from the Lower Ninth Ward. I just graduated from college at SLU in Hammond, Louisiana.

RACHEL: Where I teach. I've never lived outside the state of Louisiana. To me it's home . . .

ENSEMBLE: Uptown, French Quarter, Mid-City, Upper Ninth Ward, Lower Ninth Ward, Lakeview, Gentilly, Metairie, Garden District, Carrolton, Central City, New Orleans East.

RACHEL: . . . and I know it won't be the same. I just don't think you can go through something like this and think that it will really be the same.

[*Pause.*]

RACHEL: Part 1: Evacuation.

[ACTORS *shift, some replace chairs, set stage.*]

VIVIE: Welcome to the Katrina Disaster Tour. I'm Vivie, and I'll be your tour guide. Does everyone have a seat, 'cause the tour bus is ready to roll. OK? Good, now, listen up, here's how it works. We can't tell you every story out of New Orleans, I mean, my God, 250,000 people lost their homes. But these twelve folks you just met are gonna tell you . . .

ENSEMBLE: Exactly . . . [*Warily, each of them thinks they know best what occurred*]

. . . what happened.

VIVIE [*to* ENSEMBLE]: Now, c'mon. These people paid good money for this tour, so let's get to it.

[ACTORS *clear space. Hip-hop music in.* SISTER *and* FRIEND *dance.*]

BRIANNA: It was a beautiful Saturday. I was doing my normal chores. The sun was shining. My sister was in her junior year. She had started school two weeks before.

SISTER: I remember that Friday during my art class, somebody mentioning a storm.

FRIEND: Oh, yeah, I heard about that. It's not supposed to be much of anything.

BRIANNA: Saturday night she invited a friend over. They hung out.

FRIEND: Oh, you know, hurricanes.

SISTER: Pish posh.

FRIEND: A lot of people had evacuated at that point.

SISTER: But we hadn't decided to, and my friend hadn't decided to either.

BRIANNA: So they were just hanging out, thinking they were, I don't know . . .

SISTER AND FRIEND: Badass.

[*Focus shifts to* DESIREE *and* PRODUCER.]

DESIREE: I literally had no idea there was a storm in the Gulf. At all. I woke up Saturday, it was a beautiful day. And my producer—I'm an actor and director—I had directed a show and it was, like, a hit and it had been extended and the producer called.

PRODUCER: Should I call off the show?

DESIREE: Why? What are you talking about?

PRODUCER: Well, there's a hurricane.

DESIREE: That's not a big deal.

[*Focus shifts to* RACHEL *and* FRIEND.]

RACHEL: I was actually in Jackson, Mississippi, for a teachers' conference that Saturday. My friend called.

FRIEND: What are you doing with your house? You can't come home.

RACHEL: Well, it'll sit there.

FRIEND: I think I'm going to call your parents and go with them to evacuate.

RACHEL: Ah, all right, whatever. Have fun. I'll be home on Monday.

[TED *and* CORY *take two chairs off the wall and sit.*]

TED: I stayed for every hurricane in the last, like, seventeen years, and they've all been a waste of time driving back with the traffic.

CORY: I was in the French Quarter . . . I'd been working really hard on a bunch of different stuff. That Friday night . . . the storm coming . . . that sort of thing happens a lot. Every season there's an evacuation and nothing ever happens . . . or it gets called off at the last minute, and I thought that that's what would happen.

TED: They never left before . . . why leave now? That was a lot of the mentality. A lot of people think people were poor and couldn't leave but . . . every year you have at least one evacuation. I was working at the restaurant . . . my bosses were getting their kids and stuff ready to leave . . . and we closed the restaurant down early . . . so . . . screw it . . . make a weekend out of it.

CORY: I was tired. I was ready to take a break from everybody . . . and I had a stack of movies. A bunch of food. I like to cook. And it's like I'm going to stay all weekend in the backyard and the bedroom and cook my grill and watch movies. I'm gonna take a break.

TED: I didn't leave because . . . I'm stupid.

[*He laughs.*]

Nah . . . My parents live on the West Bank. They didn't leave.

[*Another group gathers.*]

JAMES: We had lived through hurricanes before.

JOE: Not category five, but . . . I was born and raised in Miami. I remember when I was twelve years old down at my grandmother's in Key West, Florida, boarding up her house, staying through some hurricanes in this godforsaken Ninth-Ward-type environment.

GRANDMOTHER: Don't worry, this house was built by a slaver. It'll float.

[GABE *winces.*]

JOE [*to* GRANDMOTHER]: I don't care how many slaves this guy brought across, it's not going to float . . .

GABE: Some people . . . see people have gone through hurricanes here before, and a lot of people reference Betsy . . . A lot of people stayed during Betsy in '65 and survived. And they kind of knew that if they get up in the attic and if they have a way to get out, you know, even if the water comes, eventually it would recede and that would be that. A lot of people just chose to ride the storm out.

DESIREE: My grandfather never left for hurricanes, but Grandmother always evacuated whether he came with her or not. Every hurricane. Didn't matter how little or how big. She would take all of her dogs and all the insurance papers and go to this hotel in Hattiesburg. She had this routine down over the years.

BRIANNA: It was usually this weekend holiday. We go to a hotel and go out to eat and check out this little tiny town that we've managed to find in the middle of like Mississippi or something. So my sister spent the car ride doing her homework, assuming she'd be back in school on Monday.

[FAITH *and* HUSBAND *move to one side.*]

FAITH: I had actually worked Saturday before the storm. I was supposed to work until eleven that night, but my husband ⁂ . .

HUSBAND: I want you to leave by five o'clock Sunday morning. So you can't work till eleven. I'll pick up everything in the yard that could blow away, and you pack.

FAITH: You know, when Lindsey was six months old, we evacuated to Houston. We packed up all this baby stuff and everything, and we were gone for two days and came home.

HUSBAND: Well, it sounds really bad.

FAITH [*exasperated*]: We're gonna drive for two days, and then we're gonna be home just like last time. I'm not packing all this baby stuff for two days.

[FAITH *and* HUSBAND *move off, other actors move on, forming a group center stage. They nod their agreement, share a solidarity.*]

VIVIE: 'Cause our drill is this. The storm comes. You pack up. You leave. You stay gone two, three days.

JAMES: We got word that the office should be closed up, start packing. I closed up, and I went home. The other guys went home . . . definitely, probably be seeing each other Tuesday.

RACHEL: This is a hurricane . . . the power's going to go out . . . the wind's going to come. We're going to come back, and everything'll be OK. My mother literally left with two or three days' worth of clothing. Being a Jewish mother . . . she took food . . .

SHAKIRA: I remember the year before . . . I went with my roommate to her home, and it was a beautiful sunny day, and nothing happened in Hammond but a little drizzle.

VIVIE: George, in '98, we were gone three days, and for Ivan, in 2004, we were gone for three days . . . and this was going to be another three-day trip.

BRIANNA: You tell a New Orleanian to leave for a hurricane, it's a two-day thing.

DARRYL AND GABE: Two, three days.

FAITH: We were told to pack for three days.

JOE: Our checklist did consist of only three days' worth of clothes.

DESIREE: We figured it would be three days, and then we would be back.

SHAKIRA: Except for—when Katrina came, it did a little bit more destruction than what we thought.

[ACTORS *move off.*]

VOICEOVER: "Saturday, August 28, 2005. Voluntary evacuation of the city via contra flow will begin at 4:00 P.M."

GABE: Contra flow is the method we use to evacuate—we turn the interstate into a one-way street—leaving the area.

[*He watches* BRIANNA *and* SISTER.]

BRIANNA: We managed to go all the way up to Memphis this time, which was something we'd never done. And we went with the contra flow . . .

SISTER: . . . which was really fun.

BRIANNA: They turned all the highways out.

SISTER: Look at those shirts. "Go with the contra flow." Ooh, let's get some . . .

GABE: If you think about the timing of the hurricane . . . a lot of poor people . . . it was at the end of the month . . . A lot of people get paid the first and the third . . . by way of some kind of government check or whatever. End of the month they don't have any money at all. So unless there was some assistance to get out of the city, they didn't have a way to get out. They couldn't even buy their way out.

JAMES: I went home and decided to get my wife and son out. My wife is diabetic, and the reason why I didn't go with them is because I didn't have enough money to pay for me and to get all her medications, needles, and insulin. She and my son went to her sister's in Dallas, and I stayed, thinking, "Well, you know, we may get a little water, but I'll get things cleaned up before they get back."

[*He crosses up to the wall and moves chairs, other household items.*]

JOE: On Saturday there were four of us left on this block. The two families over there, the one family over here, and myself. My wife was gone. Left to go see our daughter.

JAMES: Clean the backyard, stow everything, go out front, board up our front windows.

JOE: I had pre-positioned everything. I went down our checklist. Bank records. Any jewelry, coins, money, traveler's checks. Insurance, warrantees, important legal documents, passports. Key to safety deposit boxes, wills, all computers . . . three, I'm a computer technology specialist . . . systems backups, CD-ROMs, pictures, videotapes of family, photo albums . . .

VIVIE: No pictures. That's in my head. I rarely take a photograph . . . I don't hold on to . . . that means nothing to me.

JOE: All our cameras, prescription medicines. Um, we lost a grandson, he lasted seven days. And so his picture. Our other grandchildren are doing fantastic. Let's see, my wife has a recipe box, she wants her recipe box. That was not going to be left for hurricanes.

[BRIANNA *and* SISTER *move into the light at the wall.*]

BRIANNA: My mother had a gut feeling because she was here for Betsy. And she was like, maybe we need to leave. My sister and I just packed duffel bags with T-shirts and shorts. Then she grabbed her basketball and her trophies.

SISTER: Aren't you gonna take your diplomas?

BRIANNA: I'm leaving them. [*To audience*] I'm sorry I didn't take them, but I took my bills in case anything did happen. In case I had to call creditors or whatever.

[*She picks up her expandable file.*]

VIVIE: I have a bag packed right now, and it stays packed. I have a case of water . . . always in my car . . . always. Bare essentials. Tuna fish in the cans or pouches. Nuts, raisins . . . and toilet paper.

[*The sound of TV reports can be heard.*]

JOE: Everything was in the car. I wasn't watching the TV. I do know how to read satellite data, and I don't listen to reporters. I think they are talking heads who will do anything to get a story, and they always exaggerate. They usually don't know sh . . . squat. They just read scripts, you know, and they look so profound and empty. They don't know science, couldn't read a satellite, couldn't even find north if they had a compass. I just don't like them. Obviously. So, anyway, I got a call from a neighbor at five o'clock Sunday morning.

NEIGHBOR: We're leaving. I think Bob and Lois are going. The Sidells are leaving too.

JOE: What's going on?

NEIGHBOR: Put on your TV.

JOE: So I went to the TV, and they were hallucinating about category five and how Katrina's going to hit us straight on. And I went to my computer, and I looked at the data.

[*A group of* ACTORS *moves forward.* JOE *moves off.*]

GABE: The storm did not go where they said it was supposed to. It was sitting off the coast of Florida on Wednesday. It was supposed to cross into the Miami area and then enter the Gulf of Mexico. It was only supposed to be a category one storm. It wasn't supposed to come this way at all.

JAMES: It hit Florida, did as much devastation as a category one, then immediately got into the Gulf of Mexico. Katrina became a category five in twenty-four hours and quadrupled in size and in strength. It looked initially like it was going to come this way, then it turned back toward Mississippi.

JOE: I'm sorry for Mississippi, but . . . I hate to say it, but when you are in a hurricane zone, and you see a hurricane, you pray it goes anywhere but where you are. You know, it's not very nice. It's very selfish. But that's a fact. Because the people in Florida, the people in Mississippi, they're all doing the same thing. "Don't let it hit us!"

FAITH: Friday night when we went to bed, the storm had turned and was going back towards the east, and when we woke up Sunday morning, all of a sudden it turned again and began to come towards New Orleans.

JOE: Well, it was clear we were going to get clipped. So I got into my car. I checked my watch. Six A.M., and I'm sitting there and it was bumper to bumper.

DESIREE: So basically here we are, Sunday before the storm, the news media is predicting the very worst, you've got a mandatory evacuation of the city, everybody's got to go.

[*Sound transition.* CORY *and* DARRYL *into the light.*]

CORY: Sunday morning I walked outside. I had to go across the street to the store. Everybody's crazy, man. So I went and called Darryl. [*On the phone*] What's going on? We're supposed to record today . . . Everybody's running around . . .

DARRYL: Shit, man, it's coming.

CORY: I'm guessing we're not recording today? We're not mixing today?

DARRYL: Where you been, man?

CORY: I shut everything down all weekend.

DARRYL: I am going to be at your house in five minutes. Have your passport, your license, anything important that you can put in a bag in five minutes.

CORY [*to audience*]: I had an extra pair of boxers, these shorts right here, one pair of tennis shoes that have eaten it since, and two T-shirts. One button-down shirt . . . I didn't have time . . . I was like, do I need a suit?

[CORY *and* DARRYL *off.* DESIREE, GRANDMOTHER, BRIANNA, VIVIE *on.*]

DESIREE: I called my grandmother. She had already evacuated, and she wanted me to get out of town too. But first . . .

GRANDMOTHER: See if you can get your grandfather to leave with you.

DESIREE: Like that's going to happen. But I went over to see him after I packed up my car and made sure the house was secure. I hung out, talked, and drank a lot of coffee. He was a World War II POW. He was in a camp for about seven months, and the Germans would make him sing. He had a great singing voice. He confided in me that he wasn't feeling well and didn't want to leave because of that. He was hiding this from my grandmother. And he was also like, I don't care what happens. I've lived a life. Whatever comes, comes. Well, I said jokingly, the neighbors have a boat. If it gets really bad, jump in.

[DESIREE *moves off, watches* VIVIE *and* BRIANNA.]

BRIANNA: We didn't get to Memphis until 2:00 A.M. Traffic basically. We had a dog and a cat, so we had to find a hotel that was pet friendly.

VIVIE: We left our cat. 'Cause we were coming home in three days. So we put food and water out.

DESIREE: He wouldn't leave with me, even though I asked him a few times. So I left, and before I did, I went across the street, and our neighbor's cat Taffy was outside. And I saw the Dumonts, and we all stood on the street. It was the most beautiful sun. Then I left, and I cried all the way driving across the bridge.

[HUSBAND *takes* FAITH's *hand, pulls her center stage.*]

FAITH: Charity Hospital went on their emergency plan as of seven o'clock Saturday night, so I was able to leave and come home at seven. So I left the next morning, that Sunday morning at five.

HUSBAND: I'm reporting to work. I'm a paramedic, I have to stay. You know, I've done this several times before.

FAITH: I know. I was on the initial disaster plan at Charity too, remember? I stayed there for almost two weeks straight. But we didn't have children at the time.

HUSBAND: We've been down this road before.

FAITH: OK.

[HUSBAND *grabs* FAITH, *holds her fiercely. She resists then gives in. They move off, replaced by* SHAKIRA *and* FATHER *on one side,* TED, DARRYL, *and* CORY *on the other.*]

SHAKIRA: I was in Hammond, and my father came and got me and brought me to New Orleans. My younger brother was in a juvenile home, and so my dad went and got him.

FATHER: I'm just trying to keep everybody together . . .

[GRANDMOTHER *and* BROTHER *join them.*]

SHAKIRA: It was my grandmother, my brother, myself, and my father. We tried to leave, but traffic was too bad.

FATHER: It's taking us about an hour and a half to get to a place that usually takes us fifteen minutes. This car is a gas guzzler, and we don't have a lot of gas.

SHAKIRA: So my dad . . . we just turned back around and went home.

TED: Basically what happened . . . I went to get gas, and there wasn't any left . . . and I didn't know how I was going to be able to leave. So I went back to the restaurant and took all the ice out of the machines and took as much food as I could out of the walk-in because . . . I mean . . . it was all going to go bad. And I went back to my house in Mid-City and just rode it out with my friends.

[DARRYL *and* CORY *at center.*]

DARRYL: I was on my last gram of gas . . .

CORY: . . . That his car would ever see. It was the first time I'd ever seen anarchy.

DARRYL: Yeah, man, I was driving by the lakefront.

CORY: What you think might happen if you were told nuclear war was going to break out was what was going on in the street that day.

DARRYL: There's no gas, and the stations that did have it . . . it was like there's no way you're getting in . . .

CORY: Some people were being extra really nice and charitable. And some . . . most people are just out for themselves.

DARRYL: You saw it, man.

CORY: It came out. It came all the way out.

[*Sound transition.* DESIREE *and the* ENSEMBLE *move into light.* ACTORS *form a line of waiting drivers.*]

DESIREE: I was almost out of gas, and there were huge lines, and then the EMPTY sign comes up right in front of me, and you feel kind of desperate. So I get back on I-10 and get to the next exit, and there's a gas station and there's a line. And I'm waiting.

DRIVER: What is that guy doing?

DESIREE: He's cutting in line!

ENSEMBLE: What the fuck are you doing? Who does that guy think he is skipping ahead? Get the hell out of here!

DESIREE: I was dirty, my hair was sticking out, I felt crazy. [*To the driver*] You are NOT going to pass, you are NOT going to cut. Get back in line. [*To audience*] And I just stood on the road and refused to move until everyone got back in line. [*To the drivers*] This is a disaster, we have to work together!

GAS STATION ATTENDANT: Folks, you need to make two orderly lines. Cash only, fifty-dollar maximum.

DESIREE: There were no ATMs. If you didn't have cash, you were pretty fucked. And I got my gas, and I just decided to drive Vicky, my crown Victoria, until I dropped.

JOE: Now I knew it was not going to hit until Monday. I could see the tracking. I know distance is equal to speed times time . . . [*Laughs*] Little formulas like that pay off pretty good. It'll hit Monday early in the morning.

So even if it took me twelve to fifteen hours—you know, I'm still going to get to Dallas.

BRIANNA AND FAITH: Memphis.

DESIREE: Hattiesburg.

DARRYL AND RACHEL: Jackson.

VIVIE AND CORY: Baton Rouge.

SHAKIRA: Part 2. The Storm.

[*Period music in.* ACTORS *move downstage for the "history lesson."*]

GABE: The French Quarter was the original city. It's on high land. In 1718, when New Orleans was founded, both England and France were trying to establish settlements on the Mississippi River in order to control the middle of the country.

DARRYL [*impatiently*]: Whoever controls that river controls who and what goes in it and what comes out.

RACHEL: About 1905, the city expanded to low areas once pumps were put in place. It was a time of technology, and people were now able to do things they never did before.

[VIVIE *shakes her head, interrupts.*]

VIVIE: You had greed, you had crooked politicians that said, "Oh, yeah, come on, come on, come to our city." And they got paid off underneath the table. So what they did is they bought these huge chunks of swampland. And they said, "Oh, we're going to call this a subdivision and build houses ..."

FAITH: But it wasn't until the late twentieth century that the city became unsafe.

JOE: What has changed is the coastline. We have a lot of coastal erosion going on. The wetlands, marshes, and swamps have disappeared.

TED: And the big problem is this: without wetlands there is nothing to absorb the storm surge, that wall of water, twelve to fifteen feet high that was pushed into the city by Katrina.

[TED *points to the wall, and* ACTORS *turn upstage to watch him.*]

VOICEOVER: "Monday, August 30, 2005. Hurricane Katrina hit Louisiana's shores this morning at 6:10 A.M., crossing Plaquemines Parish. Becoming a category three storm, it proceeded on almost a northern path, across St. Bernard Parish, and made final landfall between Louisiana and Mississippi, this morning at roughly 10:00 A.M."

[ACTORS *off.* VIVIE *and* JAMES *stay.*]

VIVIE: You know, I think Mother Earth came back to claim some of her land. That's what my gut tells me. And you know this place was so broken. The schools were broken, the political system was broken. It was so broke it's like a fine piece of china that's just shattered in a million pieces . . . Katrina really just said, "You know what, you all are trying to put this fine china cup together. You know, you need to really start over. You'll never drink out of it again."

JAMES: It had gotten to the point when all this stuff was out of control. Crime and everything. God came in and just cleared the whole space.

[*Storm transition.* GABE *and* JAMES, *downstage, gradually move together.* TED *and* SHAKIRA *move upstage by the wall.*]

GABE: When we get word of a storm out in the Gulf, we go on alert. I put all my plans in place at an executive command center that was located at the Hyatt Hotel.

JAMES: The storm came . . . and it was atrocious. Hundred-plus mile-an-hour winds shook the house. Everything was destroyed after the roof came off and water came in.

GABE: The Hyatt had a lot of exterior window damage. The building rocked, and glass shattered all around. Everybody in the hotel was hunkered down in the ballroom.

JAMES: The storm lasted a good nine hours, about six o'clock Monday morning to about two, two thirty. Then the sun came out.

TED AND SHAKIRA:

It was a beautiful,	It was beautiful out . . .
clear blue sky;	we had a balcony, and I sat out there.
I mean, there wasn't a cloud	A sunny day.
anywhere.	

[ACTORS *move on.*]

FAITH: The hurricane passed . . .

BRIANNA: I remember hearing that the hurricane had gone through and that the city was fine.

FAITH: . . . and it seemed like everyone was fine.

SISTER: Let's go, let's go. Let's go. I don't know why we're hanging out here anymore.

VIVIE: So people were getting ready to return home.

JAMES: Everything was over, we took a deep breath.

[DESIREE *and* OFFICER *are downstage.*]

DESIREE: I wanted to get back to my house. And so I drove back, and the highway was just full of branches and debris, and my exit was blocked by the police. [*To* OFFICER] Is there a problem, officer?

OFFICER: We just had a storm. We've got power lines down everywhere. Where do you think you're going?

DESIREE: I'm going back home.

OFFICER: Not today, you're not. Unless you are essential personnel, you are not allowed in until further notice. Clear off like this . . . turn around and go back where you came from.

DESIREE: OK, thank you, officer.

[*Sound effect. She floors the gas pedal.*]

Good Ol' Vicky. I came home and nobody chased me. He could have got on the radio and said, "Look out for a Crown Victoria coming that way . . ." but he didn't. And I got home. Our fence was down, and my neighbor's trampoline was completely folded in half like a taco. But my home was OK.

[GABE, FACILITIES MANAGER, *and* OPERATIONS MANAGER *tentatively step forward.*]

GABE: I went outside to assess the damage with my facilities and operations managers. [*To* COLLEAGUES] OK, well, this isn't that bad. I mean, it's not a whole bunch of structural damage.

FACILITIES MANAGER: Uh . . . look at the Hyatt, I mean, windows knocked out on the north side of the building. It looks terrible with the curtains hanging out. Actually, it looks like maybe a bomb or something like that happened.

GABE: That's just windows blown out. No real structural damage.

OPERATIONS MANAGER: This is not that bad.

FACILITIES MANAGER: We'll have the city back in a week or two. As far as power to the city.

[*They look around. Staring down,* GABE *crosses the stage.*]

GABE: Man, the storm is gone, and looks like everything is OK.

[*Beat.*]

So where's all this damn water coming from?

BRIANNA: Part 3: The Levees.

[*Sound transition as the wall slowly tips forward, the props falling to the floor with a deafening crash. After a beat,* VIVIE *steps forward, picking her way through the debris. Other* ACTORS *follow.*]

VIVIE: And then all of a sudden the levees broke, and it's like holy moly. The levees broke. Now everybody told us if this happens and this happens, the city's going to fill up with water because you're thirteen feet below sea level. But we didn't take the direct hit. The scenario wasn't what they said it was supposed to be in order for us to have this disaster happen.

JAMES: I walked to the back of my house, and I saw that the water was at least a foot deep, and I came back to the front of the house, and the water was up around my waist, and before I realized what was going on, water had almost gotten to my chest.

BRIANNA: And then stories started to take a turn for the worst.

GABE: We had lost communications . . . the mayor had problems in communicating with the police and the fire folks. So basically we didn't know that the levee had broken.

DESIREE [*angrily*]: All that fucking money that the Homeland Security allotted to states like Wyoming and Louisiana, and these motherfuckers can't communicate with each other. Because that was the main thing New York wanted, because that's what happened in 9/11: they couldn't communicate with each other, and that's why so many people died. And they're talking about not having batteries and cell phones not working, and I'm thinking, what about satellite phones? Weren't they all supposed to buy these? And I thought, well, it's Louisiana, so somebody's probably got a goddamn swimming pool in their backyard instead of having satellite phones so people know what in the hell is going on.

VIVIE: The water comes in, overtops levees, breaks floodwalls. It was late August, in South Louisiana. Ninety-eight degrees, with a heat index of 105, 106. Mercy!

[GABE *and* FACILITIES MANAGER *cross to center.*]

GABE: That night . . . I remember we went to bed . . . and, uh, of course we didn't have any air conditioning or anything like that . . . so it's hot in the hotel.

FACILITIES MANAGER: You know, the windows were blown out on the north side of the building . . . so maybe we should go up there to sleep and get a good breeze or something.

GABE: Just . . .

FACILITIES MANAGER: What?

GABE: Nobody should sleepwalk, you know . . . 'cause you'll walk straight out the window.

[OPERATIONS MANAGER *comes in and wakes up* GABE.]

OPERATIONS MANAGER: Can I get on your computer?

GABE: Hmmm, what's wrong?

OPERATIONS MANAGER: Man, I heard . . . somebody said that one of the levees had broken and water's coming into the city.

[*They get the computer and log on.*]

GABE: The levee's broken.

OPERATIONS MANAGER: Oh my God!

GABE: The 17th Street Canal. The levee's broken.

OPERATIONS MANAGER [*pointing*]: And how many others?

[JOE *enters and grabs two chairs, using them to illustrate the floodwalls and levees.*]

JOE: Water comes into Lake Pontchartrain, and it begins to rise. That water comes down the canals. Now we have floodwalls along the canals. Floodwalls are sheet pilings that the Army Corps of Engineers has put in earthen levees in order to make them higher.

VIVIE: The floodwalls were supposed to be sunk twenty feet into the ground. They were sunk ten.

JOE: The canals are here. These are the walls on the canal. And the levee's down here. So water comes into the canal and rises above the levee, eventually puts pressure on the floodwalls, and the floodwalls cannot contain the water because the pressure is too great. The moving water overcomes the strength of the weak soil at the bottom of the levees. So what happens? The floodwalls collapse.

VIVIE: This was a man-made disaster. These levees broke because the Army Corps of Engineers did not do their job. Not because God said, "Oh, let there be a flood," and the land was covered with water. That people could have handled. But no. These people made a conscious effort that instead of inspecting the levees, they were out having lunch and laughing, "Oh, we don't need to fool with that." You'll see the signs HOLD THE CORPS ACCOUNTABLE. Oh, yeah. You'll see 'em.

JAMES: These people probably couldn't engineer themselves out of a paper bag.

CORY: The Army Corps of Engineers testified before Congress last year that the reason the city of New Orleans flooded is that the floodwalls . . .

ENSEMBLE: That they designed failed.

BRIANNA: We were hearing all these awful horror stories and news reporters talking about hearing screams in the night and all these dogs barking.

[GABE, FACILITIES MANAGER, *and* OPERATIONS MANAGER *climb the wall with flashlights, the only light on stage.*]

GABE: I looked out over the city of New Orleans.

FACILITIES MANAGER: It's eerie. Very, very eerie.

OPERATIONS MANAGER: No lights anywhere.

FACILITIES MANAGER: We're the power company!

OPERATIONS MANAGER: Man, I have seen outages before, but normally you see somewhere on the grid, you know . . . energized. But this is nothing, anywhere . . .

GABE [*to audience*]: The only mode of communication that we had was the Internet. We could e-mail back and forth sometimes . . . not all the time. We were trying to restore the city without communications.

[*CNN sound bite reporting on the Lower Ninth Ward.*]

BRIANNA: Mama, can you believe this? All they keep showing is the Lower Ninth Ward. You know that can't be the only area that's affected.

MOM: No news about Gentilly?

BRIANNA [*shaking her head*]: I'm not sure if we can go home.

MOM: We need to do something.

BRIANNA: Let's go to Grandma's. We need to be with people who care about us.

MOM: OK, but from Memphis to Kansas is another six-hour drive.

[DESIREE *grabs a chair and sits facing the audience.*]

DESIREE: All I could think was, "Jesus Christ, this isn't just two buildings, this is a whole city." And then when you start hearing about guns, cries for help, and water up to people's necks. It's just like, Oh fuck, nobody's in charge. And that's when I totally kicked into survival mode. Whatever's gonna happen here is not going to happen to me. I'm going to be as methodical as I need to be and get out of here.

BRIANNA: It hadn't hit me that that was my city. I think I was mostly confused and then sort of outraged. Why would you do this to me?

DESIREE: I didn't have enough gas, so our neighbor, Anthony, siphoned as much gas as he could from lawn mowers.

BRIANNA: I was finally able to check e-mail, and my friends were looking for me, "Does anybody know where she is?" like I was missing.

DESIREE: I must have just driven about ninety miles-per-hour. This time, I drove all the way to DC, where my friend was. When I got there, Good Ol' Vicky died. It was just like smoke, just, poof! And then I kind of collapsed.

RACHEL: The hurricane came to Jackson, where I was, but it came with much less force. Still, it was enough to turn the Hilton into kind of a Hotel Rwanda with water coming in, no electricity and no plumbing. And we were the lucky ones because . . . it just had to be hell on earth for all those people trapped in New Orleans literally dying in the heat.

JAMES: Part 4: Those Who Stayed.

[SHAKIRA and FAMILY gather downstage. Other ACTORS begin to wade through the water.]

SHAKIRA: We had water . . . I'm about five feet five, and the water got about to my chest area. One of our neighbors came to the house.

NEIGHBOR: You all need to leave this house, because they are going to blow the canal up to relieve some of the pressure. Just like they did with Betsy.

SHAKIRA: We walked from our house, which is right by the canal bridge to the Superdome. It took us about two and a half hours to get there. Couldn't use our cars because they were all flooded out, and there was no other way to go . . .

TED: I was at my house in Mid-City. As soon as I finished eating all the stuff that I got from the restaurant, I started eating canned food. My boat floated up to my house . . . the water was higher than all the fences . . . so anything in people's backyards was floating down the road. I just got lucky . . . the canoe floated by my house, and I grabbed it . . . I have a thirty-foot house, and the whole bottom floor was flooded . . . about thirteen feet of water . . . you could canoe right in the house through the windows and then, like, tie it up to the steps and just walk upstairs. It was pretty crazy . . . a canoe floating through your house is pretty interesting.

[JAMES shuffles through the debris, picks up a backpack.]

JAMES: I had to make some quick decisions . . . the water rose right over—you didn't know where it was going to stop. Of course, the front door was sealed from the water pressure, so I had to find a crowbar or something to open the doorway. I was feeling around with my feet to see what was there. So I finally got that front door open. We have a small dog that's a shih tzu. I put him in a backpack and put it on my back and started walking to some high ground.

[ACTORS *slowly move around the stage creating a physical sculpture of bodies in the water.*]

FAITH: My husband was initially stationed with the New Orleans Fire Department. Methodist Hospital was just a few blocks away, and they were bringing 'em there in boats. But Methodist was turning 'em away, because all of the hospital generators had flooded, and they had to evacuate their patients. So he was sent to the Superdome.

SHAKIRA: We put our belongings in trash bags and carried them ... We found a trash can on the way there, and so we just kind of stuck our stuff in there so it would float. We took turns pulling it or floating it through the water depending on water level. The closer we got to the Superdome, the water got very high ... Some areas were higher than others. One guy we passed on the way ... he had his girlfriend floating on a mattress, and he told us ...

GUY: Hey—don't go in that direction. The water's too high.

SHAKIRA: He was soaked from head to toe. He was trying to swim while pushing her.

JAMES: It took nine hours to walk about a mile. And, um, during that walk ... words really can't describe how horrible that was. Bodies everywhere, there were people drowning and dying, crying for help. Children, everything you can imagine that was so horrible that words can't describe it. People getting murdered. People getting killed right in front of me. People so desperate, they didn't know what to do.

SHAKIRA: My father's a dialysis patient. We passed the hospital, and we wanted to get him in there. They said only he could be admitted. And he didn't want to be put in the hospital without us ... He wanted to keep us together, so he wouldn't stay there. We went on ... [*To* GRANDMOTHER] Grandma, Daddy's walking in water ... He has a catheter in his chest.

GRANDMOTHER: Shh, child.

SHAKIRA: But he's really afraid of water.

GRANDMOTHER: Just keep walking, don't say nothing to him.

SHAKIRA: But the water ... it's freezing. It's like walking to your grave.

GRANDMOTHER: Try to think of good things.

SHAKIRA: Try to look like I don't know what's going on . . . I freak out if I'm out of control of things . . . I guess I can try to keep my mind off all the bad stuff . . .

GRANDMOTHER: You're the oldest. You're the pillar of this family.

SHAKIRA: The water was cold, and we walked through it. Once we got out of it . . . it was hot . . . it was a super hot day. We got to the Superdome. [*To* FATHER] Daddy, you know you walked in water?

FATHER: Yeah, I know, but I couldn't think about it. I didn't want to be fearful in front of you guys.

[ACTORS *transition from the water to the Superdome, finding places in the debris to settle in, sleep, occupy themselves.*]

TED: The Superdome is the shelter of last resort. If you have no way out of the city, go there.

SHAKIRA: We were in the Superdome from Tuesday to Friday. When we first got there . . . they kind of frisked everybody . . . make sure nobody had weapons, alcohol, drugs . . . anything like that. We stood in line for a while. I think it took about an hour and a half to get in there.

BROTHER: What do we do now?

SHAKIRA: We find somewhere to sit.

BROTHER: The twenty-yard line? Word!

[*They create a space to stay.*]

SHAKIRA: When we got there, the water and everything was running, but somewhere between that Tuesday night and that Wednesday morning, the water was cut off completely . . . so the bathrooms began to overflow.

MILITARY POLICE [*a voice out of the dark*]: You can no longer use the facilities. If you have to use the bathroom, go find a corner.

SHAKIRA: So after a while the Superdome started smelling like a big cesspool . . . um . . . we had to try to find different places to stay 'cause it started getting trashed, and more and more and more people started coming in.

TED: About 25,000 were at the Superdome. Another 20,000 at the Convention Center.

SHAKIRA: So wherever you found a spot, you got there and kept it until it was time to move.

MILITARY POLICE: You need to line up if you want an MRE meal.

SHAKIRA: Lines for the Meals-Ready-to-Eat wrapped around the Dome. If you wanted to get a meal, you had to get up fairly early, and you stood in line for a long time.

BROTHER: I see some kids from school. Can I go?

GRANDMOTHER: Let's stay together.

BROTHER: But . . .

FATHER: Don't go too far. Make sure you know exactly where we are before you leave, and check back in thirty minutes so we know you are OK.

SHAKIRA: We went to go see people we knew, and they came by us. We took turns sleeping, like taking catnaps . . . but other than that, we tried to find ways to pass the time when you have nothing to do.

[BROTHER *and another* ACTOR *play cards.*]

BROTHER: UNO!

[GRANDMOTHER *reads the Book of Jonah from the Bible. Across the stage,* JAMES *still wades through water.* SHAKIRA *sings softly, "This Little Light of Mine."*** *See note on copyright page at the beginning of the play.*]

GRANDMOTHER: "But the Lord hurled a great wind upon the sea, and there was a mighty tempest so that the ship seemed likely to be wrecked. Then the sailors were afraid and cried . . ."

JAMES: Lord, I know you don't want me to die like this. In this water. Lord, help me find a way out, guide me to safety.

GRANDMOTHER: "But Jonah had gone down into the recesses of the ship, and he lay down, and was fast asleep."

JAMES: I got to a point where I got so tired. By that time I was about a mile from my house, and I didn't know which way to go, it was so desolate . . . it was getting dark. Water was up to my neck.

FAITH: His supervisors decided that my husband and his colleagues needed to leave the Superdome. Because at times they were getting calls for help . . .

VOICE IN THE BACKGROUND: Somebody over here needs medical assistance!

FAITH: . . . and when they would go to see that person, their lives were being verbally threatened by somebody else.

ANOTHER VOICE: Help me or I'll kill you.

OTHER VOICES: Help me first! My mother is elderly, and she can't stay here. She needs to get out. Help me first or else . . .

FAITH: The situation had turned violent. So all the medical people ended up leaving the Superdome and walking to the Convention Center. The conditions weren't any better there.

[GABE *wanders through the people in the Superdome, stopping to absorb the conditions around him.*]

GABE: We had guards with us, and we walked past the Superdome . . . the sights and the stench and everything there was just like something in a third world country. You had people that were sick, you know . . . this elderly lady . . . she had to use the bathroom, and the only thing that she could do was have a few of her family members stand around her while she squatted to use the bathroom . . . in the middle of everything . . . I'm saying, whoa . . . this is for real.

VIVIE: There was a police officer I know who was in the Superdome. She said a mother came up to her with a baby in her arms and said . . .

[MOTHER *and* COP *move upstage.*]

MOTHER: Can you help me?

VIVIE: The baby was dead. She was walking around with a dead baby in her arms. I said, "What did you do, Roberta?"

COP: All I could do was tell her to follow me. Let's just lay the baby down right now.

[SHAKIRA *huddles on a bench.*]

SHAKIRA: I didn't really eat or sleep for five days. We saw a couple of guys get beat up . . . um . . . They were taking kids or like young girls like thirteen, fourteen, and taking them into the bathroom, because we didn't have any lights in there, and raping them. It was like . . . Nobody was going in there 'cause it was funky. So it was like . . . open area . . . just go ahead and do whatever. Nobody was going to catch you. But I guess some guys actually caught one of the guys trying to do it, and they beat him up like right in front of us.

[VIVIE *strides down center and confronts the audience.*]

VIVIE: *Time* magazine took a picture of an old lady outside the Superdome covered up, still sitting in her wheelchair. I can tell you that was absolutely the truth. One of my employees says she saw people being raped in there. And when she brought it to the people's attention . . . they did nothing. The police were overwhelmed. Absolutely. You got six bullets in your gun. Whatcha gonna shoot one of 'em? And you got thousands of people on top of you? Thousands of hungry, scared, poor, hot, sick, dying people. Nothing. For days.

GABE: By the time the National Guard came in, the police were so tired. Most of those policemen had to deal with their families as well as the flooding in their own homes. I would let them come into our center and just get a cold bottle of water . . . and that was like giving them . . . five hundred dollars. You could see the look on their faces and what they had to deal with. One of the policemen who killed himself was sitting right in our center the night before.

[FAITH *and* HUSBAND *appear in light, opposite sides of the stage, and speak on cell phones.*]

FAITH: I had lost communication with my husband for roughly a week. I had no idea what was going on. And then he called.

HUSBAND: Sweetheart . . .

FAITH: Oh my God. Are you all right?

HUSBAND: We've all been moved to a safe location . . .

FAITH: I heard that paramedics were in danger. Is it true?

HUSBAND: Yeah . . . But we've left the Convention Center . . . all the paramedics are in a hotel with some police. Well, we were. Did you hear the story about the police confiscating vehicles from a Cadillac dealership? Well, it's true, because I was with those guys.

[POLICEMAN *approaches* HUSBAND.]

POLICEMAN: We're going out to get vehicles.

HUSBAND: You're going to just leave us here?

POLICEMAN: What can we do? All our cars are flooded.

[HUSBAND *grabs* POLICEMAN *roughly.*]

HUSBAND: We need your protection.

[POLICEMAN *pushes* HUSBAND *away.*]

POLICEMAN: Sorry. You'll have to fend for yourselves.

HUSBAND [*to* FAITH]: Good thing I brought my own gun. So every night we have to assign people to sit and watch, because we're still having people who drive by and just randomly shoot.

FAITH: For what reason?

HUSBAND: Nobody really knows.

FAITH: I saw on the news that the jails flooded, and there's no place to put people that are breaking in and robbing stores. So the police are just telling them, "Drop what you have, and get out of here." So they're going to places where there's no police.

HUSBAND: Most of the stores in the city have had everything taken out. Not a shoe left in a shoe store. Not a ring left in a jewelry store. Not a camera left in an electronics store.

FAITH: The city's gone crazy . . .

GABE: One night there at the hotel . . . We're asleep and the police barged in . . .

[*The* POLICEMAN *rushes in and shakes* GABE.]

POLICEMAN: Get up, get up. I need every available man . . . I need every available man. They're not going to take our food, they're not going to take our food. I need everybody up. They're not going to take our food.

GABE: Now wait a minute . . . we're not policemen. You lock that door right there.

[GABE *grabs a baseball bat and is in* POLICEMAN's *face.*]

If anybody comes here, we'll take care of that. But I'm not going looking for them. That's not my job.

POLICEMAN: Well, we got some looters trying to take our food from the delivery truck outside. I'm just trying to protect that.

[DESIREE *and* FRIEND *move into light near* DARRYL, *who watches them.*]

DESIREE: We were watching CNN, and it was showing the black people in New Orleans, and my friend said some just shitty racist things, and I just wanted to wring her fuckin' neck, and I just hate that stuff.

FRIEND: The black people are going crazy, and they're taking over the city.

DESIREE: Yeah, of course they're looting. Probably everybody's starving and it's like 112 degrees there.

[DARRYL *crosses downstage.*]

DARRYL: I went to Jackson, Mississippi. I had to go there and watch the damn TV portraying people of this city as animals. And it's like, OK, when people . . . if you think that your life is in jeopardy, you're going to become something else. You're going to click into survival mode.

JOE: Part 5: Getting Out.

[ACTORS *drag themselves up, negotiate the debris, and begin to form lines to exit the Superdome.*]

TED: We got with the fire department in Mid-City and helped people get out. We had small boats, and we'd go down the side streets and . . . we'd find people and bring them to the big boats on the big streets, and they'd take 'em out of the city. It was hard because there's only so much you can do in a day. We would go out at sunup, and we would come in at sundown, because you can't be out in the streets after dark. They're arresting because of looting. No matter what you're doing. Even if you're helping. So . . . you just canoe around . . . you just keep moving people . . . and bringing people food and water.

JAMES: I got out of the water . . . Onto a parking garage. It was just the dog and me. Some Tulane medical people found me. They helped me. They gave me shots and everything. Eighty percent of the city was inundated with water, so the Guard had to evacuate us by helicopter.

SHAKIRA: So Thursday everybody was trying to get out of the Superdome. There was supposed to be buses. We stood in line.

[BROTHER *stands in line with* SHAKIRA *and* GRANDMOTHER.]

BROTHER: But Dad's not here.

GRANDMOTHER: He left with the medical staff to get dialysis. He hasn't had it since last Friday—that's almost a week.

MILITARY POLICE: Men over here and women and children on the other side. [*To* BROTHER] Men over here.

[BROTHER *looks to the* MILITARY POLICE *then his* GRANDMOTHER.]

GRANDMOTHER: He's seventeen so he's not an adult. [*To* BROTHER] Where we go you'll go . . . we're not separating from you. [*To* MILITARY POLICE] We're already separated enough.

MILITARY POLICE: OK, keep them together.

SHAKIRA: The buses weren't coming. So Thursday night we slept right on the outskirts of the Superdome . . . I finally got a little bit of sleep. And I dreamed that water was coming in . . .

FAITH: The National Guard were finding people that were dead on the street. And those people were left there because the morgue had flooded, so there was nowhere to bring them.

TED: A lot of people were calling for help. Some of them were on their roofs or on their balconies in the front. They had been waiting four or five days with no food or water. They'd try and drop you water . . . the helicopters . . . they threw some stuff out and they'd mark your house, but, I mean, there were so many people stuck there . . . So they would come and look at you and be like, "We'll take your grandmother, but we'll come back for you." They were taking them down to Interstate-10 where the ramps were . . .

VIVIE: Some waited there for days. And what did they sleep on? The concrete. How much shade do you have up there—not a whole heck of a lot.

[ACTORS *listen to* RACHEL *and begin to step out of the story, moving into the argument. Some sit down wearily. All ad-lib responses to the argument.*]

RACHEL: People died on that overpass. It wasn't even like they had food and water . . . Where was the Army? How could you not have a helicopter dropping food and water down for them . . . someone actually would have to explain to me how you could airlift to Iraq and you can't airlift to an overpass in New Orleans?

JOE [*angrily*]: This blows my mind. A couple of Black Hawks, one loaded with food and one loaded with water, dump it! I'm a retired military officer, colonel in the United States Army reserve. I'm a logistics officer, OK, I've done this stuff in faraway lands, you know, where you stockpile this stuff for emergencies, and you have it pre-positioned for both civilians and military. The National Guard should've been kicking butt.

DARRYL: I've been in the military, too. I was in a unit that could be dropped off anywhere in the world, twenty-four hours later we would supply them with running water, housing, latrines, runways for aircraft to land and take off. Not long before Katrina the tsunami happened. Twenty-four hours later everybody was rescued. Why the hell did it take *three weeks* to come here and rescue people who were on their fucking roofs with water beneath their feet and a hundred something degrees? All of this aid—housing, food, water—just sat there for weeks and weeks while people were *dying*. They were *dying*! I don't understand this shit!

RACHEL: It was a lack of leadership on every level. Mayor Nagin and the governor were so completely overwhelmed that they just became frozen. And my God, look at FEMA.

DARRYL: I know one thing, the mayor, he did something that I didn't do. He stayed here—the whole time. He never left. Do you know of any mayor who would have put his life in jeopardy and stayed in a city that was under water?

[DESIREE *jumps up and confronts* DARRYL, *other* ACTORS *either agree or disagree with her.*]

DESIREE: Nagin was in a hotel room doing coke in the bathroom!

GABE: He had a command center right next to ours. We were locked at the hip. We ate together, we slept together, we did everything together.

RACHEL: School buses that were sitting in the Lower Ninth Ward could have been a way for people to get out. If they had had a real evacuation plan. They didn't have the keys. Can you imagine? That nobody had the keys to the school buses.

[*The* ENSEMBLE *voices opinions and feelings, chaos erupts.*]

GABE: Let me tell you about this . . . It happened right there in front of me. You had people on those buses without a policeman or anybody assigned to them. So the people that were driving the buses came back and told the city . . . I can't do this because you have people there smoking pot on the bus, having sex on the bus . . . cursing us out . . . and the National Guard hadn't gotten here yet. So that whole bussing people out of the city sounds good, but you didn't have the protection for the bus drivers.

JOE: Let me just interject here. One of my major critiques in this entire operation is failure of leadership. The governor, the mayor, Brownie, all deer in the headlights. When the federal force came in, Lieutenant General Honoré, 82nd Airborne, told the governor, just sit down, you know, just sit down.

DARRYL: The "Ragin Cajun."

[JOE *and* GABE *face off.*]

JOE: But it was weeks before the federal force actually got here. Politicians and leaders are just not the same thing.

[VIVIE *steps forward, reminds them of the audience, and guides them back to the "Disaster Tour," urging them to continue with the story.*]

VIVIE: Now, c'mon. C'mon.

SHAKIRA: We got up at like two o'clock in the morning, and we went and stood outside. We didn't get on a bus until three in the afternoon.

[HUSBAND *and* MOTHER *climb the wall. The sound of a helicopter is heard.*]

FAITH: I saw my husband on the news. There was this family and this mother . . . and she had like six kids.

MOTHER [*to* HUSBAND]: I'm not leaving. I'm too scared.

HUSBAND: It's OK.

MOTHER: I'm not getting in that little basket.

HUSBAND: Take my hand.

MOTHER: I'm too scared.

HUSBAND: Look, it's a one-stop shop. You get one chance. I'm sorry, but you're going to be better off with me than you're going to be sitting in this house with no food or water.

[*The* MOTHER *takes his hand.*]

FAITH: They finally got her into that thing. Then the roof caved in, and he had to be rescued by helicopter.

JAMES: I was put on a bus to Lafayette. They had a medical camp when we got there. I stayed in shelters and everything for about two and a half months while we were waiting to come back home.

TED: A lot of older folks who didn't have husbands or wives anymore weren't leaving without their pets. So we loaded all the boats with the old people and their animals, and we just pulled the boats out till we got to higher ground. They had like seventeen Black Hawk helicopters lined up, and they just started taking everybody out. That was nine days after the storm.

SHAKIRA: We ended up in Dallas, where we stayed with my sorority sister for a week and a half. We didn't have anything to do there, so we volunteered at the Dallas Convention Center, where evacuees were staying.

[TED *crosses downstage, pours a little water over his face to cool off.*]

TED: We got dropped at the airport. It was hot . . . there were people hanging around everywhere . . . They had minimum power . . . not enough for air conditioning. There were . . . dead people everywhere. There were people on stretchers. There were old people that were dying, you know . . . you couldn't do anything. There was nobody . . . there was this huge line that like zig-zagged on the tarmac . . . it had water and like some little snack fruits, and that was it. They just put you on planes and . . . didn't tell you where you were going . . . People brought their animals on the plane. There were dogs running up and down the aisle . . . it was just a . . . it was a madhouse. [*Beat.*] I got off the plane in Little Rock, Arkansas, and I was still soaking wet . . . They gave us Red Cross cards. And then I just . . . I went traveling. I went and met my friends in DC and started working.

[ACTORS *cross to the walls of the theater and draw large X's. They fill in information, date house searched, by whom, what was found. They write "2 dead bodies."*]

DESIREE: I thought my grandfather was fine. I thought he went into the attic and he was fine. That's what you do. You axe out a hole in your roof, and somebody comes and rescues you.

BRIANNA: I have a friend who lost two cousins . . . They were up in the roof, in their attic, and they couldn't hack their way out and they drowned.

[JAMES *points to the drawings on the theater wall.*]

JAMES: They are finding people every day. People come back and find their relatives in their homes. My next-door neighbor was supposed to have gotten out with his wife. They were both dead in the house when we got back.

GABE: The last count that I remember was something around eleven hundred . . . officially. But I don't remember the death toll.

FAITH: The last I was told, there were more than sixteen hundred, but I'm pretty sure that there's more unofficial deaths.

JAMES: Eight to ten thousand. It's been a big hidden thing. It was an election year, and they didn't want that to come out. If they found a body that they could identify, then that went into the official count. Problem is, once a body is in the water for three days, it's almost impossible to identify, and so many people, thousands of people, were in the water for weeks. They had a vast morgue in Gonzales, and they buried probably about four thousand people in a mass grave.

DESIREE: Then my grandmother called to tell me that they found my grandfather. The 82nd Airborne got to the house, which was under water up to the roof, so that's about twelve feet. They put a hole in the roof and put a flashlight in, but they didn't see anything. Then when the water had gone down, a friend of the family, Tommy, posed as my grandfather's nephew and got a group of National Guardsmen to take him to the house in a boat.

[TOMMY *crosses down and faces* DESIREE.]

TOMMY: I came in, and there was stuff everywhere. I tried to find your grandfather. Then I saw him underneath a pile of debris. I found him on the sofa in the den. He was the whitest, cleanest human being I'd ever seen, which is what I think happens to people when they're in water, they turn white. We left a Guardsman on duty with the body that night, which is a real honor because it's like one of their own.

DESIREE: So they took him out with the flag over him, and I think he would have really liked that . . . and of course all the press his story got—his picture was everywhere, POW decorated soldier. He was such a celebrity. And I kind of love the fact that in his death, so many people got to know about him, because he was really kind of terrific.

FAITH: Part 6: Returning Home.

[SHAKIRA *sings "Do You Know What It Means to Miss New Orleans."** See note on copyright page at the beginning of the play. The* ENSEMBLE *slowly enters and begins to pick through the debris, finding various items.*]

ENSEMBLE: Mementos, diplomas, antiques, computers, sports jerseys, scrapbooks, family pictures, recipes, musical instruments, wedding photos, legal documents, my cat, family heirlooms, artwork, kiddy books I used to read to my children. [*Beat.*] My shoes. I came back to a dozen pairs of fuzzy shoes. [*Beat.*] You know, some shoes were your favorite shoes, whether your dress shoes or whatever, and you can't find those shoes anymore. [*Beat.*] Gone, all gone.

JOE: To come back here in New Orleans you needed to have one of three things. Maybe all three. You needed to have money, that's for sure. You needed to have a desire to *be here.* So in many cases that's family in the area. And the last thing is that you could not be old. My wife and I came back, and everything was gray. There was no grass; all the tree branches were down . . . I can't say it was a war zone . . . but it was still . . . not many people around. It was *very* strange.

[WIFE *crosses to him with two carbon masks. They put them on.*]

WIFE: We're going to have to destroy the house if we can't get rid of that smell.

JOE: Fridge full of food. Three weeks without power in all that heat.

WIFE: It's not pretty.

JOE: The mold is at least three feet high.

WIFE: Is that a plant growing in our carpet?

JOE [*to audience*]: We'd get up in the morning, we'd put our nasty clothes on and the masks, and we'd de-mold. I, well, my wife and I, took out wet carpet, pulling up wet, dirty vinyl, and gutted the walls and all this, from seven o'clock to seven o'clock . . . My hands. You should've seen my hands.

WIFE: We never had a FEMA trailer. We washed dishes for eight months in our bathtub. That's not fun. We didn't have a stove for about ten months.

JOE: The living room had to be entirely gutted. Unfortunately we lost about two hundred fifty books, give or take. Some of those books were 1890s. They swelled up. Plus, the water was disgusting, even if you had a book you loved. I mean, I hate to say it, but there were dead people in that water.

DESIREE: I was driving back to New Orleans. Driving really insane just thinking maybe I'd blow up or something. I got stopped by the cops. Again.

[*She hands her driver's license to the* COP.]

COP: You're from New Orleans?
DESIREE: Yeah, man, I'm from New Orleans.
COP: Are you OK? How'd you do in the storm?
DESIREE: No, man, I'm not OK. My grandfather died.

[*Beat.*]

COP: You drive carefully.

[BRIANNA, SISTER, *and* MOM *stand behind a door frame in the wall upstage. They "push" it and fall into their house.*]

BRIANNA: Oh my God. The ceiling's collapsed.
SISTER: This is our house . . . ?
BRIANNA: Look at our hardwood floors. Warped. All warped. Mama. Mama, aren't you going to say anything?
MOM: It's all right, girls.
BRIANNA: No, it's not. How can you stand there stone-faced? I know you are trying to protect us, just like you did when Daddy died, but it only makes it worse.

[MOM *picks up remnants of a damaged picture frame.*]

MOM: I don't have any of you all's pictures. I don't have your First Communion. Your daddy's picture . . . We don't have any of our pictures. None. None of us.

[HUSBAND *and* FAITH, *on opposite sides of the stage, speak on phones.*]

HUSBAND: The house is still here. Flooded, but here.
FAITH: When can we move back? I've been in Tennessee for three weeks!
HUSBAND: Well, it's like this . . . the mold was four feet high, so basically everything had to go.
FAITH: Go?
HUSBAND: It's all out in front of the house.
FAITH: Who . . . ?
HUSBAND: One crew was from Chicago and one was from New Jersey—they came and we cleared everything out of our house and my mom's. Volunteer firemen. But, um, yeah, I think it's time you came home.
FAITH [*to audience*]: I thought that was the longest drive coming home, not really knowing what to expect and what not to expect, but I guess it really hit me when I couldn't even see my house because the pile in front was so high.

[FAITH *crosses stage, turns to see* HUSBAND, *and they kiss.*]

I can see straight through from my front door to my back fence.

HUSBAND: All the Sheetrock, the insulation, we had to gut all that.

FAITH: How are we gonna afford all this? How am I going to go back to work? What are we going to do with the baby? And it's not like I can ask my mom to watch her, because her house flooded too.

HUSBAND: Right now what we need is a place to live.

[JAMES *and* TED *move to one side.*]

JAMES: The water stayed in my house for five weeks. Just the weight of the water must have collapsed the floor. There was nothing of my house, just a shell. It's a real sight to sit there and watch people throw all your things away. That's your life, your history.

TED: When the restaurant opened up, I moved back to New Orleans, but for the first month or so ... every place I went I had a flashback of what it was like. I couldn't even go in the airport for like two months. You come back into something ... where you saw these people that were just dead ...

[DARRYL *and* CORY *see each other across the stage and grab each other in a bear hug.*]

DARRYL: So should we continue to do the band? We had a little momentum running.

CORY: I don't know. We've splintered up pretty bad. It was like there was a rubber band around us, and now everybody's doing what they can ... I don't know anymore what "continue" means ...

DARRYL: But are we going to get together in New York? Are we going to move to Austin? You know ...

CORY: I don't know if there's going to be anything to come back to. We've been gone for three months.

DARRYL: Three fucking months, man.

CORY: You gotta make plans for three months. You end up having a life somewhere. You have to make money. You have to work. So I took the first job somebody offered me. It's sort of good for me ... this nine-to-five thing.

DARRYL: Everyone is evaluating their lives, man ... you're trying to figure out what to do next. You got a little break from life for a second. You know?

CORY: It takes so long to build. Then when everything gets stripped away like that, do you really want to go and build it from scratch? Or do you want to go and do something else? I think I'm ready to hang it up.

DARRYL: What are you saying, man?

[*Pause.*]

We started this together. You can't back out now.

CORY: OK ... I'll tell you what ... let's go back and get the band together, but it's got to be real from now on ... no bullshit. You know? ... Don't just do it to do it.

DARRYL: All right. Let's make something happen, man. Inspire some of these fuckers ...

[*They shake hands and slap each other on the back.*]

JAMES: People gave us money, clothes—people of all cultures and races. I still have shirts that folks gave me at work. Underwear and stuff, I mean everything. Religious groups from Ohio came out and gutted our house. We wouldn't have been able to pay for that ... White people. Volunteers. Not the government. The folks who were supposed to step up didn't, and the folks who you didn't think would did.

RACHEL: My parents' house was destroyed, but for five months my friend let them stay with him while they rebuilt. They slept in his bedroom, and he slept on a futon. He would never have had it any other way.

JAMES: FEMA didn't give us anything. They told us we had too much insurance. Everything we did was pretty much out of pocket. We took it all out of savings. It absolutely broke us. We're broken.

RACHEL [*to audience*]: I had students to worry about ... many of them were from the Lower Ninth Ward.

[*Members of the* ENSEMBLE, *including* SHAKIRA, *form a circle.*]

WHITE STUDENT #1: I really don't want to be in school. A lot of us don't want to be here ... a lot of us.

RACHEL: OK, this is what's going to happen. Everybody's going to have a chance to talk, whatever comes out.

BLACK STUDENT #1: I want to be in New Orleans, but the crime there is too bad ... some people kill and take what you have ... but like they're killing for fun. They're just killing because they can do it. There's not enough police ... or they're crooked. So ... I just don't want to do this right now.

BLACK STUDENT #2: I didn't know where my brother was until it was almost Christmastime. He ended up in San Antonio, and we went to Dallas.

BLACK STUDENT #3: We lost ... um ... anything we had downstairs. And we don't have any place to live.

WHITE STUDENT #2: A lot of people lost everything. The truth of it is that you had the richest of the rich and the poorest of the poor. And Katrina absolutely had no sympathy on either of them.

WHITE STUDENT #3: That's the thing that is really so upsetting. When the politicians tried to make this a racial issue.

[*Silence. Tension. Black students look at one another.* RACHEL *looks to* SHAKIRA, *whose turn is next.*]

RACHEL: You know, the other day, a girl I know was working on her bat mitzvah speech, and she said, "I'm not using the K word. I swear to you, I am so tired of everybody saying my bat mitzvah was affected by Hurricane Katrina." Let's not use it as a crutch.

SHAKIRA [*looks at* RACHEL]: I've had far worse things happen in my lifetime. To me this was a learning experience. I'm graduating, but I'll be moving to Texas.

[*The circle of students disperses.*]

BRIANNA: My mom gave my sister a choice to come back with us or stay in Kansas at private school and finish high school there. She stayed. Mind over heart, I guess. It killed me.

VIVIE: My god . . . I was sixteen months out of my house. The first adjuster came out.

[ADJUSTER *enters and looks around.*]

ADJUSTER: This house is one hundred twenty-eight years old. Well, the roof certainly has to be repaired. The structure is compromised. What kind of tree is that?

VIVIE: A hundred-year-old pecan tree smashed down the center of the house. It's OK. I'm over it. But every day I would call these people. Literally every day. It was as if they could have cared absolutely less. Because they weren't here. They were . . . somewhere where the grass is green, like the guy in *A Prairie Home Companion,* and people are happy all day. And then you'd get his name and you'd fax him everything he wanted and then you'd call back and leave messages and two months would pass . . .

ADJUSTER #2: I'm sorry, he's no longer with the company. I'm so-and-so, and I'm taking over your claim.

VIVIE: OK. Where would you like me to start?

ADJUSTER #2: Well, we have to send out another adjuster.

[ADJUSTER #3 *comes out.*]

ADJUSTER #3: Blah blah blah, no problem.

VIVIE: About six months later the fourth adjuster came out.

ADJUSTER #4: There's no damage here. This is worth about $10,000.

VIVIE: A hundred-year-old pecan tree smashed down the center of my house, and the roof was a $40,000 slate roof. $10,000? No, can't do that.

[*Beat.*]

Then the fifth adjuster came.

[ADJUSTER #5 *just shakes his head and walks away.*]

Now my time was running out to file a lawsuit. So I talked to a friend of mine who is a secretary for a president of a major corporation. [*To* FRIEND] I have to write a letter. I need you to get me the e-mail address of a corporation president. 'Cause I went on the website to try and find it, and I mean I'd click on a link and it'd send me to Peru or some shit.

FRIEND: Give me a minute . . . Done.

VIVIE: Within four days I had a check in the mail. And the adjuster who stopped calling us back for six weeks all of a sudden called us.

ADJUSTER #5: What can I do to help you?

VIVIE: Besides let me shoot your ass, I can't really think of a whole lot. Oooh, did I say that?

[DARRYL *grabs a chair, crosses downstage, and speaks to audience.*]

DARRYL: I'm laying it down. I'm telling the truth. I'm in a FEMA trailer. Since '98 I've been paying for a $150,000 flood insurance policy. Now my mortgage company is trying *not* to pay me anything, and they are foreclosing on my home because I have no proof. [*Beat.*] The game is this—they know that everybody's home is underwater, so how they gonna retrieve a mortgage statement? That's what's really going on here. I don't want a handout. I never did. I don't want shit from the government. I hustled. I finished high school, I went to college, got a degree, I joined the Air Force. I did what society says to do to be a successful person . . . And I'm getting screwed . . . that really messes up my state of mind. All I want is what the hell I paid for. I'm an American! That's the truth, Ruth. If I didn't have my music to keep my mind stable . . .

[JOE *crosses in and puts his hands on* DARRYL's *shoulders.*]

JOE: I have had tremendous bouts of depression.

VIVIE: I've never taken any medication in my whole life. Now you open our medicine cabinet, and it's like holy shit. What do I feel like doing today?

DARRYL: I'm so glad I have my music.

[ENSEMBLE *gathers downstage and faces the audience. One by one they deliver lines.*]

ENSEMBLE:
  Racial discrimination.
  Rental price gouging.
  Who can afford housing?
  Rising insurance costs.
  Contractor fraud. $50,000 lost.
  Hearing about crime all the time.
  You loot, we shoot.
  An ax in your attic and a gun under your bed.
  Killing because you can, people shot in the head.
  It's tough when police are not enough.
  It's a world of strife when police are crooked.
  And corruption's a way of life.
  No medical care, hospitals empty mortar and brick.
  As they tell you in the 'hood, "Don't get sick."
  Can't be old to live here. They'll be gone before long.
  Our senior citizens die of broken hearts.
  Obituary column's now six pages long.
  Suicide rates have tripled, and there's clinical depression.
  There's no mental health, and I just have to mention.
  Our psychologists and psychiatrists have not come back.
  Just more substance abuse, drinking, drugs, and crack.
  I'm having an American existential crisis.
  And you know I might just . . .
  Well, I'm brokenhearted. We don't elect good politicians,
  But why not Nagin, if we let Bush finish what he started?
  I want to believe in something so badly. I want a flesh and blood
  Somebody to have a big idea, someone I can trust since the flood.
  We're still waiting for the second coming of somebody.

VIVIE: I think a revolution needs to come out of this. We have relied on "they" too many times. We have to start teaching people how to help themselves.

Because "they" never came. I think this is a wake-up call. Stand up and say what needs to be said.

[JOE *is hanging a tattered American flag on the wall upstage.* ENSEMBLE *faces him.*]

JAMES: Is it a holiday?

JOE: Nope.

JAMES: Someone passed away?

JOE: No . . .

JAMES: Then what are you doing with that flag?

JOE: This here is my battle flag. It stays up until my house is rebuilt. Until then, and not a day sooner.

ENSEMBLE [*softly*]: I pledge allegiance to the flag of the United States of America, and to the Republic for which it stands . . .

[VIVIE *and* CORY *step forward.*]

VIVIE: They've lost everything, and yet some people still want to come back. Go figure.

[ACTORS *throw confetti and hug each other in celebration then freeze.*]

CORY: 'Cause we're still gonna party. New Orleans is about celebration when there's nothing to celebrate . . .

VIVIE: We know how to party. I can tell you we know how to put a party on. But you know, it's like any party. The guests leave, and we still got to clean up the mess. We had a grand party, and thank you very much, but we still gotta clean up the mess.

[*The* ACTORS *begin to clean up the debris on the stage.* JOE *takes the flag off the wall.*]

TED: We're gonna get a hurricane this year . . . it could turn or go straight. It's either Louisiana, Texas, or Florida.

GABE: The biggest thing is the levees . . . even though the Corps repaired those levee breaks . . . nothing was done to other parts of the levees.

JAMES: Everybody sleeps with one eye open and the car running. The trunk full, so you can get the hell out of here.

JOE: Everybody says, you know, "Don't rebuild the city." They are not taking into consideration how important New Orleans is . . . I mean all the stuff coming down the Mississippi ends up here. But not everyone should rebuild where they were. They should take their money and go to higher ground.

BRIANNA: But this is home. Regardless of where you go, you're going to be subjected to something. You know all you can do is prepare. My sister decided to stay in Kansas. So she left hurricanes to go to tornadoes.

SHAKIRA: My father is now in school. My grandmother started a senior citizens program. There's a lot of things they didn't have the opportunity to do before that they're able to do now that they are living in Texas.

DESIREE: Nothing made me feel more like a New Orleanian, a local, than the storm. For the first time in my life, I don't have an escape plan or a goal. It's just, it's Sunday in New Orleans and I'm going swimming.

DARRYL: We're still "refugees." As a musician they love me. As a homeowner I'm nobody.

FAITH: Now I have a three-month-old son, and my husband's on his second deployment to Iraq. How do I deal with it? I have no choice. Some days are better than others. Some days I just want to stay at home and cry, but I just do what I have to do.

CORY: Even if half the population is gone and does not come back . . . even if it's a small town. If there's five people living here, it's still the spirit of New Orleans . . .

RACHEL: Home is a sacred place.

ENSEMBLE: With liberty and justice . . .

VIVIE: This Disaster Tour is not something Hollywood could do, because the ending would be a cliffhanger—you don't know how it's gonna . . . It's a cliffhanger. It's like "to be continued." Which just pisses ya off when ya see "to be continued." I remember as a kid to see that on a movie was like, goddammit, I'm not going to be able to watch the rest of this shit. And that's what this is. It's to be continued.

ENSEMBLE: . . . for all."

[*A trumpet plays "A Closer Walk with Thee."** See note on copyright page at the beginning of the play.* JOE *helps the* ACTORS *drape the tattered American flag over debris to create a coffin. They lift the coffin and face the audience.*]

[*Blackout.*]

AFTERWORD

Aimée Hayes, Artistic Director,
Southern Rep Theatre, New Orleans

The mantra we live by in New Orleans is that it wasn't the hurricane—it was the failure of the federal levees. The bitterness and anger I still feel six years later surprises me with its potency and unrelenting constancy. A good child of the sixties and seventies, I used to trust in a positive system of resolution—problems have solutions if you work hard enough. Six years later I find old beliefs useless and rage and grief still wherever I go. In the aftermath, returning to New Orleans was not what I wanted to do at all. I had resolved to stay away and never go back. I was ashamed of the horrors and inequities revealed that week after the storm—ashamed of my country and most of all ashamed that I didn't stay and save my grandfather from the water.

My last day in New Orleans before evacuating, I visited him in the Gentilly home I grew up in. He was my legal guardian throughout most of my young life and was most like a father to me. My grandmother instructed me to make sure he had bought enough bottled water and filled the bathtub with water. We spent all afternoon talking about his crazy WWII stories and reminiscing about our quirky Hoosier ancestors. He walked me down the driveway to my car. I can acutely recall the way the setting sun angled through the giant oak trees on our street, dappling the lawns with a sharp relief of cool and warm. The orange cat across the street, Skittles, lolled about on a neighbor's lawn, oblivious to his family's hurried packing of a small U-Haul trailer. My grandpa and I stood in the driveway and sort of took it all in. Everything seemed captured or frozen for an instant—watching neighbors tape and board their windows, Skittles basking in the sun, Grandpa next to me, the motor boat parked next door, and the endless afternoon light reaching down to us from the bluest, clearest sky. It's a simple wish, but I just want that one small moment back, because it was the last one we would ever have together.

When I came back to New Orleans in December 2005, I was numb, in shock, and like everyone else a little batshit crazy, going through the motions.

It became clear I had to do something about my anger and grief. I make theater, so that's what I did, creating a late-night variety show as an outlet for the constant outrage and hate I seemed to feel for the politicians, Washington, the Army Corps of Engineers, and for myself and my actions. That led to some manageability and helped me be here and want to stay. As a native who kept looking for home anywhere but here, I finally "came out" as a New Orleanian ready to equally embrace the dirt and corruption, along with the easier parts to love like bike rides along the Mississippi, Mardi Gras day in the Quarter, the music, and shrimp po-boys.

I was also fortunate enough to become a part of Southern Rep Theatre, getting hired as its managing director in 2007, and a little over one year later becoming its artistic director. The previous artistic director, Ryan Rilette, had the vision to commission two productions related to the storms, *Rising Water*, from local playwright John Biguenet, and *The Breach* from three playwrights not from New Orleans—Catherine Filloux, Tarell Alvin McCraney, and Joe Sutton—the idea being to get both a local and a national response to what happened to the city and its people. About this same time, Lisa Brenner, a terrific dramaturg I worked with in New York City, and her colleague Suzanne Trauth came to New Orleans to understand what happened here. Many folks shared their stories with them, and *Katrina: The K Word* grew from that process. Tim Maddock and Lotti Louise Pharriss's *Because They Have No Words* was also based on one individual's experience in New Orleans after the storm, aiding in the animal rescue. Our neighborhood cat Skittles did not make it through Katrina, but so many folks I know had their animals successfully rescued. I am still amazed by the rescuers' heroics and valor without which so many of our animal companions would have not made it through. In fall 2008, I was invited by John Pietrowski, artistic director of Playwright's Theatre of New Jersey, to direct a staged reading there as part of a festival of plays about Katrina. Samuel Brett Williams's play *The Trash Bag Tourist* was also included in that series.

The city continues to explode with artistic responses to the events of 2005—visual art, novels, music, and theater—a mass attempt at articulating what folks either experienced firsthand or were forced to watch from afar. Honestly, I absolutely believe that any artistic reaction to a horrific event like what happened here in New Orleans is valid. One doesn't have to be a native to get it. We all know suffering, and I think we all know it when we see it. The empathy and compassion that make us human are what allows art to happen. This anthology's very existence supports this. Yet how do New Orleanians move forward? Do we want to? How do we define or free ourselves from the bitter hold that the past has on our hearts and imaginations? For me it is in the small steps of recovery: a school reopens, a family returns home, Saints fans celebrate a winning game, a lemon tree blossoms for the first time since the storm, and theater and art thrive amidst the weariness, hope, and euphoria.

So, may the work continue to come forth, and may we continue to honor the need to tell our stories. May our remembrances of that time never fade or fully leave us. May art and memory serve as peaceful balms for the hurt we will forever know and the suffering we've endured. Amen.

ABOUT THE PLAYWRIGHTS

JOHN BIGUENET has published six books, including the widely acclaimed *Oyster*, a novel, and *The Torturer's Apprentice: Stories*. Biguenet's radio play *Wundmale* premiered on Westdeutscher Rundfunk. *The Vulgar Soul* won the 2004 Southern New Plays Festival and premiered in 2005 at Southern Rep Theatre. *Rising Water*, the first play in his award-winning trilogy about the collapse of levees in New Orleans and its aftermath, was followed in 2009 by *Shotgun*, set four months after the flood. His new play, *Night Train*, was developed on a Studio Attachment at the National Theatre in London. An O. Henry Award recipient and *New York Times* guest columnist, Biguenet is the Robert Hunter Distinguished University Professor at Loyola University in New Orleans.

LISA S. BRENNER's published articles include "Storming the Nation: Post Katrina New Orleans, Documentary Theatre, and Civic Responsibility," *Transformations* (March 2010); and "Beyond Words: Producing Palestinian–Israeli Dialogue at the Galilee Multicultural Theatre," *Theatre Topics* (September 2009). She has worked as a professional dramaturg, including her work at Vital Theatre in New York City, garnering two OOBR Awards for Excellence. *Taking Names*, a play she co-wrote with three other playwrights, won Best New Play in the 2000 All Out Arts Festival in New York City. Brenner is currently assistant professor of Theatre Arts at Drew University in Madison, New Jersey. In 2009, Drew granted her the Faculty Leadership Civic Engagement Award for her work on *Katrina: The K Word*, among other projects.

CATHERINE FILLOUX is an award-winning playwright who has been writing about human rights and social justice for the past twenty years. Her plays have been produced in New York and around the world. Filloux is the author of two music theater pieces, *Where Elephants Weep*, produced in Phnom Penh, and *The Floating Box*, produced in New York. Her plays are published by Playscripts, Inc., and her anthology *Silence of God and Other Plays* was published by Seagull Books, London Limited. She has received awards from the O'Neill, Kennedy Center, Omni Center for Peace, and New Dramatists.

TIM MADDOCK grew up in suburban Kansas City and went on to obtain a B.S. in theater from Northwestern University. He is also a graduate of the midsummer program at the British American Drama Academy in Oxford, England. Before moving to Los Angeles, Tim performed in regional theater in Chicago and Kansas City, in such shows as *Tony 'n' Tina's Wedding* and *A Few Good Men*. Since moving to Los Angeles, he has worked in various stage productions including Emilie Beck's critically acclaimed play *And Let the Skies Fall!* at the El Portal Theatre. Tim appeared in *Because They Have No Words* in its Los Angeles premiere and also appeared in the spring 2008 production at the prestigious Piven Theatre in Evanston, Illinois. Tim is also a member of the Dramatists Guild of America.

TARELL ALVIN MCCRANEY is the Royal Shakespeare's Company's international writer-in-residence and the 2009 Hodder Fellow at Princeton University. His *The Brother/Sister Plays* have been performed by the Public, Foundry Theatre, London's Young Vic, Alliance Theatre, and McCarter Theatre. *Wig Out!*, developed at Sundance Theatre Lab and produced at the Vineyard Theatre in New York and at the Royal Court in London, won the GLAAD Award for Outstanding Play. McCraney has garnered several distinguished accolades, including the 2009 Steinberg Playwright Award, the inaugural New York Times Outstanding Playwright Award, the London Evening Standard Award for Most Promising Playwright, and the Whiting Writing Award.

LOTTI LOUISE PHARRISS is a writer, producer, and partner in Weirdsmobile Productions, Inc. She produced the world premiere of *Because They Have No Words*. A native of the San Francisco Bay Area, Lotti holds a B.A. in performance studies from Northwestern University and an M.A. in theater from the University of Illinois at Chicago. During her years in Chicago, Pharriss produced several new plays and had her writing produced by theaters such as Live Bait and Tellin' Tales. She is a proud member of the Dramatists Guild of America and has volunteered as an adult theater artist and mentor with the Virginia Avenue Project in Santa Monica since 1994.

JOE SUTTON's plays include *Voir Dire, As It Is in Heaven, The Third Army,* and *Restoring the Sun*. They have been produced by such theaters as the New York Theater Workshop, Seattle Rep, BAM, and most recently the Old Vic, which produced his play *Complicit*. Joe is a recipient of fellowships from the New York Foundation for the Arts and the National Endowment for the Arts and has been nominated for the Pulitzer Prize. He resides in Montclair, New Jersey, with his wife, Anne, and their sons, James and Nicholas.

SUZANNE M. TRAUTH is a professor of theater at Montclair State University, where she coordinates the BFA acting program. She directed *Katrina: The K Word* at Montclair State as well as staged readings of the play at Playwrights Theatre of New Jersey and Drew University. Trauth has produced and directed productions at the Ensemble Studio Theatre in New York, the Whole Theatre, 12 Miles West, and TheatreFest. As part of a global initiative, she directed *The Crucible* for the Theatre-on-Podol in the Ukraine. She coauthored *Sonia Moore and American Acting Training* and *Producing Musical Theatre,* has written on acting theory and Soviet theater, and served as assistant artistic director of the Sonia Moore Studio in New York.

SAMUEL BRETT WILLIAMS hails from Hot Springs, Arkansas, where he was raised in a strict Southern Baptist environment. Brett's plays have been developed at the Eugene O'Neill National Playwrights' Conference, the John F. Kennedy Center for the Performing Arts, the Lark Play Development Center, Naked Angels, Yale University, and P73 Productions. His plays have been produced at Cherry Lane Theatre, Ars Nova, Stageworks/Hudson, Mile Square Theatre, the D.C. Arts Center, and New Orleans Theatre Experiment. Brett is published in *Best New American Plays 2004–2005, Best New American Plays 2006–2007,* and by Playscripts, Inc. Recently, he received the Helen Merrill Emerging Playwright Award and a National New Play Network Commission. In September 2010, Project Y produced his play *The Revival* on Theatre Row in New York City.

INTERVIEWS WITH THE PLAYWRIGHTS

JOHN BIGUENET, AUTHOR OF *RISING WATER*

LB: What is your personal connection to New Orleans?

JB: My family has lived in New Orleans for centuries.

LB: How did the idea for a Katrina play happen?

JB: *Rising Water* began with a series of columns I wrote and videos I shot for the *New York Times* about the destruction of New Orleans (http://biguenet .blogs.nytimes.com/). The more I learned about the suffering and death of my fellow New Orleanians in this needless man-made catastrophe that occurred when defective levees designed and built by the U.S. Army Corps of Engineers crumbled in conditions well below their intended capacity, the angrier I got. But when I tried to write about it, I wound up telling a love story about a couple who'd been together thirty years.

LB: How did you go about writing *Rising Water*?

JB: I was so angry as I composed the early drafts that I kept killing off both characters in the first act, creating a rather serious problem when it came to the second act. The more I considered the structure of the play, though, with a first act set in an attic crowded with souvenirs of a couple's life together and a second act on a moonlit rooftop overlooking a drowned city, the more I realized the first was about memory and the second about dream. One act would look back, and the other would look forward, asking whether the flood might not be the end of the world but a new world just beginning.

LB: How did you use your firsthand knowledge of New Orleans to develop the play?

JB: Having returned to our ruined house just a few weeks after the levee collapse, I was in the city as survivors began to tell their stories about the flood and its aftermath. Interviewing individuals for my column in the *New York Times,* following the developing investigations in the national press and in the *New Orleans Times-Picayune,* and simply trying to find housing and rebuild our lives in a devastated city provided me with the research I needed to write *Rising Water.*

LB: What changes did you make during the revision process?

JB: *Rising Water* was given a staged reading by the National New Play Network, which had commissioned the play, at the 2006 National Showcase of

New Plays at the New Jersey Repertory Company on December 2, 2006. In a talkback following the performance, audience members encouraged further development of the absurdist elements of the play, and, perhaps most importantly, one person suggested that, considering its subject, I needed to give the audience permission to laugh. On the flight home to New Orleans the next day, I decided to make the play not more absurdist but more local. It would be a play by a New Orleanian presented by New Orleanians for New Orleanians. I changed the names of the characters to Camille and Sugar and had already begun the rewrite by the time the plane touched down at Louis Armstrong International Airport. The revisions continued right up to opening night three months later.

LB: The play was first produced in New Orleans. How was it received?

JB: Ryan Rilette directed the premiere on March 17, 2007, at Southern Rep Theatre in New Orleans with Cristine McMurdo-Wallis playing Camille and Danny Bowen playing Sugar. *Rising Water* became the best-selling show in the twenty-year history of Southern Rep Theatre (despite the fact that the previous record was set when New Orleans had twice the population as the city did at the time of the play's run). David Cuthbert of the *New Orleans Times-Picayune* declared *Rising Water* "a rich mixture of tragedy and humor . . . The play grabbed the audience in its first tense moments and never let go . . . *Rising Water* is more like cream, rising to the top."

LB: What is it like for you as a New Orleans playwright now?

JB: I continue to choose to live in New Orleans, despite the difficulties of daily life in the city. It is a deeply wounded place populated by people with a great deal of grit.

CATHERINE FILLOUX, TARELL ALVIN MCCRANEY, AND JOE SUTTON, AUTHORS OF *THE BREACH*

LB: How did the idea for *The Breach* happen?

JS: I was watching television images of Hurricane Katrina, and I couldn't believe what I was seeing. I felt like I had to do something. I'm a playwright, so my first thought was to write a play. But I realized that this story was so big I couldn't write it alone. I called Catherine Filloux, a playwright who had written about issues like human rights and genocide, and she quickly agreed to join me. Catherine suggested we also involve Lynn Nottage, but she sadly had to pull out of the project a few months later, because her schedule just got too demanding. Then we found Tarell McCraney.

TM: I was away in England at the time of the call, but I immediately said yes, and the first day back I met with Joe and Catherine to see if I would work with them to begin this project.

LB: What was it like having three playwrights collaborating on a piece?

CF: Three playwrights don't often embark on writing a play together. We spent a lot of time shaping the piece after we wrote our separate sections. We listened to each other a lot. We did a lot of revisions throughout the process.

JS: We each wrote our narrative line, and our dramaturg, Mark Lutwak, helped us pull together the composite. The device of double-casting also helped to make it a united piece. We further developed the piece through a series of staged readings around the country, in New Orleans and Baton Rouge, but also places like Bay St. Louis, Mississippi; Manalapan, Florida; Washington, D.C.; and New Haven, Connecticut.

TM: It took a moment, I am guessing, to make an indelible mark, but it would take, will take, a lifetime of shifting, changing, coloring, undoing, going back and revising to try and get right what the experience did and how it came to happen.

CF: My section of the play creates a theatrical role for an actress who embodies Water. I have always been drawn to water, having grown up by the Pacific Ocean. I love to swim, and my father sailed a catamaran across the Atlantic to get to this country and built the first fiberglass sailboat, though this story of the fiberglass sailboat ended in tragedy. When I went to New Orleans after Hurricane Katrina, the shadow of water was everywhere. Werner Herzog made a documentary called *Grizzly Man*. Nature, the bear, and water are as brutal and savage as they are cuddly and playful. Water is everywhere. In New Orleans and Biloxi—and on the road in between—when we looked at the aftermath of the storm, water *was* everywhere. What does Man have over Nature? What does my character Mac have over Water? Mac is sick, he has a disease, but he's still a fighter. I met many fighters in New Orleans. Sometimes, when I was there, the whole city seemed a city of fighters. And New Orleans was/is also a city fighting for its place in our nation. Who wins? My story is about Man winning. Iraq and the war came up a lot when I was in New Orleans. Where was all the aid and help during the Katrina flood? We were fighting a war in Iraq. Ryan Rilette, the artistic director of Southern Rep, in New Orleans, who opened up his house to us, told me that sometimes when New Orleanians heard news footage about Iraq, it sounded like news footage about New Orleans after Katrina. My play places Mac in a fight with Water. It's so much fun to create a role like Water, as it opens up a theatrical world.

LB: What are some of your memories of New Orleans?

CF: I'd been there as a kid when my parents drove us four children across the country in an old Pontiac and we stopped to hear jazz in a small room—Preservation Hall. I'll never forget that night. New Orleans was romantic, and since we were French, we conversed with some French people in the French Quarter. It was delightful to hear their Cajun accents. It seemed the kind of city one might have a honeymoon in. Now my personal connection to New Orleans is the time I spent there after Katrina. It is impossible to know the scope of the devastation unless you were there after the storm. The smell, the air which made your throat scratch, the signs everywhere advertising getting rid of mold; houses that seemed like they'd been sucked to their guts. There were tours of people in vans coming to see the devastation. The broken levees. People cleaning up. Trailers in the middle of nowhere. The joy somehow of having survived in the best city in America. Walking through weeds and slabs of foundations in the Ninth Ward much later when the neighborhood had completely disappeared.

TM: First Ryan Rilette, then artistic director of Southern Rep in New Orleans, asked that I come down and see the city. The hurricane had hit, and the city was slowly trying to rebuild from the destruction that was caused by the levee's breach. I came down to the city and found it still in very bad shape: crime spiking, despair and anger still boiling . . . And yet . . . there was so much respect and love there, too. So much kindness mixed right in with the suffering. People having hard stories to tell but also having a great time telling 'em. If you want to hear a story told right, have someone from New Orleans tell it! I listened to those stories, and I began to write what was said how it was said, weaving together the real-life account with what only the imagination could bind into reality. I talked to people my age. I made friends with them. They are still my friends.

LB: How was the play received in New Orleans?

CF: Southern Rep, being in New Orleans and where we developed the play, held a very important place for us. Seattle is far away from New Orleans, so it was a different feeling to have the play there.

TM: When we did the first reading of the play at Southern Rep, we knew we had something. Partially by the way the crowd at the reading told us point blank that the theater stood the chance of being leveled to the ground if we put some of the scenes that were fearless and hard for those who had lived through it to see/talk about into the play, but also because we knew our charge: We had a play that did what we had set out to do, which was focus attention and add to a steadily quieting dialogue about the disaster that befell one of America's most gifted and beautiful cities—one that I loved.

LB: Did you research for this play?

JS: We worked with Ryan Rilette, artistic director of Southern Rep, and Jearlean Osborne, a community organizer and social activist from Biloxi. They both helped us plan our research. They took us on tours of the devastation, but also to hear people's stories. I traveled on my own around the state of Louisiana, gathering as many perspectives as I could.

CF: My research happened in New Orleans, where I listened to many people and witnessed the aftermath of Katrina. I also did a lot of reading.

TM: I visited a place called Tipitina's and bars up and down Bourbon Street. I walked around the Ninth Ward and Elysian Fields and drove to Chalmette and St. Bernard Parish. I cried, I stared, I laughed, I hoped, I prayed, I clichéd, I cursed, I moaned, I fell in love.

LB: What is your connection to New Orleans now?

JS: Unfortunately, I have not been back since that very intensive two-year-plus period. That said, I still follow the news about the Gulf Region and the recovery very closely.

CF: I've been part of a theater and peace-building project with the American theater artist and civil rights leader John O'Neal, who is from New Orleans.

TM: I cannot pinpoint the moment I fell in love with this city, nor what I would do if I couldn't visit it the once a year that I try to do. I am leaving out tons of small moments that shaped and changed the way I see things even unto this very day. And even as I tried to fashion that love into a play set on a rooftop in the dark of those days after Katrina . . . every day I find I have more to say.

TIM MADDOCK AND LOTTI LOUISE PHARRISS, AUTHORS OF
BECAUSE THEY HAVE NO WORDS

ST: Where did the idea for the play come from?

TM: The play is essentially the real story of what happened to me when I went to New Orleans as a volunteer with the Humane Society of the United States after Katrina. Upon my return I sat down with Lotti and told her the whole story. Lotti was so struck by what she heard that she suggested we do "something" with it. After batting around several ideas, we settled on a play, as it is a medium with which we are both comfortable. (Lotti and I met as theater majors at Northwestern University many years ago.)

LLP: I was so amazed by the stories Tim came back with after his journey—they were very personal and were nothing like what we were hearing on the news about New Orleans and Katrina. At first I thought I might try to write about his experiences as a series of articles to pitch to a newspaper or magazine, but a play quickly emerged as a more natural format for us to tell the story. And my first thought for the play was a one-man show for Tim, but we decided that having other actors onstage to play the people and animals he encountered was the more compelling choice.

ST: Did either of you have a personal connection to New Orleans?

TM: In the spring of 1991, I went on spring break with a bunch of my fraternity brothers to New Orleans. I left them behind and found myself in a gay bar, where I met a man and fell quickly in "love." This was the impetus for my coming out and changing my life forever. New Orleans held a special place in my heart.

LLP: I am somewhat ashamed to say I have never been to New Orleans, pre- or post-Katrina. In both respects, it continues to loom large in my mind as a mythical place—not fictional, mind you, but legendary or archetypal. Someday I will definitely visit, and it will be interesting to see how that sense of myth is either dispelled or confirmed by the reality of the place.

ST: How were you two able to work together to create the play?

TM: Lotti and I began by recording all our conversations about my experiences. Then we tediously transcribed them all. Lotti took those and put down the first third of the play, adding her artistic flourish as she did so. At that point, we brought in a third collaborator (the director), who thought we should expand the scope of the play to include other events of my life which could be tied thematically to the Katrina experience. I wrote several scenes that centered around the death of my mom and my relationship with my partner. I also wrote out some of the more complex stories about individual animals (with the bureaucracy involved in the HSUS rescue operation—the "hows" and "whys" of what happened were a little overwhelming and difficult to follow). Once we had a whole play, Lotti and I went back and forth with cuts, additions, and suggestions until we felt we had it right.

LLP: Tim explained our process well, so I will add that there were three things that were ultimately very important to me in the creation of this play: (1) find humor wherever possible so that the audience would not become numb to the more emotionally difficult material; (2) make the story personal and specific in order to make it universal (i.e., Tim could be any of you in the audience); and (3) honor the people of New Orleans. People have asked me, "With all the human suffering, how could you write a play about the *animals*?" Well, it was about both—animals are the inroad to the people's emotional journey. Tim and I both love our pets as members of our families, and that was such a big part of what Tim witnessed—when people had lost everything, just being able to reunite with a beloved animal was enough to give them hope.

ST: Besides your personal experiences, Tim, was there other research you had to do?

TM: Not much. There was a bit of verifying the information I had heard in New Orleans versus the information I was hearing from the media upon my return, collecting some statistics and looking up some names (neighborhoods, streets, etc.).

LLP: Exactly. Tim's memory of the people and animals he met was my research!

ST: Where was the first production?

TM: The Lounge Theatre in Los Angeles, California. We opened September 2, 2006 (just a year after Katrina).

LLP: It was a whirlwind year, putting it together in time for the anniversary. Besides writing and rewriting even during the rehearsal process, I produced the play and Tim played himself. I'm amazed we emerged sane!

TM: We received a glowing review from *Backstage West* and a Pick of the Week review from *LA Weekly*. Additionally, we received two Ovation Award nominations (Best Ensemble and a Best New Play nomination for Lotti and myself).

LLP: The audience response was also thrilling—I only wish we could have extended the run, as word of mouth had really started to build, and we completely sold out our last two weekends.

ST: What were the primary changes made during the revision process?

TM: At the time we had cast the play and begun rehearsal, the real-life events hadn't yet resolved. We still had owners fighting for the return of an animal and two cats that were missing. Additionally, as we got the play up and on its feet, we continued to rewrite jokes, trim the fat, etc. Also, in order to bring down the overall running time, the play underwent a major cut before its second production at the Piven Theatre in Evanston, Illinois, in May 2008. Again, we continued to make small changes all the way through that rehearsal process.

LLP: A play is always a living, breathing thing if it's being performed, so I wouldn't be surprised if this published version isn't even the last!

ST: Have you been back to New Orleans?

TM: I am still good friends with several of the rescuers with whom I worked in Louisiana. I also reconnected with the man I met at that gay bar way back in 1991. As for the city itself, I have, sadly, not returned. I can't bring myself to return to the site of so much pain. There is nothing left of the New Orleans I fell in love with in college. When I remember the city now, I remember the desolation and destruction. I see the anguish and suffering of the people and animals I encountered. I remember my anger and frustration. I remember what it is to feel helpless. I have no doubt that I will go back someday. But not today.

LLP: I still read every news article about New Orleans, fascinated by the place and angered by how slow the recovery process has been. My heart will always be with the people and animals there. As for my own eventual journey to the Big Easy? To be continued . . .

SAMUEL BRETT WILLIAMS, AUTHOR OF *THE TRASH BAG TOURIST*

ST: How did you decide to write the play?

SBW: My stepfather is the Garland County administrator for the Department of Human Services in Arkadelphia, Arkansas. Shortly after Hurricane Katrina hit New Orleans, an influx of poor, newly homeless victims were shipped into Arkansas for food and shelter. My stepfather oversaw an entire community center filled with thousands of displaced Louisianans. I came home from graduate school to visit my parents at this time, and I was shocked at the way the town was talking about the victims. I literally heard someone say they were "rapin' babies" and "makin' the lines too long at the Wal-Mart." There was another part of the community that was very concerned about the victims, but only as long as they were considered "victims," which turned out to be a few months. And, of course, there were some people who were genuinely heartbroken and attempted to help on a daily basis. As a playwright I wanted to explore the first two groups of people in a way to hopefully better understand myself and my community. This was my attempt at that.

ST: Had you spent much time in New Orleans?

SBW: Growing up in Arkansas, my friends and I found ourselves in New Orleans a lot—enjoying the music, the food, the sporting events. New Orleans is by far my favorite city in the United States. It's a wonderful mixture of the South and Europe and even Africa.

ST: How did you approach the writing?

SBW: My goal throughout was just to maintain the integrity of the story and the people portrayed in the story. That's all I ever really hope to do when writing. A close friend of mine (Teresa Stephenson, who was first to be cast in the role of Molly) lives in New Orleans. So I went down there with her and visited her family before and during the show. Also, since it is technically set in Arkadelphia, Arkansas, I feel like I have been researching it my whole life.

ST: Where was *The Trash Bag Tourist* produced?

SBW: The play was first produced at Mason Gross School of the Arts (Rutgers University, New Brunswick, New Jersey). I had the director (Michole Biancosino) and an actress (Teresa Stephenson) who would later go to New Orleans with me. It was well received, but that production lacked in emotion. I took another pass at the script, and then we went down to Louisiana with the New Orleans Theatre Experiment. The play was produced at the New Orleans Arts Center. It was by far the best theater experience of my life. The crowds were out the door, the local paper gave us a great review, and the community really seemed to appreciate us coming to them so soon after Katrina. We even had an actual Katrina victim in the cast. Now, I can't pretend any of that would have been possible without Michole, Teresa, and Teresa's very welcoming family.

ST: Have you visited New Orleans since then?

SBW: I try to get to the city of New Orleans as often as possible. Like I said, it's one of my favorite places in the world. And, recently, I have been asked to write another Katrina play—looking at the situation now, years later—for the same theater company (New Orleans Theatre Experiment) that produced *The Trash Bag Tourist*. I can't wait to get started!

LISA S. BRENNER AND SUZANNE M. TRAUTH, CREATORS OF
KATRINA: THE K WORD

What follows is a description of our process in creating *Katrina: The K Word.*

LB: I was at home, listening to the radio, and they were reporting about a new documentary film being made about Katrina and Rita. I remember pausing and thinking that there was a strong response to Katrina by filmmakers (Spike Lee, Jonathan Demme), but at that point I hadn't heard of any plays about this topic. I wondered what my response and even my responsibility as a theater practitioner should be.

ST: Once we agreed to write the play—this was September 2006, the first anniversary of Hurricane Katrina—I started to read all kinds of articles and reports. I just found myself immersed in the world of the storm. I had only been to New Orleans as a tourist, twice before Katrina hit. My experience was mostly the French Quarter, wonderful restaurants and spectacular music. During that week in 2005, I was in Texas, and I remember hearing about survivors coming to Houston and San Antonio. I watched CNN, as others in this country did, and was shocked and appalled by what I saw. August 29 through September 1 seemed like an eternity.

LB: It was quickly apparent that we needed to go down to New Orleans and speak to people directly. Even in 2007, the French Quarter did not seem that affected by Katrina. But several people we met took us to places where we could see the extensive devastation firsthand. None of the images I had seen on television prepared me for my gut-wrenching response of shock, anger, and dismay at what I was seeing. At the same time we were so inspired by the spirit of the people and the impression that, despite the destruction, New Orleans was still home.

ST: Though we initially planned to write a fictional piece about Hurricane Katrina, once we interviewed actual residents, we realized we had to use their words. We could not "make this stuff up."

LB: I remember we first arrived at the hotel in the heart of the French Quarter, and the woman at the front desk shunned us: "No one here wants to talk about it. We are tired of talking about Katrina. We just want to move on." So on our first day in New Orleans, we were already asking ourselves, "Had we made a mistake?" But that night we met with the woman who would later become the character Desiree. She said, "Are you kidding? I feel like screaming it from the rooftops!" And we soon found out she wasn't alone.

ST: We began this project because we felt that the story of Katrina needed to be told. However, we discovered that the story doesn't exist, for every person who was affected by the storm has his or her own version of what happened. We had a few contacts, and each contact introduced us to other contacts—whether a volunteer who knew a drummer in a band playing that night, or a teacher who had students from the Lower Ninth Ward, or a restaurant owner whose chef had chosen to ride out the storm. They all really wanted people to understand what they had gone through.

LB: During the summer of 2007, we transcribed the interviews, began to create a structure for the material, and did an informal reading before casting in September. Along the way, we researched New Orleans, Hurricane Katrina, and its aftermath, and read Tom Piazza's book *Why New Orleans Matters.* We also read blogs that offered a variety of individual reactions to the storm, but the interviews formed the basis for the play and were the primary source for our material. After transcribing them, we created this text by cutting, editing, and rearranging the words.

ST: And changing the names. Some of the characters are composites of various people we interviewed. Some of the stories were simplified for the sake of clarity, yet none are fictional. All of the narratives are true as far as they were told to us.

LB: While we may not agree with every comment nor do we present every claim as fact, we have tried to stay true to the opinions expressed and to the spirit of the amazing people who felt that what happened in New Orleans in 2005 and since deserves our attention.

ST: The revising process continued into the fall . . . right up until the week we opened. We had many scenes and characters that had to be cut in order to tell the story in a coherent fashion. To keep the arcs of the characters moving and strong, we had to eliminate some beautiful moments. It felt like losing good friends!

LB: There is one story that we both felt had to be cut in the interest of time and dramatic tension. However, I don't think I will ever forget when we first heard it. A woman in a wheelchair told us about going through her ninety-year-old mother's belongings after the storm. A set of dishes had survived—their holiday dishes. But despite all of the happy memories these dishes had had before, now they just reminded her of dead people. "I could never eat off of them again," she said.

ST: And now? Our dramaturg, Nancy Tichenor, has led groups of students to New Orleans during spring break to participate in the rebuilding effort. I have not been back to New Orleans since our trip in 2007. But not a day goes by that I don't think about the people we interviewed and wonder how they are doing. During hurricane season, every year since 2005, I hold my breath.

LB: In 2010, I returned to New Orleans and had the pleasure of meeting the organizers and some of the children involved in The Porch 7th Ward Cultural Organization. I'm looking forward to developing our relationship with them.

FOR MORE INFORMATION

For more information on supporting post-Katrina New Orleans, see the following:

http://www.ccstb.org/

http://www.commongroundrelief.org/

http://www.habitat-nola.org/

http://www.handsonneworleans.org/

http://www.lakewoodbeacon.org/

http://www.levees.org/

http://www.njwaterwatch.org/spring-break/

http://www.stbernardproject.org/v158/

http://www.therootsofmusic.com/

For a sampling of arts organizations in New Orleans, see:

http://www.artspotproductions.org/

http://www.ashecac.org/

http://www.beatitudesinneworleans.blogspot.com/

http://www.jazzandheritage.org/

http://www.junebugproductions.org/

http://www.nolaproject.com/

http://ny2no.net/homeneworleans/home/

http://www.sankofamarketplace.org/

http://www.southernrep.com/

http://www.theporch-7.com/

http://www.thevestigesproject.org/

http://www.transformaprojects.org/

http://www.torrestama.com/

For information on animal rescue, see:

http://www.humanesociety.org/

http://www.idausa.org/

http://www.fullmoonfarm.org/

RECOMMENDED READING

Eggers, Dave. *Zeitoun.* San Francisco: McSweeney's Books, 2009.

Horne, Jed. *Breach of Faith: Hurricane Katrina and the Near Death of a Great American City.* New York: Random House, 2008.

Piazza, Tom. *Why New Orleans Matters.* New York: ReganBooks, 2005.

Roahen, Sara. *Gumbo Tales: Finding My Place at the New Orleans Table.* New York: W. W. Norton & Co., 2009.

STATEMENT ON THE PORCH 7TH WARD CULTURAL ORGANIZATION

By purchasing this anthology, you have made a donation to The Porch 7th Ward Cultural Organization in New Orleans, Louisiana. Its mission is to promote and sustain cultures of the neighborhood, city, and region, and to foster exchange between cultural groups. This organization holds to the belief that empowerment through culture is their primary tool for positive change within the community and the city. The Porch 7th Ward Cultural Organization conducts diverse creative programming for all ages. For more information, please visit their website: www.theporch-7.com.